Basic English Grammar

FOR DUMMIES®

A Wiley Brand

by Geraldine Woods

FOR DUMMIES®
A Wiley Brand

Basic English Grammar For Dummies®

Published by: **John Wiley & Sons, Inc.,** 111 River Street, Hoboken, NJ 07030-5774, www.wiley.com

© 2015 John Wiley & Sons, Inc., Hoboken, New Jersey.

Media and software compilation copyright © 2015 by John Wiley & Sons, Inc. All rights reserved.

Published simultaneously in Canada

For general information on our other products and services, please contact our Customer Care Department within the U.S. at 877-762-2974, outside the U.S. at (001) 317-572-3993, or fax 317-572-4002. For technical support, please visit www.wiley.com/techsupport.

Wiley publishes in a variety of print and electronic formats and by print-on-demand. Some material included with standard print versions of this book may not be included in e-books or in print-on-demand. If this book refers to media such as a CD or DVD that is not included in the version you purchased, you may download this material at http://booksupport.wiley.com. For more information about Wiley products, visit HYPERLINK "http://www.wiley.com" www.wiley.com.

Library of Congress Control Number: 2015941963

ISBN 978-1-119-06347-6 (pbk); ISBN 978-1-119-06349-0 (ebk);

ISBN 978-1-119-06348-3 (ebk)

Manufactured in the United States of America

10 9 8 7 6 5 4 3 2 1

Contents at a Glance

Table of Contents

Introduction

You want to send a letter to your aunt. She is very strict about proper grammar and spelling. This is what you write:

Dear Aunt Louise,

~~I wanted I would like I want to thank~~

Thank you for ~~you're your~~

Thank you for the ~~presant pressent~~ gift.

By now, the notepaper is a mess, and so are you. If this sounds like your life, you are not alone. Many people struggle when they must write or speak formally. Fortunately, help is on the way. In fact, it is already here, in the book you are reading.

English grammar is not a mystery. It is a set of traditions and patterns of language handed down through the years. Anyone can learn the rules of Standard English. *Basic English Grammar For Dummies* explains what you need to know. With practice and the information in this book, you can express yourself confidently and correctly. Even Aunt Louise will be pleased!

About This Book

As I wrote this book, I followed For Dummies traditions. I also made some patterns myself. Every time I introduce a grammar term, I italicize and explain it. If I write *noun,* for example, I tell you a *noun* is the name of a person, place, thing, or idea. Do not be afraid! In *Basic English Grammar For Dummies,* I use very few grammar terms. As often as possible, I explain what you need to know in normal, nonteacher language. I also underline some words or phrases that you should pay close attention to.

To help you pick up important points quickly, I frequently place information in lists. Every item in a list begins with a little check mark. The key idea appears in boldface (extra-dark type). Examples illustrate every rule. Keep an eye out for these examples, centered alone on a line. If I mention an idea but do not explain it immediately, I direct you to a chapter that contains more information.

Although this book focuses on grammar, I could not resist throwing in some vocabulary builders. A strong vocabulary makes your writing more interesting. Look for gray boxes, called sidebars, if you want to learn new words. If your vocabulary is already in good shape, ignore the gray boxes and go right to the text.

Foolish Assumptions

I do not know who you are, but I have already spent some time with you — the reader I imagine. When I write, I keep you, the reader, in my mind. I imagine you holding a yellow For Dummies book or an e-reader. This is how I see you:

- ✔ You know the language, but you are open to learning more.
- ✔ You want a firmer grasp of the rules of Standard English, the formal language of educated people.
- ✔ You are busy. You do not want to waste time memorizing facts you will never need.
- ✔ You enjoy a little humor.

That is everything I assume about you. Have I described you accurately? I hope so.

Icons Used in This Book

Flip through *Basic English Grammar For Dummies*. Many little drawings appear in the margin. Those pictures are called *icons*. Icons alert you in these ways:

This icon signals a shortcut or an extra bit of information. A tip is a whisper in your ear, helping you master a grammar rule.

This icon tells you where errors often pop up, so you can avoid mistakes.

For every topic, you find a few questions labeled with this icon. Take the quizzes to check whether you have mastered the material. Answers follow every quick quiz. (No peeking allowed.)

Key ideas appear with this icon.

Beyond the Book

Like me, you probably spend a lot of time on the Internet. I have placed extra material there, to add to what you find on the screen of your e-reader or between the paper covers of *Basic English Grammar For Dummies*. Here is what you get, all for free:

- ✔ **Cheat Sheet:** Yes, I know you are honest. You do not cheat on tests or at work. You could use a little help sometimes, though. The Cheat Sheet lists essential information from this book. Print it out and tape it to your desk or put it in your pocket. Glance at the Cheat Sheet at www.dummies.com/cheatsheet/basicenglishgrammar when you want to refresh your memory about key grammar rules.

- ✔ **An extra Part of Tens:** All For Dummies books, including this one, end with the Part of Tens. Two chapters in this book explain ten ways to improve your writing skills and ten mistakes that wreck your sentences, respectively. You can read an extra Part of Tens online at www.dummies.com/extras/basicenglishgrammar. That one lists ten ways to polish your writing. With this online Part of Tens, you move beyond grammar and into style. You see how to create sophisticated sentences. Like designer clothing, well-made sentences attract positive attention.

- ✔ **Articles:** I love language, and I have more to say about every topic in this book. Plus, the rules of Standard English are not carved in stone. They are changing right now, adapting to new means of communication such as smartphones, tablets, and the like. Fortunately, the Internet gives me space for in-depth discussions of old grammar rules and reports of new developments. Look for articles that tell you a little bit more about parts of speech, parts of a sentence, new media, and other topics. For example, do you know how to combine words and images for a presentation? Would you like to learn whether to capitalize school years, seasons, and historical eras? Check www.dummies.com/extras/basicenglishgrammar to find articles on these topics, and more.

Where to Go From Here

You do not have to read *Basic English Grammar For Dummies* in order. Nor do you have to read the entire book. You can, of course. If you do, you will be my favorite reader.

I realize, however, that you are busy. You probably want to select just what you need. To get started, take a close look at the Table of Contents. Mark off topics that interest or puzzle you. You should also take a look at the table at the end of Chapter 2, which presents common grammar issues and tells you which chapters explain them. Read the chapters you have selected.

Another way to personalize your approach to grammar starts with the quizzes in each chapter. Try some. If you get every question right, feel free to skip that section. (Also, take a moment to pat yourself on the back for a job well done.) If the quiz stumps you, spend some time in that section of the book. Read the explanations, and glance at related material in other chapters.

If you are facing a specific task — a school report or a work presentation, perhaps — turn to Part V. There you find information about common writing formats. Check out the online material, too.

No matter which path you choose to follow through *Basic English Grammar For Dummies,* you will arrive at the same place. You will be a stronger, more confident writer and speaker.

Part I

Getting Started with Basic English Grammar

In this part . . .

- ✔ Identify the elements of proper English.
- ✔ Explore the format of everyday writing tasks.
- ✔ Become familiar with common errors.
- ✔ Learn when breaking the rules of Standard English is acceptable.
- ✔ See how to take advantage of computer programs that check your spelling and grammar.

Chapter 1

Getting a Grip on Grammar

*L*ots of people groan when they hear the word grammar. They think that grammar is just a long list of picky rules. Who cares if you say *had gone* or *went?* Why worry about the choice between *I* and *me?* These issues can seem silly. Wouldn't it be better to spend time searching for a cancer cure?

Yes, grammar is often picky. Certainly, the world needs more than grammar — much more! Yet proper language does matter. Rightly or wrongly, many people judge your intelligence and ability based on the way you speak and write. Better jobs and higher grades often go to those who follow the rules. In this chapter, you survey key elements of Standard English — grammar, spelling, and much more.

Getting to Know the Elements of Proper English

When you bake a cake, you need all the right ingredients. If you forget one, the cake is tasteless. English has a number of ingredients, too. You cannot ignore any if you wish to express yourself correctly. Here are the ingredients of proper English:

> ✓ **Parts of speech:** Words are like people. Both base a portion of their identity on the work they do. Words that name people or things, for example, are *nouns.* English teachers call the identity of a word the *part of speech.* Understanding how to select the appropriate part of speech is an important aspect of grammar.

Did you go to grammar school?

In the Middle Ages, the word *grammar* meant education. The term applied to all sorts of learning, not just to rules of the language. This old definition lasted a long time. When I was a child, quite a few centuries after the Middle Ages ended, I attended *grammar school*. I did study English grammar during grades one through eight. I also had lessons in math, history, science, and many other subjects. Now, children enroll in *elementary* or *primary* school, not grammar school. Even so, the link between proper English usage and education remains strong.

- ✔ **Parts of a sentence:** Words seldom like to be alone. (This is another quality that words and people have in common.) When words join together, they form *sentences.* Complete sentences are essential in formal writing.

- ✔ **Mechanics:** Surprised? Usually, mechanics repair cars and other machines. In language, the term *mechanics* refers to the little things that help readers understand what you mean. Spelling and capitalization are included in mechanics. So is *punctuation,* the placement of periods, commas, question marks, and other symbols. Without proper mechanics, your writing suffers.

- ✔ **Word order:** In English, location partly determines meaning. *The dog bit John* is different from *John bit the dog.* In the first version, the dog is in trouble. In the second, John has a problem. You should know the rules that govern the placement of words.

- ✔ **Word choice:** Some words sound alike (*eye* and *I,* for example). Others are nearly twins (for instance, *affect* and *effect*). Selecting the wrong word can wreck your writing.

- ✔ **Word forms:** Today *I walk.* Yesterday *I walked.* The form of the word *walk* changes to reveal the time period of the action. Knowing the correct form is essential.

These are the main ingredients that cook up proper English.

Building Language, Block by Block: Parts of Speech

According to one survey, the English language includes more than one million words. All those words can be sorted into one of eight boxes: the *parts of speech.* Take a look at the Big Eight:

- ✔ Nouns
- ✔ Pronouns
- ✔ Verbs
- ✔ Adjectives
- ✔ Adverbs
- ✔ Prepositions
- ✔ Conjunctions
- ✔ Interjections

Not every box has the same number of words in it. The *interjection* container is light. The *noun* and *verb* containers are huge. The other boxes fall somewhere in between.

Just to give you an idea how these parts of speech look within a sentence, here are some examples. The parts of speech are underlined and labeled:

Nora likes algebra. (*Nora* and *algebra* are nouns.)

I told you the story already. (*I* and *you* are pronouns.)

The baby shook the rattle. (*Shook* is a verb.)

Great speeches require intense practice. (*Great* and *intense* are adjectives.)

Glen wrote his name carefully and correctly. (*Carefully* and *correctly* are adverbs.)

A play by that author received great reviews from the critics. (*By* and *from* are prepositions.)

Nora and Fred like opera, but Sal prefers jazz. (*And* and *but* are conjunctions.)

Wow, those tickets are cheap! (*Wow* is an interjection.)

You may ask, "Why should anyone bother labeling parts of speech?" Good question! Most of the time, you think about the meaning of a word, not its part of speech. Most of the time, your writing is correct. However, some important grammar rules depend upon knowing the difference between one part of speech and another. For example, an *adjective* is a word that describes people, places, or things. An *adverb* is also a description, but it cannot do an adjective's job.

Take a look at these examples. Pay close attention to the underlined words:

WRONG: Today the weather is beautifully.

WHY IT IS WRONG: *Beautifully* is not the proper part of speech for this spot in the sentence. *Beautifully* is an adverb. You need an adjective here.

RIGHT: Today the weather is <u>beautiful</u>.

WHY IT IS RIGHT: The adjective *beautiful* works well here.

WRONG: Bill and Tina <u>agenda</u> the next meeting.

WHY IT IS WRONG: *Agenda* is a noun. You need an action word (a verb).

RIGHT: Bill and Tina <u>wrote</u> the agenda for the next meeting.

WHY IT IS RIGHT: The verb *wrote* provides the action. *Agenda* correctly appears as a noun.

WRONG: The puppy lifted <u>it's</u> paw.

WHY IT IS WRONG: You need a pronoun in this spot. *It's* means "it is."

RIGHT: The puppy lifted <u>its</u> paw.

WHY IT IS RIGHT: *Its* is a pronoun.

WRONG: The rumor spread <u>threw</u> the class.

WHY IT IS WRONG: *Threw* is a verb. You should not have an action word here.

RIGHT: The rumor spread <u>through</u> the class.

WHY IT IS RIGHT: The verb is gone. In its place you have a preposition, a word that relates ideas. In this sentence, it relates *spread* and *class,* showing where the rumor *spread.*

In Part II, you find in-depth information on every part of speech. Well, every part of speech except for *interjections.* An *interjection* is a word that briefly comments on the rest of the sentence. *Ouch, wow,* and *oh* are interjections. I do not provide in-depth commentary on interjections. They have no depth! They simply add a little interest to your conversation.

 Every dictionary tells you the part of speech of the word, usually right in front of the definition. Some words may have several labels, because they change their identity in different sentences. For more information on how to understand every part of a dictionary definition, see Chapter 21.

Making Sentences

A judge sentences criminals to prison. There, criminals must follow many rules. You may feel that English sentences are prisons, too. So many rules apply to them! I am just kidding. English sentences are definitely *not* prisons.

They are structures to hold your thoughts. They help your reader pick apart one idea from another. Take a peek at this paragraph:

> going to the beach bad idea no pets allowed want take the dog he does not bite you know kind and friendly he is to the park instead

Oh, my! In that paragraph, all the ideas are jumbled together. It resembles a closet with no hangers. The clothes are impossible to find.

Take another look at the same paragraph, this time with proper sentences:

> Going to the beach is a bad idea. No pets are allowed. I want to take the dog. He does not bite. You know how kind and friendly he is. We should go to the park instead.

This one is easier to understand, isn't it? The extra words, capital letters, and punctuation are like hangers. They organize your thoughts into complete sentences. In doing so, they sort out ideas the way hangers sort out clothing.

Complete and proper sentences are not always necessary. When you speak with your friends, for instance, you may use half-sentences.

Read this conversation. Imagine that Joe and Barbara are speaking to or texting each other:

> Joe: Want to go to the beach?
>
> Barbara: Not without my dog.
>
> Joe: Okay, the park instead.

These comments work well because Joe and Barbara are not in a formal situation. To find out when formal English is necessary and when conversational English will do, turn to Chapter 2. For more about grammar and texting, see Chapter 18.

When you do want to create grammatically correct sentences, you must pay attention to several issues. The sections that follow briefly show you these issues.

Action or being words

Every sentence has at least one word that expresses action or being. That word is a *verb*. In these sentences, the verbs are underlined:

> Candice <u>loves</u> her engagement ring. (*loves* = action word)
>
> Duke <u>ate</u> every dog biscuit in the box. (*ate* = action word)

She <u>will be</u> pleased with your work. (*will be* = being words)

<u>Were</u> the lights on? (*Were* = being word)

Selecting the right verb form is important. Glance at these examples. Notice the underlined verbs:

WRONG: You <u>was</u> wrong.

WHY IT IS WRONG: The verb form *was* does not pair properly with *you*.

RIGHT: You <u>were</u> wrong.

WHY IT IS RIGHT: *Were* is the verb form that matches *you*. (To learn more about this topic, see Chapter 9.)

WRONG: The mayor <u>speaked</u> to voters yesterday.

WHY IT IS WRONG: *Speaked* is not correct in Standard English.

RIGHT: The mayor <u>spoke</u> to voters yesterday.

WHY IT IS RIGHT: *Spoke* is the irregular verb form you need in this sentence. (For more information about irregular verb forms, see Chapter 10.)

WRONG: John <u>studying</u> for his exam.

WHY IT IS WRONG: The verb form *studying* is not complete.

RIGHT: John <u>is studying</u> for his exam.

WHY IT IS RIGHT: Now the verb is complete. (See Chapter 9 for more about these verb forms.)

As you see, you can make many mistakes with action and being words. Verbs are complicated! Do not panic. The chapters I mention in the preceding examples explain the rules you must follow.

Subjects

In a sentence, someone or something does the action or exists in the state of being. That word is the *subject*. Notice the underlined subjects in these example sentences:

<u>Cindy</u> arrived at ten o'clock. (*Cindy* = subject)

<u>We</u> had sandwiches for lunch. (*We* = subject)

The <u>sandwiches</u> were delicious. (*sandwiches* = subject)

Do <u>you</u> like peanut butter? (*you* = subject)

<u>It</u> is smooth and sticky. (*It* = subject)

<u>Jelly</u> and <u>jam</u> go well with peanut butter. (*Jelly* and *jam* = subjects)

Most times, you know who or what you want to write about. The subject, in other words, is usually easy to select. When the subject is a pronoun, errors often occur. Examine these examples. The underlined words are important:

WRONG: <u>Him</u> and John failed the Latin test.

WHY IT IS WRONG: *Him* cannot be a subject.

RIGHT: <u>He</u> and John failed the Latin test.

WHY IT IS RIGHT: *He* is a proper subject.

WRONG: Are <u>youse</u> ready?

WHY IT IS WRONG: *Youse* is not the plural of *you.* <u>*Youse*</u> is not a Standard English form.

RIGHT: Are <u>you</u> ready?

WHY IT IS RIGHT: *You* is Standard English. *You* is both singular (one) and plural (more than one).

WRONG: <u>Us</u> friends should stick together.

WHY IT IS WRONG: <u>Us</u> is not a proper subject.

RIGHT: <u>We</u> friends should stick together.

WHY IT IS RIGHT: *We* is a proper subject.

Chapter 4 explains which pronouns work as subjects.

Pairing subjects with verbs can also cause trouble. Check these examples. Pay attention to the underlined words:

WRONG: Mr. Smith and Ms. Jones <u>has been promoted</u>.

WHY IT IS WRONG: *Has been promoted* pairs up with one person. In this sentence, you have two people, *Mr. Smith and Ms. Jones.*

RIGHT: Mr. Smith and Ms. Jones <u>have been promoted</u>.

WHY IT IS RIGHT: The verb *have been promoted* matches well with *Mr. Smith and Ms. Jones.* Both are plural (more than one).

WRONG: The list of grammar rules <u>are</u> too long.

WHY IT IS WRONG: The subject of the sentence is *list,* a singular word. It cannot pair with *are,* a plural verb form. Did you focus on *rules? Rules* is not the subject of this sentence. It is part of a description, *of grammar rules.*

RIGHT: The list of grammar rules <u>is</u> too long.

WHY IT IS RIGHT: The singular verb form, *is,* pairs correctly with the singular subject, *list.*

To find out more about matching singular subjects to singular verb forms and plural subjects to plural verb forms, check out Chapter 11.

Complements and descriptions

Your thoughts are rich and varied. You want to say more than "Mary is" or "I run." Some elements, called *complements,* complete ideas. Take a peek at these example sentences. The complements are underlined:

Mary is <u>happy</u>.

Deborah mailed the <u>letter</u>.

Cathy and Drew are always <u>nervous</u> in the dentist's office.

Give <u>Jean</u> her <u>pizza</u>.

Did you tell <u>Barbara</u> the <u>secret</u>?

Usually, complements fall into place correctly. Pronouns can cause problems when they act as complements. (Have you noticed that pronouns are trouble-makers?) For more information on complements, check out Chapter 12. To sort out pronouns, see Chapter 4.

Your writing would be very boring without descriptions. Notice the underlined descriptions in these examples:

<u>Every morning</u> I run <u>through the park</u>.

<u>Pink</u> paint covered the <u>bumpy</u> wall.

<u>Silk</u> thread is <u>more expensive</u> than <u>cotton</u> thread.

Wind <u>in that area</u> blows the <u>fallen</u> leaves <u>away</u>.

The book <u>of speeches</u> helped me prepare <u>for graduation</u>.

<u>Singing</u>, the choir entered the church.

As you see, descriptions come in many shapes and sizes. Chapter 6 explains what type of description is best for every situation.

Small but Important: Punctuating, Capitalizing, and Spelling

Punctuation marks, capital letters, and spelling may seem unimportant. Do not overlook these little things, though. They add more to your writing than you may expect. Take punctuation, for example. Some years ago, senators in a state government debated the placement of a comma for several hours. With the comma, the law had one meaning. Without it, the law was completely different! This section gives you an overview of punctuation, capitalization, and spelling.

Punctuation

I once saw a television show in which something similar to this conversation took place:

> Angel (waving a thick stack of paper): I am writing a book.
>
> Angel's friend (looking at the first page): What is this? I cannot read it. There is no punctuation.
>
> Angel: Oh, I will worry about that stuff later.
>
> Angel's friend: I do not think so! You need punctuation now!

Angel's friend is right. You cannot read without punctuation, the little marks that show the reader where to pause, when someone is speaking, and so on. These are the basic punctuation marks that you should know:

✔ **Apostrophe:** This is a little curved hook above the line. An apostrophe, along with the letter _s,_ shows possession:

  - Elle<u>n's</u> car (Ellen owns the car.)
  - the boy<u>s'</u> locker room (The locker room belongs to the boys.)
  - my cous<u>in's</u> shoes (My cousin owns the shoes.)
  - the Vice Presi<u>dent's</u> staff (The staff belongs to the Vice President.)
  - state<u>s'</u> rights (The rights belong to the states.)

Apostrophes also shorten words:

  - Annie doe<u>sn't</u> ice skate. (Here, _doesn't_ is short for _does not_)
  - <u>I'm</u> excited that vacation is finally here. (_I'm_ is short for _I am._)
  - Olivia coul<u>dn't</u> go on the roller coaster. (In this sentence, _couldn't_ is short for _could not._)
  - Is<u>n't</u> that lemonade too cold? (_Isn't_ is short for _is not._)

To learn more about apostrophes, turn to Chapter 14.

✔ **Period, question mark, exclamation point:** These three punctuation marks signal the end of a sentence. A _period_ is a little dot. It follows a sentence that makes a statement. A _question mark_ is made from a curve and a dot. It follows a sentence that asks a question. An _exclamation point_ is a vertical line and a dot. It shows emphasis — the punctuation mark that shouts. Look at these punctuation marks in action:

- Mary's socks are blue. (The period ends the statement.)

- Are Tim's shoes blue also? (The question mark ends the question.)

- No, they are not! (The exclamation point adds emphasis.)

To learn more about these three important punctuation marks, see Chapter 13.

✔ **Comma:** This little curved hook starts on the line and reaches below. A comma tells the reader to pause. Notice the commas in these sentences:

- Katie, my friend, is visiting from Chicago.

- Katie arrived yesterday, but she has to leave tomorrow.

- Chicago, which is in the state of Illinois, is a large city.

- Tim, have you ever visited Chicago?

If you read these sentences aloud, you can hear the short silences that appear at each comma. If commas trouble you, check out Chapter 15.

✔ **Quotation marks:** Quotation marks are pairs of curved marks that appear above the line. Their most common job is to mark off the exact words that someone said or wrote. Notice the quotation marks in these examples:

- "Be quiet," said the librarian.

- The children cried, "We were not very loud."

- "In the library," replied the librarian, "any noise is too loud."

To use quotation marks properly, you must follow many rules. Turn to Chapter 16 for everything you need to know about quotation marks.

Capitalization

Have you ever seen a very old piece of writing? Capital letters show up in strange places. The Declaration of Independence is more than 200 years old. In the middle of one sentence, you see a famous phrase:

the pursuit of Happiness

These days, *happiness* would appear in lowercase (noncapitals). The Founders of the country could place a capital wherever they wanted. You do not have the same freedom. You must follow the rules. Glance at these situations, which require capital letters:

✔ **Speaker or writer:** The pronoun *I* always refers to the person who is writing. It is always capitalized. Check these examples:

- When I am asleep, I do not snore.

- Gene and I love to sail on the lake.

- Do I have to pay extra for my suitcase?

By the way, poets sometimes place the pronoun *I* in lowercase. Poets break rules whenever they wish. Outside of a poem, however, use a capital letter for *I*.

✔ **First word in a sentence:** A capital letter begins every sentence. The letter serves as a signal that one sentence has ended and another has begun. Read these examples:

- Nana sings to the baby. She has a terrible voice! The baby does not mind. He loves her anyway.

- Palm trees grow in my yard. Warm weather suits them. Rain storms water the trees. They require little care.

Are you curious about numbers? You cannot capitalize *22* or *15* or any numeral. So what happens when a number appears at the beginning of a sentence? Good question! The answer is that you should not begin a sentence with a numeral. If you need a number there, use the word:

- WRONG: 22 people live in that building.

- RIGHT: Twenty-two people live in that building.

✔ **Names:** I am *Geraldine Woods,* not *geraldine woods.* Nearly all names require capital letters. (Some companies choose lowercase letters for products. The *iPad* is an example of a name that does not begin with a capital letter.)

Of course, these are not the only rules that govern capital letters. Turn to Chapter 17 for more information.

Spelling

In silly television shows, *spell* is a magic word. In grammar, *spell* is also a magic word. Spelling — placing every letter in the right spot — is important. Take a close look at the following paragraph. Can you identify five misspelled words?

Jenny enjoys sewing. She pushs the needle into the cloth with her thum. Tina, who is makeing a new skirt, offen chats with Jenny wen they sew.

Before you check your answers, think for a moment. The preceding paragraph contains proper sentences. It clearly states the facts. Yet it is not a good piece of writing. The misspelled words turn a good paragraph into a bad one. Here are the correctly spelled words: *pushes, thumb, making, often, when.*

In Chapter 21, you find some rules for English spelling. Unfortunately, many, many English words do not follow those rules. To check your spelling, you may need help from the dictionary. Chapter 21 also explains how to understand and use the dictionary.

Many words sound the same but have different spelling and meaning. Other words are nearly alike in appearance or sound, but their definitions are not alike. Check Chapter 22 for help with these confusing words.

Facing Everyday Writing Tasks

Do you spend a lot of time sitting at a desk? If you do, you probably face writing tasks such as these:

- ✔ **School assignments:** You write an essay on an exam or for homework. You answer questions basked on a reading assignment. Perhaps you have to write a book review or a lab report. Your teacher may ask for a research paper or a short story. All these writing jobs call for good grammar. All follow patterns that are easy to learn. Knowing proper English and formatting will raise your grades.

- ✔ **Work-related writing:** You send a memo to your co-workers or to your supervisor. The boss wants a report or a presentation. Perhaps it is your responsibility to answer emails or letters from customers. In the business world, good writing is expected — and often rewarded. Grammar rules apply to every writing task in the working world. Knowing the best format for each type of writing is also important.

- ✔ **Personal writing:** Outside of school and work, you may write a note to a friend. Perhaps you must send a letter to a landlord or a government official. You probably email or text friends and family members. In many situations, informal language and nonstandard grammar are fine. In others, you need your best writing skills.

When you face an everyday writing task, you should understand the rules and traditions that apply to it. Chapters 18, 19, and 20 tell you everything you need to complete your writing work easily and effectively. Explanations of the newer forms of communication — texts and slide presentations, for example — appear in these chapters also.

Sometimes it is fine to bend the rules of grammar and to use informal language. For example, would you send this text to a friend?

Would you accompany me to the cafeteria at your earliest convenience?

Or, is this your reply when your friend asks, "Who's there?"

It is I.

If you answered "yes," you probably eat alone and receive very few phone calls. With friends, proper grammar may turn a fun social occasion into something more formal. To find out more about when proper English is required and when you should relax the rules, see Chapter 2.

Mom and Dad

Because the ancient Romans once ruled a huge empire, babies are born in *maternity* wards. For the same reason, fathers may take a *paternity* test to prove that they are, indeed, fathers. These words come from Latin, the language of ancient Rome. *Mater* and *matr* are word parts associated with motherhood. *Pater* and *patri* are word parts associated with fatherhood. Here are some members of this word family:

Maternity means "motherhood." "Pregnant women go to the <u>maternity</u> ward."

A **matriarch** is the "female head of a family." "The aunts and uncles often went to Great Grandmother, the <u>matriarch</u>, for advice."

Maternal means "motherly, relating to the mother." "Her <u>maternal</u> feelings grew as she held her new baby."

A **matron** is "a married woman, a woman in charge of children." "The children in the audience were afraid of the <u>matron</u>, who watched them carefully."

Paternity means "fatherhood." "The <u>paternity</u> test showed that he was the baby's father."

A **patriarch** is the "male head of a family." "Every Sunday, they had dinner with Oliver, the <u>patriarch</u> of their family."

Paternal means "fatherly, relating to the father." "Her <u>paternal</u> grandfather was ill, so she immediately flew to Florida, where her father's family lived."

Keep your eye out for "mom and dad" words as you read. Add any you find to your personal vocabulary list.

Chapter 2

Language in Action

• •

In This Chapter

▶ Choosing the correct level of formality

▶ Using computer programs and smartphone apps to improve your writing

▶ Identifying your grammar strengths and weaknesses

• •

*E*nglish, like every language, has plenty of rules. In some situations, you must follow all the rules. In other situations, you can break a few rules. Yes, I am a grammarian. Even so, I believe that *some* rules are meant to be broken in *some* situations.

In this chapter, I explain when proper English is necessary and when it is not. I also explain how to use computer and smartphone programs to improve your command of English. Finally, in this chapter you find a checklist, so you can make a personal grammar improvement plan.

Adjusting Language to Suit Your Audience

Sometimes people speak of good and bad English. I stay away from those terms. I do not like them, because I do not believe that they are accurate. I prefer the label *Standard English* for speech and writing that follows every rule. Any other level of English breaks some rules.

You may wonder what other levels of English exist. You may also worry about learning them. You have no reason to be concerned, though. You already speak and write. You already know the language on some level.

For convenience, I sort English into three levels of formality. Take a look at this message, sent three different ways:

> Gotta go. Wanna come?
>
> I have to go. Do you feel like coming with me?
>
> I must leave. Would you like to accompany me?

These examples climb the stairs of language. Each step is a bit more formal. The first statement, the basement of English, is the sort of language people use when they are chatting with friends. I call this level *friendspeak.* (This is not an official term. I made it up.) The second level is also friendly, but the sentences follow more rules that those in the first. I call this level *conversational English.* The third example is grammatically correct. The language hits the highest level of formality. This level is *Standard English.* The name, which many English teachers use, comes from the fact that a standard is a rule. Standard English obeys every rule. In this section, you examine each level of language.

You may not yet know every rule of Standard English. Therefore, it may be hard at first for you to see the difference between one level of English and another. Do not worry. As you work your way through *Basic English Grammar For Dummies,* the rules will become clear.

Friendspeak

When you relax, you probably change your clothes. You take off your school or business outfit. You put on comfortable clothing. Sweats and an old t-shirt signal that you have no obligations. You can do whatever you like. You are in charge. Language works the same way. *Friendspeak,* my term for the language you use when you are off duty, shows that it is time for fun.

Friendspeak works well when the power level is balanced. The people you are talking with or writing to are your peers. Look at these two conversations. Both actually took place in my classroom:

> STUDENT to TEACHER: He and I went to the gym. He did 60 push-ups. I can't do as many push-ups as he can.
>
> TEACHER to STUDENT: He exercises regularly. That's why he is strong.
>
> SAME STUDENT to ANOTHER STUDENT: Me and him went to the gym. He did 60 push-ups, and I'm like, no way.
>
> OTHER STUDENT: Dude, he like, lives in the gym.

These two conversations say the same thing, but not in the same way. In speaking with a teacher, the student knows that he should follow the rules. The teacher also follows grammar rules. Why? The teacher–student relationship is a formal one. In the second conversation, breaking the rules is the point. The original speaker shows that he and the other student have nothing to prove to each other. They are comfortable with each other's mistakes. In fact, they make mistakes on purpose, to show that they have a personal, friendly relationship.

Excellent grammar usually gives you an advantage in life. When you speak with friends, though, perfectly proper sentences may sound snobby. For this reason, more casual language (either *friendspeak* or *conversational English,* which I cover in the next section) is sometimes more suitable than Standard English.

I do not deal with *friendspeak* in this book. Chances are, you already know it. This level of language is fine in these situations:

- ✔ Talking with friends
- ✔ Chatting with close family members, especially those who are the same age
- ✔ Writing to friends in emails and texts

Many people use this level of English for posts on social media. This practice sounds harmless. After all, you are writing to people who, on that website, are your friends. Be careful! Employers and school officials sometimes check social media when they are considering your application for a job or for admission to a school. True, they understand that you are not aiming for perfect grammar when you post. However, if you come across as offensive or ignorant, you may hurt your chances for acceptance.

Employ *friendspeak* only when you are sure that the people you are addressing are comfortable with this type of language.

Conversational English

One step higher on the ladder of correct language is *conversational English.* Instead of sweats and t-shirts, think of conversational English as well-fitting jeans and a reasonably nice shirt. The language is comfortable, but not as messy as *friendspeak.* Conversational English is the language just about everyone uses for — surprise! — conversations. In this level of language, the people speaking probably know each other. They relax, but not completely.

I use conversational English in this book. As I write, I imagine that I am speaking with you, the reader. I pretend that I know you and that we are spending some free time together. I do not see myself as a teacher in a formal classroom situation.

Conversational English is suitable for these situations:

- ✔ Chats with friends and family
- ✔ Conversations with neighbors and other acquaintances
- ✔ Notes, emails, instant messages, letters, and texts to friends and family
- ✔ Comments posted on social media
- ✔ Informal conversations with teachers
- ✔ Remarks to co-workers

The last two items on this list are tricky. In a school or business situation, you can be friendly, but not too friendly. Suppose a teacher is in the middle of a lesson. In this situation, do not employ conversational English. Questions and remarks during class are best phrased in Standard English. If you are chatting with a teacher after class, though, you do not need formal language. At work, conversational English is fine for lunch and coffee breaks. During meetings at work, you should be more careful to follow the rules of grammar.

At work or at school, check the level of language before you speak. How formal are others' remarks? Listen, and adapt your own language to match the group's preferred style.

Standard English

Standard English is similar to the clothing you select when you want to look your best. Imagine a business suit or an outfit you would wear to a dinner party. When you employ Standard English, your readers or listeners grasp that you know the rules of grammar. You demonstrate that you have a strong vocabulary.

You should speak and write in Standard English when you are addressing someone who has more power and authority than you do. This level of English adds dignity to every interaction. It signals that you are taking things seriously and putting forth your best effort. Use Standard English for these situations:

- ✔ Business letters
- ✔ Emails to clients or colleagues

✔ Letters to the editor or to government officials

✔ Written reports (on paper or on websites)

✔ Memos

✔ Homework assignments

✔ Notes or emails to teachers

✔ Speeches, presentations, and oral reports

✔ Important conversations (job interviews, admissions interviews, and the like)

In any situation in which you are being judged, begin with Standard English. You can always ease up if you discover that your reader or listener prefers a different, less formal style.

In the preceding section, perhaps add "or emails." Many students today communicate with their teachers via email. (Mine do all the time, and most of the time their grammar is atrocious!)

You have to know the rules of Standard English before you decide that it is okay to break them. As you read *Basic English Grammar For Dummies,* keep track of the rules. Practice, so you can be perfect when the need arises.

Check whether you understand the right level of English for every situation. In the first column is a remark. The second column identifies the audience for the remark. Fill in the third column.

Remark	*Listener or Reader*	*Suitable? Not Suitable?*
1. Wanna explain that again?	math professor	
2. I did not answer the customer yet.	supervisor at work	
3. A little help, please!	your cousin	
4. He's gotta ton of work now.	customer	
5. Profits and losses should be posted today.	co-worker	

Here are the answers: 1. not suitable 2. suitable 3. suitable 4. not suitable 5. suitable.

Getting Help from Spelling and Grammar Checkers

Do you type on a computer or a smartphone? If so, you write with a *word processing program.* This sort of program allows you to type, delete, and insert words. It also checks spelling and grammar. When you are typing, you probably see a wavy red line or another signal when you spell a word incorrectly. If you make a grammar mistake, a green line or something else pops up.

Spelling and grammar checkers can be helpful. If I type *teh* instead of *the,* I may not notice the error. The computer's alert helps me see the mistake. Then I can type *the* correctly.

However, these checkers carry risks. Here are some of them:

- Spelling checkers are loaded with lists of properly spelled English words. Not every word is on the list. If you try to correct every error that the program flags, you may make unnecessary changes. Check the dictionary if you think a word identified as wrong is actually correct.

- You can add words to the program's dictionary. For example, every time I type *smartphone,* the computer underlines it. If I type *smart phone,* the computer accepts my spelling. However, *smartphone* is now the accepted term for phones that act as mini-computers. To avoid the red line, I have to add *smartphone* to the program's list of acceptable words.

  Check the help function of the program you use for word processing. Follow the directions to add words to the program's dictionary.

- Spelling programs cannot tell the difference between words that sound alike, such as *hole* and *whole.* If you write *hymn* (a religious song) instead of *him* (a word referring to a male), the computer accepts the mistake. (For help with these word pairs and other words often used incorrectly, see Chapter 22.)

- Many computer programs have an *autocorrect* function. The computer sees *aslo* and turns it into *also* automatically. Autocorrect is great — when it is right. When it is wrong, you end up with a message you never intended. For example, once autocorrect changed *I don't* into *Idiot.* The person who received the text was not happy to be addressed as an idiot! You can usually turn off autocorrect on your phone or computer. If you leave it on, check everything. Correct the corrections if you see a mistake!

- Most spelling and grammar programs have language and country settings. If you have the wrong setting, the program will find many errors that do not exist; it will not detect many actual mistakes. Be sure to select the right language and country before you begin to write.

- Grammar checkers detect some mistakes, but they do not catch everything. For example, if I type

> He do the work.

the computer accepts the sentence. The proper sentence is

> He does the work.

Computers are not as smart as people. Use your own knowledge of grammar to write properly.

The dictionary is the final authority when it comes to spelling. However, it is hard to look up a word if you don't know how to spell it. Here is where computer programs can help. If you have the right app (program) on your phone or tablet, you can say the word, which then pops up on the screen. Before you accept the spelling, take a look at the definition. Be sure the definition matches your intended meaning.

No program is perfect. Check spelling with a dictionary. Proofread your work to catch and fix grammar errors.

How sick is your grammar?

No, I am not talking about a sore throat. I am not checking whether you have to visit the doctor. Instead, I am using a slang word. *Sick,* which usually means not healthy, means awesome or fun in slang. *Slang* is language that a group uses to talk with each other. In fact, the group creates slang. Few outside the group understand it. That quality is the whole purpose of slang. When you make up words, you unite the group. You push others away because they do not know what you are saying. Once a slang word becomes widely known, it loses its purpose. The old word drops away, and a new slang term takes its place.

Because slang changes quickly, you must be very careful in using it. Remember, people outside the group will not understand you. Inside the group, you have to keep up. Slang that works today may be outdated by tomorrow. You will not sound cool (an older slang word). You will sound old-fashioned.

Needless to say (though I am going to say it anyway!), slang is not the right choice when you are speaking to anyone in authority. Keep slang out of business and school settings. It is for fun events only.

Recognizing Your Grammar Profile

No one else in the universe is exactly like you. Even your identical twin, if you have one, differs from you in some way. Your biology and experiences are unique. So is your grammar profile. Some parts of grammar you know very well. Other aspects of grammar may puzzle you. When you are writing a sentence with many descriptions, for example, you may wonder where to place them. Perhaps pronouns are your personal devils. Your strengths and weaknesses form your grammar profile.

Table 2-1 is a checklist of common grammar problems. These problems may stump you when you are writing. Next to each problem is a chapter number. If you say, "I know that already," consider skipping that chapter. If you say, "I need help with this one," you probably need to read the chapter listed in the "Help Needed?" column. Once you have filled out the checklist, you have a road map through *Basic English Grammar For Dummies* and a clear route to a better command of the English language.

Table 2-1	Checklist of Common Grammar Problems	
Problem	*Chapter(s) Covering This Topic*	*Help Needed?*
The *amazon river* or the *Amazon River?*	3 and 17	
One monkey and two *monkies? monkeys?*	3	
That boxes or *those* boxes?	3	
You *was?* You *were?*	4	
John and *I* went? John and *myself* went?	4	
Should you go over *their* or *there?*	4	
It's snowing? *Its* snowing?	4	
He told *me?* He told *I?*	4	
the book about *I?* the book about *me?*	4	
Yesterday he *walk?* Yesterday he *walked?*	5	
I *is?* I *am?*	5	
they *jumps?* they *jump?*	5	
we *does?* we *do?*	5	
Will you *had?* Will you *have?*	5	
May be nearby? *Might* be nearby?	5	
Real good? *Really* good?	6	
Henry feels *bad?* Henry feels *badly?*	6	

Problem	Chapter(s) Covering This Topic	Help Needed?
An apple? *A* apple?	6	
easier? more easier?	6	
less difficult? least difficult?	6	
since Tuesday? *after* Tuesday?	7	
between you and *I?* between you and *me?*	7	
both strict *but* kind? both strict *and* kind?	8	
John sang, I danced? John sang, and I danced?	8	
It snowed, *however,* I went anyway. Correct? Incorrect?	8	
Cuting? Cutting?	9	
John *slips?* John *is slipping?*	9	
Had been asked? *Has* been asked?	10	
Had *gone?* Had *went?*	10	
Have *did?* Have *done?*	10	
She *gone?* She *has gone?*	10	
River *flow?* River *flows?*	11	
pen and pencil *was?* pen and pencil *were?*	11	
stick or stone *is?* stick or stone *are?*	11	
Everyone *are?* Everyone *is?*	11	
Here *are* three books? Here *is* three books?	11	
some of the pie *was?* some of the pie *were?*	11	
any of the nails *is?* any of the nails *are?*	11	
It is *I?* It is *me?*	12	
Call Roger and *he?* Call Roger and *him?*	12	
John is. Complete sentence? Incomplete sentence?	13	
the *childrens'* clothing? the *children's* clothing?	14	
I *dont* know? I *don't* know?	14	
boys, *girls, and* parents? boys, *girls and* parents?	15	
No I will not? *No, I* will not?	15	
Go *home, Bob?* Go *home Bob?*	15	

(continued)

Table 2-1 *(continued)*

Problem	Chapter(s) Covering This Topic	Help Needed?
Sally said, *I love that movie.* Sally said, "*I love that movie.*"	16	
Director of Security? director of security?	17	
mts.? Mts?	17	
Text *LOL?* Text *I am joking?*	18	
The problem *is:* Correct punctuation? Incorrect?	19	
Sincerely Yours? Sincerely yours?	20	
recieve? receive?	21	
Affect your mood? *Effect* your mood?	22	
Sometimes? Some times?	22	
The reason is *because?* The reason is *that?*	22	
Bought *only* one shirt? *Only* bought one shirt?	23	
Sealing the envelope, the letter . . . Correct? Incorrect?	23	
Can't hardly? Can hardly?	23	
Can't help *but think?* Can't help *thinking?*	23	
Didn't do *nothing?* Didn't do *anything?*	23	

C U L8TR: Texting

Does this heading confuse you? It is a text I received. The message, translated into words, is *see you later.* Texting is awkward. The screen is tiny, and the letters are even smaller. Probably because typing on a phone is uncomfortable, people often take shortcuts when they text. The abbreviations in the heading are an example of a shortcut.

I understand the need for speed. I live in New York City, where everything moves along quickly! However, texting abbreviations are risky. Often, the person receiving the message does not understand that *g2g* means *got to go* and *imho* is short for *in my humble opinion.*

Also, these abbreviations may give the impression that you do not know proper English. When you send a text, pause before you hit Send. Think about the person you are communicating with. Then decide how formal you should be. (For more information on grammar and electronic media, turn to Chapter 18.)

Part II
The Parts of Speech

Building blocks of language

You cannot build a sentence without the basic elements of language, what English teachers call the *parts of speech*. In this part, you meet all eight:

✔ **Nouns and pronouns:** To name people, places, things, and ideas, you need nouns, which I explain in Chapter 3. Chapter 4 addresses *pronouns,* words that replace nouns (*he, she, us,* and so forth).

✔ **Verbs:** Life is often filled with action, and action is expressed by a verb. Life sometimes simply *is.* Words that express states of being are also verbs. To discover everything you need to know about verbs, see Chapter 5.

✔ **Adjectives and adverbs:** Life — and language — would be very boring without descriptions. Chapter 6 shows you two types of descriptive words, *adjectives* and *adverbs,* and explains when each is correct.

✔ **Prepositions:** This part of speech creates a relationship between one idea and another. With *before, during, of, by,* and other prepositions, you show all kinds of relationships. Chapter 7 discusses prepositions in the context of your sentences and shows you how to locate them properly so that they say what you intend.

✔ **Conjunctions and interjections:** *Conjunctions* unite, and *interjections* inject emotion or commentary into your sentences. Turn to Chapter 8 for information on *and, because, but, although,* and other conjunctions, as well as information on interjections.

For a bonus article on Parts of Speech, go online and take a look at
www.dummies.com/extras/basicenglishgrammar.

In this part . . .

✔ Place nouns and pronouns where they belong in your sentences.

✔ Discover how to indicate past, present, and future time with verbs.

✔ Learn how to insert descriptions and create comparisons.

✔ Add meaning with prepositions and interjections.

✔ Find out how conjunctions link ideas.

Chapter 3

People to See, Places to Go, Things to Remember: Recognizing Nouns

....

In This Chapter

▶ Spotting nouns

▶ Forming plurals

▶ Using *this, that, these,* and *those* with nouns

....

Watch very young children learning to speak. Their first words are usually the names of important people, places, or things: *Mama, Dada, home,* or *toy.* I imagine that language started in the same way. Our ancient relatives probably talked about what mattered to them — *cave, fire,* or *bear,* and, of course, *Mama* and *Dada.* Parents are always important people.

In this chapter, you learn about the first part of speech that young children use — nouns. You identify nouns and sort out those that name one (singular nouns) from those that name more than one (plural nouns). You also see how to attach other words — *that, this, those,* and *these* — to nouns.

Identifying Nouns

Important people, places, and things need names. The part of speech that names them is a *noun.*

Before you do anything with nouns — change them from singular to plural or the other way around, capitalize them, or place them in sentences — you have to find them. In this section, you search for nouns when they name people, places, things or events, and ideas or emotions. Happy hunting!

Naming people with nouns

Who are you? You are, right now, a <u>reader</u>. You are also some of these: a <u>man</u>, a <u>woman</u>, a <u>student</u>, or a <u>worker</u>. You may be a <u>mother</u> or <u>father</u>, a <u>son</u> or <u>daughter</u>, a <u>cousin</u>, and a <u>grandparent</u> or a <u>grandchild</u>. Perhaps you are a famous <u>actor</u>. (If you are famous, please autograph something for me. I can make a lot of money selling autographs. Thank you!)

Every underlined word in the paragraph above is a general term for a person. Those words are *nouns*. Here are some other nouns for people:

> singer
>
> writer
>
> New Yorker
>
> lawyer
>
> neighbor

Can you guess which nouns apply to me? I can't sing, and I know nothing about the law. I do write, and I live in a crowded building in New York. I can use <u>writer</u>, <u>New Yorker</u>, and <u>neighbor</u> to talk about myself. All these nouns refer to me, a <u>person</u>. (The word *person,* by the way, is also a noun.)

Of course, I can also use my name to talk about myself. I'm <u>Geraldine Woods</u>. My friends call me <u>Gerri</u>. (People who don't like me have names for me, too. I will not print those names here!) All names are nouns, including these:

> Barack Obama
>
> Queen Elizabeth I
>
> Peter Popper
>
> Mary Watson
>
> Spider-Man

Do I have to tell you that nothing on the list applies to me? I am sorry to disappoint you, but I am not a queen (like Elizabeth I), a president (like Barack Obama), or a superhero (like Spider-Man).

 Did you notice that the names in the preceding list begin with capital letters? Specific names *(John Smith)* are capitalized. General names *(customer)* are not capitalized. To find out more about when a name should be capitalized, turn to Chapter 17.

See whether you can identify the nouns in the following paragraph:

> Jenny is a plumber. She told William that her last customer, Arthur Smith, was cheap. He wanted to pay her less than Gene Muller did, and Gene is a poor man.

You should have found eight nouns: *Jenny, plumber, William, customer, Arthur Smith, Gene Muller, Gene, man.* All these words name people, so all are nouns.

Both general and specific names for people are nouns.

Naming places with nouns

Where are you? I am in my bedroom, in the corner that I use as an office, in an apartment in Manhattan in New York State in the United States of America. Recently I visited London and Madrid after retiring from my school, which is located in another area of the city.

The underlined words in the preceding paragraph are places. Words that name places, even when they are general terms, are nouns. Here are several more:

river

mountain

continent

theater

street

Names of specific places are also nouns:

Amazon River

Antarctica

Greenwich Village

Sierra Nevada

Jupiter

The places that nouns name can be very large (the *universe*) or very small (my *closet*). Size doesn't matter. (Well, size doesn't matter in grammar! You decide whether it matters in other areas.)

Capital letters do matter. The name of a specific place is capitalized *(Atlantic Ocean)*. General names of places are not *(island)*. For more information about capitalizing the names of places, see Chapter 17.

See whether you can identify the nouns in the following paragraph:

> In Canada, which is a large country in North America, he often visits Montreal, a beautiful city on the Saint Lawrence River, near Mont Tremblant, a great place to ski.

You should have identified eight nouns: *Canada, country, North America, Montreal, city, Saint Lawrence River, Mont Tremblant, place.* All these words name places (including the word *place* itself), so all are nouns.

Naming things with nouns

As I look through my <u>window</u>, I see many <u>things</u>: <u>buildings</u>, <u>cars</u>, an occasional <u>bus</u>, and <u>construction</u> on the <u>terrace</u> nearby, where someone has planted a tiny <u>garden</u> — three <u>bushes</u> with pink <u>flowers</u>.

Yes, even in the middle of New York City, you can find a garden! A garden is a thing, and so are all the underlined words in the preceding paragraph. Words that name things are nouns.

When I say "thing," I don't mean only things that you can buy in a store and put on a shelf. You probably noticed that one of the underlined nouns *(construction)* is an activity. Nouns can name activities as well as objects. Here are other nouns that name things:

> tables
>
> mustard
>
> marriage
>
> chat
>
> conferences

The names of events are also nouns:

> vacation
>
> New Year's Eve
>
> birthdays
>
> World War II
>
> exams

As you see, nouns may name events in general terms *(birthdays).* Other nouns name specific events *(New Year's Eve, World War II).*

The name of a specific event is usually capitalized *(Great Depression)*. General names for events are normally written without capital letters *(anniversary)*. The name of an object may be capitalized if it is a brand *(Cadillac)* unless the company decides not to use a capital letter *(iPad)*. To find out more about when you should capitalize the name of an event or object, see Chapter 17.

See whether you can find the nouns in the following paragraph:

> Nearly everyone who enjoys crafts buys glue, crayons, and cloth to make decorations for holidays and other celebrations, such as Halloween and Thanksgiving.

You should have found nine nouns: *crafts, glue, crayons, cloth, decorations, holidays, celebrations, Halloween, Thanksgiving.* All these words name things, so all are nouns.

The names of things, activities, and events are nouns.

Naming ideas and emotions with nouns

I feel <u>loyalty</u> to those I love and <u>gratitude</u> to everyone who has ever helped me. I believe that <u>love</u> and <u>friendship</u> are always better than <u>hatred</u> and <u>rejection</u>. Do you agree with these <u>thoughts</u>, or is your <u>opinion</u> different?

Ideas and emotions are real and extremely powerful, even though you can't touch them. The names for ideas and emotions are nouns. All the underlined words in the preceding paragraph are nouns. Take a look at more nouns that name ideas and emotions:

    confusion

    patriotism

    viewpoint

    joy

    anger

The names of belief systems, such as a religion *(Catholicism,* for example), are nouns. The names of causes, such as *environmentalism,* which means concern for the environment, are also nouns.

Sometimes you need a capital letter for a particular system of belief *(Islam* or *Judaism,* for example), and sometimes you do not *(democracy,* for instance). For more information on capitalizing the names of ideas or beliefs, turn to Chapter 17.

See whether you can find the nouns in the following sentence:

He was filled with happiness when she explained her thoughts on freedom, because he also worked to bring about justice and equality in society.

The noun connection

Four letters — *tion* — often appear at the end of nouns. In fact, these letters have the power to change words that tell what you do (which grammarians call verbs) into nouns. Take a look at these pairs. In each pair, the first word is a verb. The second word in each pair is a noun:

- ✔ **connect – connection** George and his partner <u>connect</u> the pipes. The <u>connection</u> is tight, so no water leaks out.

- ✔ **prepare – preparation** Please <u>prepare</u> for the party. Food <u>preparation</u> is especially important because our guests will be hungry.

- ✔ **inform – information** The postal workers must <u>inform</u> their supervisors when a package is missing. The <u>information</u> is passed along to the customer who sent the package.

- ✔ **direct – direction** Many police officers <u>direct</u> traffic. Without proper <u>direction</u>, cars may crash.

- ✔ **act – action** Jane and Joe will <u>act</u> surprised, but they are, in fact, expecting a party. They appreciate the kind <u>actions</u> of their friends.

Four other letters — *ness* — also show up at the end of nouns. These letters change descriptions into nouns. In these pairs, the first word is a description, and the second is a noun.

- ✔ **kind – kindness** Henry is a <u>kind</u> man who helps everyone. His <u>kindness</u> has earned him many friends.

- ✔ **helpless – helplessness** A newborn baby is completely <u>helpless</u>. Parents react to their infant's <u>helplessness</u> by handling the baby carefully.

- ✔ **hard – hardness** A diamond is a <u>hard</u> stone. Because of its <u>hardness</u>, a diamond can cut glass.

- ✔ **soft – softness** Dry the glass with a <u>soft</u> cloth. Test the pillow for <u>softness</u>.

- ✔ **rough – roughness** <u>Rough</u> play is not allowed in the playground. If the teacher sees <u>roughness</u>, recess is over.

Sometimes the spelling changes a little when you add one of these endings, but the result is the same. The addition of *tion* or *ness* creates a noun. Have a glance at these pairs. The second word in each pair is a noun.

- ✔ **participate – participation** Students <u>participate</u> in every meeting, offering comments and suggestions to the teachers. This <u>participation</u> involves everyone in the planning process.

- ✔ **devote – devotion** Do not <u>devote</u> too much time to that project. We recognize and appreciate your <u>devotion</u> to duty.

- ✔ **lovely – loveliness** The <u>lovely</u> little girl smiled. The camera captured her <u>loveliness</u>.

- ✔ **lonely – loneliness** A <u>lonely</u> person needs friends. <u>Loneliness</u> is not good for your health.

- ✔ **happy – happiness** A <u>happy</u> clown makes us laugh. The audience feels <u>happiness</u> at the circus.

Watch for words with these endings. When you see one, you have probably found a noun.

You should have found six nouns: *happiness, thoughts, freedom, justice, equality, society.* All these words name ideas or feelings, so all are nouns.

Many words that describe feelings and ideas have other forms that are not nouns. For example, *equality* is a noun, but *equal* is not. The noun *(equality)* names the concept. The other form *(equal)* describes something else *(equal rights, equal opportunity).*

Sorting Out Singular and Plural Nouns

Smile! You are having a <u>baby</u>. Smile more! You are having three <u>babies</u>.

Baby is a singular noun. *Babies* is a plural noun. When you become a parent, the difference between singular (one) and plural (more than one) is rather important. It's important in grammar also. Why? Within a sentence, singular nouns match up with other singular words, and plurals pair with other plurals.

If you'd like to know more about these matches, see the section "Attaching 'This', 'These', and Other Words to Nouns," later in this chapter. You can also read Chapter 4, where I tell you how to pair up nouns and pronouns, and Chapter 11, where you see how to match nouns properly with either singular or plural verbs.

In this section, you discover the singular and plural forms of nouns.

Adding the letters "S" or "ES" to form plurals

Take a look at these singular and plural nouns. Notice the difference between them:

Singular	*Plural*
fork	forks
television	televisions
shoe	shoes
infant	infants
horse	horses
officer	officers
photo	photos

As you see, these nouns change from singular to plural when you add the letter *s.*

If all nouns formed plurals this way, your life would be much easier. Sadly, some nouns follow a different pattern. Check out these singular and plural nouns. Notice how they differ:

Singular	*Plural*
brush	brushes
match	matches
kiss	kisses
tax	taxes
witch	witches
loss	losses
bush	bushes

The rule for these words is simple: When the singular noun ends in *sh, ch, ss,* or *x,* add the letters *es* to form the plural noun.

See whether you can write the form that is missing in the following table. You should add or take away either *s* or *es:*

Singular	*Plural*
mess	
	lions
switch	
	boxes
zoo	
	gorillas
eyelash	

You should have added the following words to the table: *messes, lion, switches, box, zoos, gorilla, eyelashes.* The words *mess, switch, box,* and *eyelash* employ the letters *es* to form the plural. The other words form plurals with the letter *s* alone.

Words that end with the letter *o* sometimes add a simple *s* (*zoos, avocados*) and sometimes *es* (*potatoes, heroes*). Check your dictionary if you are not sure whether to add *s* or *es* to form a plural.

Creating plurals of words that end with the letter "y"

Read these sentences, paying special attention to the underlined words:

Bill has one <u>key</u> for his house and two <u>keys</u> for his car.

Diane lives in a <u>city</u>, and she enjoys visiting many other <u>cities</u> when she is on vacation.

Did you notice that in the first sentence, the singular word *key* becomes plural when you add the letter *s?* In the second sentence, the singular word *city* changes when it becomes plural. The *y* changes to *i,* and then *es* is tacked on. Why the difference? The letter before the *y* is the *key* to these *mysteries* of grammar.

When you are forming the plural of a word that ends with the letter *y,* pay extra attention. If the letter before the *y* is *a, e, u,* or *o* (letters that are called *vowels*), add an *s* to the end of the word to form the plural:

Singular	*Plural*
monkey	monkeys
tray	trays
toy	toys
way	ways
boy	boys
essay	essays

If the letter before the *y* is not a vowel, change the *y* to *i* and add *es* to form the plural:

Singular	*Plural*
reply	replies
enemy	enemies
salary	salaries
university	universities
baby	babies
lily	lilies

See whether you can make plurals correctly. In the second column, write the plural form of each word in the first column.

Singular	*Plural*
turkey	
bunny	
berry	
delay	
daisy	
journey	
valley	

Here are the correct plural forms of these words: *turkeys, bunnies, berries, delays, daisies, journeys, valleys.* The words that end in *ay, ey,* and *oy (turkey, delay, journey, valley)* form plurals with the letter *s.* Words ending with a different letter before the final *y form plurals by* changing the *y* to *i* and adding *es (bunnies, berries, daisies).*

You may hear this rule explained in a different way: To make the plural of a noun ending in a vowel (the letters *a, e, i, o,* or *u*) followed by the letter *y,* add the letter *s.* I did not include one vowel, *i,* in my explanation because that vowel does not appear in front of the letter *y.* I like to keep things simple.

Plurals that break the rules

Are you a rebel, or do you usually follow the rules? I wrote *usually* because my experience tells me that no one follows the rules all the time. The English language also breaks the rules occasionally and creates strange plural forms. Read these sentences, paying attention to the underlined words:

> Help! One little <u>sheep</u> is eating my lunch! I am just joking. Only a few <u>sheep</u> live near me, and they are all in zoos.

The first underlined word, *sheep,* is singular. The clues are *one,* which always signals a singular noun, and *is,* a singular verb. The second underlined word looks exactly the same. However, this time *sheep* is plural, indicating more than one animal. The clues are *a few,* which signals a plural noun; the word *live,* which is a plural verb; and the word *they,* which refers to *sheep* and is a plural form. English is odd, isn't it? Sometimes the same word can be either singular or plural, depending upon how the word is used.

You can't memorize every plural form in the English language — not if you want to have time to eat, sleep, and have a real life. However, you should know some common irregular plurals:

Singular	*Plural*	*Singular*	*Plural*
half	halves	moose	moose
loaf	loaves	deer	deer
knife	knives	mouse	mice
leaf	leaves	goose	geese
man	men	tooth	teeth
woman	women	information	information
child	children	editor-in-chief	editors-in-chief

Your best path through the world of irregular plurals is to remember those you use often. You may want to keep a list of your personal favorites. You can look up other plurals in the dictionary when you need them.

See whether you can write the irregular plural form of each word. If you are not sure, check the dictionary.

Singular	*Plural*
ox	
hoof	
scarf	
runner-up	
crisis	
aircraft	
foot	

Answers: *oxen, hooves, scarves, runners-up, crises, aircraft, feet.*

When you come across a word with a hyphen (a short line separating two words, such as *runner-up* or *brother-in-law*), look at the most important part of the word — the section that carries the main meaning *(runner, brother)*. Make that word plural *(runners, brothers)* and leave the rest of the word alone *(runners-up, brothers-in-law)*.

The dictionary is your friend when you are writing plural forms. Look up any noun to find the plural form or instructions for creating the plural.

Attaching "This," "These," and Other Words to Nouns

Nouns often come with descriptions attached. In some languages, every description has a singular and a plural form. You are lucky, because descriptions in English usually keep the same form when they join up with nouns that are singular (one) and plural (more than one). You can correctly write about one *fine day* and five *fine days*. The description *fine* never changes. You do have to pay attention to a few words, though. Take a look at these examples:

> <u>this</u> book (singular)
>
> <u>these</u> books (plural)
>
> <u>that</u> orange (singular)

those oranges (plural)

this country (singular)

these countries (plural)

that dog (singular)

those dogs (plural)

As you see in this list, *this* and *that* pair up with singular nouns. *These* and *those* pair with plural nouns.

I often hear people attach the word *them* to nouns (*them books* or *them cars*). In proper English, *them* always stands alone and never joins a noun in this way.

Here's an example, which comes from a conversation I had with my cousin a few years ago:

WRONG: Are you still writing them grammar books?

WHY IT IS WRONG: The word *them* never attaches to other words. In my cousin's question, *them* is improperly attached to *grammar books*.

RIGHT: Are you still writing those grammar books?

WHY IT IS RIGHT: *Those* may attach to other words. In the new sentence, *those* is attached to *grammar books*.

In case you are wondering, I am still writing *those grammar books.* You are reading one right now. And no, I did not correct my cousin. When I am at a party, I leave my grammar work at home!

Two tiny words, *a* and *an,* attach only to singular nouns. You can say *a rug* or *an apple,* but not *a rugs* or *an apples.* (If you are curious about the difference between *a* and *an,* turn to Chapter 6.) I am happy to tell you that another common word that attaches to nouns, *the,* works for both singular and plural nouns.

In the following paragraph, underline the correct word from each pair:

Alex put (this/these) folder in (that/those) drawer. He locked up all (this/these) files because all (that/those) information is secret. Anne took (them/those) keys and opened (that/those) drawers. She was very interested in (this/these) file about salaries.

Here are the words you should have underlined, along with the words they attach to: *this folder, that drawer, these files, that information, those keys, those drawers, this file.* The singular nouns (*folder, drawer, information, file*) pair with these singular words: *this, that.* The plural nouns (*files, keys, drawers*) pair with these plural words: *these, those.*

Chapter 3: People to See, Places to Go, Things to Remember

Are you 'mis' -ing something?

When you tack three letters — *mis* — onto the beginning of a word, you show that something is wrong. For example:

You *count* the number of clean socks in your drawer. You say, "I have two pairs of socks. I do not have to do the laundry today." One day later, you search for a pair of socks. You find nothing! You *miscounted.* Now you have to do the laundry — barefoot!

To *count* is to add up. To *miscount* is to add incorrectly. Here are other examples of words with *mis:*

✔ **behavior – misbehavior** Parents often judge *behavior,* looking for polite, calm, respectful actions from their children. If parents see *misbehavior (wrong behavior),* they may punish their children. Example: The parent sees a child spill milk, toss toys across the room, and scream loudly. The parent says, "I do not approve of your *misbehavior.* You may not watch television tonight!"

✔ **lead – mislead** Correct information *leads* you to the truth. If someone *misleads* you, on purpose or by accident, you receive *wrong* information. In other words, someone *leads* you to the *wrong* conclusion. Example: "I am lowering taxes by $10," says the politician, not explaining that

he is also replacing the $10 tax with a $15 fee. The politician is *misleading* the voters.

✔ **understand – misunderstand** When you *understand,* you grasp the correct meaning. When you *misunderstand,* you pick up an incorrect, or *wrong,* meaning. Example: "I *understand* how busy you are, and I am grateful that you will wash the dishes tonight," says Helen. Bob replies, "No! You always *misunderstand* what I say! I cannot wash the dishes because I have to work."

✔ **step – misstep** You take a *step* when you place your foot on the floor or when you take action. A *misstep* is a wrong *step* or *action.* Example: Andy's first *step* was to make a list of things to buy at the grocery store. One *misstep* in the parking lot changed his plans, because he spent the evening in the emergency ward instead of in the kitchen. Forgetting to call his friends to cancel the dinner party was another *misstep.*

Keep an eye out for *mis* words, such as these: *misfortune* (bad luck), *misplace* (put in the wrong place, lose track of), *misquote* (report the wrong words), *misspell* (spell wrong), *mistreat* (treat wrong or treat badly), and *mistake* (take wrongly, make an error).

Chapter 4

Practicing Pronouns

● ●

In This Chapter

▶ Understanding the role of pronouns

▶ Selecting the proper pronoun for each sentence

▶ Expressing ownership with possessive pronouns

● ●

*L*ittle words should be easy, right? One, two, or a few more letters should cause no trouble.

I hate to bring bad news, but I must. Some short words — pronouns — can give you a headache faster than a screaming child on a crowded bus.

Do not worry, though. Help is on the way! This chapter explains what you need to know about pronouns.

Replacing Nouns with Pronouns

Read this paragraph:

> John took John's best friend, Alice, to Alice's house after the party. John asked Alice if Alice would give John the recipe for the cookies John and Alice had eaten at the party. Alice gave the recipe to John.

What a boring piece of writing! I suspect that you wanted to change the paragraph so that the same words do not appear over and over again. So do I, and because I am writing this book, I can change the words. Here is a new paragraph:

> John took <u>his</u> best friend, Alice, to <u>her</u> house after the party. <u>He</u> asked <u>her</u> if <u>she</u> would give <u>him</u> the recipe for the cookies that <u>they</u> had eaten at the party. <u>She</u> gave <u>it</u> to <u>him</u>.

That paragraph is not very exciting either, but it does not repeat as many words. The words I removed from the first paragraph are nouns. The underlined words I substituted in the second paragraph are *pronouns*. Pronouns have an important job: They take the place of nouns. The trick is to insert the right pronoun by matching it to the noun it replaces. In this section, I explain what you need to check before you select the proper pronoun.

Pronouns for the speaker or writer

Do you like to talk about yourself? Most people do. To talk or write about yourself, you need pronouns. Take a look at the underlined words in these sentences:

> I love to play the piano.
>
> Andrew gave me a piano.
>
> I practice on my piano every day.
>
> I have taught myself five new songs.
>
> Do not take the piano! That instrument is mine!

Every underlined word in the preceding sentences is a pronoun. These pronouns take the place of the name of the person speaking or writing. It does not matter whether the speaker or writer is a man or a woman. The same pronouns work for both sexes.

The pronouns *I, me, my, myself,* and *mine* are singular. They refer to one person only.

If you talk or write about yourself as part of a group, you need a different set of pronouns. Read these sentences and notice the underlined pronouns:

> May we play music in the show?
>
> George told us that the show is too short.
>
> "The audience will enjoy our music," we said.
>
> George finally gave us permission to play.
>
> We told ourselves not to be nervous.
>
> After the show, the applause will be ours.

The underlined words are all pronouns, and all refer to a group that includes the person speaking or writing. Don't worry about whether members of the group are male or female or some of each. The same pronouns work for both sexes.

Pronouns that refer to one person (singular pronouns) differ from pronouns that refer to a group (plural pronouns). Always check singular and plural when you select a pronoun.

See whether you can sort out these singular and plural pronouns and write them underneath the correct headings "Singular" and "Plural" listed below: *us, myself, me, I, mine, ourselves, we, our, my, ours.*

Singular   **Plural**

The singular pronouns are *myself, me, I, mine,* and *my.* The plural pronouns are *us, ourselves, we, our, ours.*

Here is something else to try that is a little harder. In each of the following sentences, you see a blank. Write a pronoun that refers to the speaker or writer in the blank. The letter *S* after a blank tells you that you need a singular pronoun. The letter *P* means you need a plural pronoun.

_____ (S) am going to work now. _____ (S) told _____ (S) that _____ (S) must hurry, because _____ (S) boss told _____ (S) that lateness is a problem. _____ (S) spoke with my friends in the office. _____ (P) all agreed that _____ (P) want _____ (P) boss to leave _____ (P) alone. _____ (P) prefer to be by _____ (P).

Here are the pronouns you should have listed: *I, I, myself, I ,my, me, I, We, we, our, us, We, ourselves.* All these words are pronouns referring to the person or people speaking.

Did you remember to capitalize the pronoun *I?* That pronoun is always capitalized. For more information on capital letters, see Chapter 17.

Pronouns such as *I, me, my, myself, mine, we, us, our, ourselves,* and *ours* refer to the person or people speaking or writing. These pronouns don't have masculine (male) or feminine (female) forms. They may represent both males and females.

Pronouns that speak to others

In this book, I am talking to *you*, the reader. To talk to someone, or to refer to the person you are speaking with, you need pronouns. In the following sentences, the underlined words are all pronouns:

Do <u>you</u> want to take a walk?

<u>Your</u> shoes look very comfortable.

Did <u>you</u> buy those shoes for <u>yourself</u>?

Usually, the three of <u>you</u> buy clothing and shoes by <u>yourselves</u>, without help.

Jean forgot her sweater and wants to borrow <u>yours</u>.

The underlined words are pronouns. They replace the name of the person you are addressing (speaking or writing to). These pronouns do not have different masculine (male) and feminine (female) forms. They work for both males and females.

The pronouns *you* and *your* may replace the name of one person or the names of more than one person. In other words, *you* and *your* may be either singular or plural. Very convenient! Use *yourself* for one person and *yourselves* for more than one.

Sometimes people try to change the pronoun *you* into a different form to show that it is plural. I often hear *y'all, you guys, youse,* and other expressions. These terms are not correct in Standard English. Use them with friends, if you like, but stay away from these words when you are in a business or school situation. The pronoun *you* is both singular and plural.

See whether you can write the following pronouns underneath the correct headings "Singular", "Plural" and "Singular and Plural" listed below: *yourself, you, your, yourselves, yours.* Check for singular (referring to one person), plural (referring to more than one person), or singular and plural (works for one or more than one).

Singular	*Plural*	*Singular and Plural*

In the singular column is *yourself.* In the plural column is *yourselves.* In the singular-and-plural column are *you, your,* and *yours.*

Now insert a pronoun into each blank in the following paragraph, always referring to the person or people being addressed. After each blank, look at the letter in parentheses. The letter *S* means that the pronoun in the blank is singular. The letter *P* means that the pronoun in the blank is plural.

_____ (S) walked the dog last night. I want to thank _____ (S) for ____ (S) help with the dog. Give _____ (S) time to rest today. _____(S) and _____ (S) friends were up very late, and _____ (P) all need time for _____ (P).

Here are the pronouns you should have added: *You, you, your, yourself, You, your, you, yourselves*. These words are pronouns that replace the name of the person or people being addressed.

Pronouns that speak about other people or things

Do you like to gossip? Almost everyone does! English has many pronouns that replace nouns that name the person or people you are speaking or writing about. Read these sentences. Notice the underlined words:

He placed his painting on the wall. He had done all the work himself. Now he waited to hear their opinions. They cheered! One of them said it was great. He looked at Mary. Did she like his art? If she said it was good, he would give the artwork to her. The painting would be hers forever.

The underlined words are pronouns. All these pronouns help you talk about someone or something else. Some pronouns that talk about other people or things are singular, and you should use them when speaking or writing about one person or thing. Some pronouns that talk about other people or things are plural, and they refer to more than one person or thing. Here is a table that shows singular and plural pronouns:

Singular	*Plural*
Male: he, him, his, himself	they, them, their, theirs, themselves
Female: she, her, hers, herself	
Thing: it, its, itself	

Did you notice the labels *male, female,* and *thing?* The pronouns *he, him, his, himself* refer to one male. The pronouns *she, her, hers, herself* refer to one female. The pronouns *it, its,* and *itself* take the place of any noun that names one thing. (For more information on nouns, turn to Chapter 3.)

Lucky for you, plural pronouns do not have different forms for males and females. *They, them, their, theirs,* and *themselves* may refer to a group of males, a group of females, groups with both males and females, or groups of things. These pronouns do many jobs! (I do not think they are paid very much, though, for all their work.)

In the second column, write a pronoun that may replace the underlined words.

Word Replaced   *Pronoun*

1. The telephone rang.

2. William and Ellen wrote letters to each other.

3. William's and Ellen's letters were always interesting.

4. James told Anne about the letters.

5. Anne read one letter.

6. Max hates Ellen and Anne.

7. Max's problem is that Max has no confidence in Max.

8. Ellen and Anne told Ellen and Anne not to worry about Max.

9. Max and Roger took Ellen's phone and fixed the phone's speaker.

10. Ellen needed the phone to call Max and Roger to tell Max and Roger to bring Max's and Roger's toothbrushes.

Here are the answers: 1. *It* 2. *They* 3. *Their* 4. *He, her, them* 5. *She, it* 6. *He, them* 7. *His, he, himself* 8. *They, themselves, him* 9. *They, her, its* 10. *She, it, them, them, their.*

When you use a pronoun, think about the noun the pronoun replaces. Decide between singular and plural pronouns. Also match masculine (male) pronouns with male nouns, and feminine (female) pronouns with female nouns. Use *it, its,* or *itself* for things.

Avoiding errors with two common pronouns

The pronoun *their* is not the same as *there* or *they're.*

✔ *Their* shows group ownership:

- The students read *their* books.

- *Their* clothing was wet when the students came in from the rain.

- Do the students have *their* umbrellas?
- The designers described *their* ideas to Philip.
- I need *their* approval before I plan my vacation.

✔ *There* refers to a place:

- Put the book *there*.
- Over *there* is my favorite piano.
- Do you know who is *there?*
- Leave your suitcase *there* for now.
- I will not visit *there* until the war ends.

✔ *They're* is a shortened form of *they are:*

- *They're* in the library now.
- Nina and Oscar said that *they're* ready when you are.
- Andrew and his son moved to Scotland, where *they're* very happy.
- I heard noise from the yard, so *they're* not in the house.
- *They're* planting vegetables.

You also have to be careful not to confuse the pronoun *its* with *it's*. Look at these sentences:

✔ *Its* is a pronoun that shows ownership or belonging:

- The book had a stain on *its* cover.
- *Its* short leg makes the table wobble.
- Lily placed the meat in *its* pan.
- *Its* gravy is in a separate dish.
- Is the problem the computer or *its* software?

✔ *It's* is a shortened form of *it is:*

- *It's* a blood stain!
- Stop searching, because *it's* not here.
- The tourist went to London because *it's* an interesting place.
- He likes New York, too, because *it's* a big city.
- When *it's* completed, the film will win many awards.

See whether you can choose the proper word from the parentheses and write it in the blank.

1. _____ (Its, It's) snowing today, so students will stay in _____ (they're, there, their) homes.

2. The school is covered with ice, and no one will go_____ (they're, there, their).

3. The driver does not trust the car or _____ (its, it's) brakes.

4. _____ (They're, There, Their) slipping on the snowy streets.

5. Are you (they're, there, their), or are you watching the television reports of the storm and _____ (its, it's) dangers?

6. When _____ (its, it's) over, please tell the children to complete _____ (they're, there, their) homework assignments.

Here are the answers: 1. *It's, their* 2. *there* 3. *its* 4. *They're* 5. *there, its* 6. *it's, their.*

Solving the Case of Pronouns

I love mystery stories. I enjoy searching for clues and solving the case. Here is a mystery for you. Can you figure out the difference between *I* and *me, she* and *her, he* and *him, they* and *them,* and similar pairs?

Each pronoun pair refers to the same person, but each half of the pair is in a different case. *Case* is a grammar term. This section helps you become a better detective so that you can solve the mystery of pronoun case.

Subject pronouns

What do the underlined pronouns in the next paragraph have in common? Figure it out! You are the detective, and this paragraph is your crime scene:

> <u>She</u> told <u>George</u> that the necklace was missing. <u>He</u> claimed that <u>she</u> was lying, because <u>he</u> knew that the necklace was in the bank. <u>He</u> explained, "<u>I</u> spoke with two bank clerks. <u>They</u> gave me a chance to see the necklace. <u>You</u> upset us all for no reason!" <u>He</u> left her alone then.

Do you see that each underlined pronoun is doing an action expressed by a nearby word or words? To help you grasp what I mean, here are the underlined pronouns and the action word (or words) matching each underlined pronoun:

<u>She</u> told

<u>He</u> claimed

<u>she</u> was lying

<u>he</u> knew

<u>He</u> explained

<u>I</u> spoke

<u>They</u> gave

<u>You</u> upset

<u>He</u> left

In this list, the underlined pronoun is connected to a "doing" word, what English teachers call a *verb*. (For more information on verbs, turn to Chapter 5.) The pronoun doing the action is a *subject*. Every underlined word on the list and in the paragraph is a subject pronoun. Here are the most common subject pronouns:

Singular Subject Pronouns	*Plural Subject Pronouns*
I	we
you	you
he, she, it	they
who	who
whoever	whoever

Because you have sharp eyes, you probably noticed that the pronouns *you, who,* and *whoever* may be either singular (referring to one) or plural (referring to more than one). The other pronouns have different singular and plural forms.

See whether you can figure out which subject pronoun goes into each blank. To help you decide, I have placed a noun in parentheses after each blank. The pronoun you write in the blank replaces that noun.

_____ (Angela) loves peaches and pears.

_____ (Richard) hates fruit.

Yesterday, _____ (Angela and Richard) had lunch.

_____ (all of us) were at the next table.

____ (Richard) pushed a peach off his plate.

_____ (The peach) fell on the floor.

_____ (The speaker) think that _____ (Richard) should apologize.

Here are the answers: *She, He, they, We, He, It, I, he.* All these words are pronouns. All are subjects. They pair with verbs: *She loves, He hates, they had, We were, He pushed, It fell, I think, he should apologize.*

Subject pronouns can also pair up with words that express a state of being. Look at the following paragraph. Examine the underlined words:

> <u>She</u> was scared of the ghost, but <u>they</u> were excited. <u>We</u> were sorry that <u>she</u> was not amused by our trick. <u>We</u> were wrong to think that <u>she</u> was in the mood for a joke. Now <u>she</u> is angry with us. <u>They</u> will be interested in hearing more about ghosts the next time we see them, but <u>she</u> seems too frightened to come for another visit.

Do you see that every underlined pronoun is connected to a word that expresses a state of being? Here are the connected pairs:

> <u>She</u> was
>
> <u>they</u> were
>
> <u>We</u> were
>
> <u>she</u> was
>
> <u>We</u> were
>
> <u>she</u> was
>
> <u>she</u> is
>
> <u>They</u> will be
>
> <u>she</u> seems

The underlined words are subject pronouns. The other words are words that express a state of being. They are verbs. (For more information about these verbs, turn to Chapter 5.)

See whether you can select a pronoun for each blank. The word that the pronoun replaces is in parentheses.

> _____ (Mary and Joe) are going on vacation next week. _____ (the person speaking) will take care of their plant. _____ (The plant) needs water every day, or _____ (the plant) will die. _____ (Mary and Joe and the person speaking) have been neighbors for many years. Usually, _____ (Mary and Joe and the person speaking) travel together. This year, though, _____ (Joe) wants to be alone with Mary. _____ (Mary) thinks that _____ (Joe) will ask her to marry him during the vacation!

Here are the answers: *They, I, It, it, We, we, he, She, he*. All these pronouns are subject pronouns. Subject pronouns pair with verbs. The subject–verb pairs from the preceding paragraph are *They are going, I will take, It needs, it will die, We have been, we travel, he wants, She thinks, he will ask*.

Object pronouns

Okay, Detective, here is another case for you to solve — the case of object pronouns. Read this paragraph and look carefully at the underlined words:

The nanny read <u>her</u> stories every night. The child heard <u>them</u> all. Years later, the young girl told <u>us</u> that her favorite story was about a magic bean. The girl read <u>it</u> to her brother. The nanny also read <u>him</u> stories. The children knew <u>her</u> well, and soon they wrote stories for their nanny. The nanny was very pleased to hear <u>them</u>.

The underlined words are all pronouns. Here is a table showing the most common object pronouns:

Singular Object Pronouns	Plural Object Pronouns
me, myself	us, ourselves
you, yourself	you, yourselves
him, her, it, himself, herself, itself	them, themselves
whom	whom
whomever	whomever

Grammarians think of these pronouns as "receivers." The traditional explanation is that an object pronoun "receives" an action. You have to stretch your imagination a little to see how the pronoun is "receiving" the action, either directly or indirectly. Here is an explanation for each pronoun that is underlined in the paragraph at the beginning of this section:

her — receives the action of reading (from the verb *read*)

them — receives the action of hearing (from the verb *heard*)

us — receives the action of telling (from the verb *told*)

it — receives the action of reading (from the verb *read*)

him — receives the action of reading (from the verb *read*)

her — receives the action of knowing (from the verb *knew*)

them — receives the action of hearing (from the verb *hear*)

In these examples, each object pronoun receives action from a verb. Object pronouns may also follow words that express the relationship between two things, a part of speech that grammarians call *prepositions*. Notice the underlined object pronouns in these examples:

a story about <u>him</u> (the preposition is *about*)

three letters from <u>me</u> (the preposition is *from*)

a book written by <u>themselves</u> (the preposition is *by*)

the park near <u>us</u> (the preposition is *near*)

the sky above <u>it</u> (the preposition is *above*)

English has many, many prepositions. Maybe too many! To discover more about prepositions, see Chapter 7.

See whether you can figure out the correct object pronoun for each blank in the paragraph below. The words in parentheses tell you the noun that the pronoun replaces.

The workers repaired _____ (the roof) yesterday, but the homeowner told _____ (the workers) that rain came through _____ (the roof) anyway and fell on _____ (Ann). Big drops splashed _____ (Robert) too. The homeowner wants _____ (the roof) replaced. He recently bought a new bedroom set, and he wants protection above _____ (the set). The workers told _____ (the writer of this paragraph) that they will do _____ (the work) next month.

Here are the answers: *it, them, it, her, him, it, it, me, it.* These words are all object pronouns. The pronoun *it* receives action from the verb *repaired; them* receives action from the verb *told; it* follows the preposition *through; her* follows the preposition *on; him* receives the action of the verb *splashed; it* receives action from the verb *wants; it* follows the preposition *above; me* receives action from the verb *told;* and *it* receives action from the verb *will do.*

Sorting subject and object pronouns

Many people mix up subject and object pronouns. These mistakes may be common, but they are still mistakes. These two groups do different jobs in a sentence. Subject pronouns act as subjects, and object pronouns as objects. What a surprise! English grammar is actually logical, for a change.

I must admit that subject pronouns may sometimes do one more job in a sentence. Very rarely, they follow and complete the meaning of a verb that expresses a state of being, such as *am, is, are, was, were, has been, will be,* and so on. This situation does not appear very often. Do not worry about these sentences.

You should worry — or at least pay close attention to — subjects and objects when they are doing their usual jobs. Specifically, never send an object pronoun to do the job of a subject pronoun! Here are some examples:

WRONG: James and me are hungry.

WHY IT IS WRONG: The pronoun *me* is an object pronoun. In this sentence, you need a subject pronoun.

RIGHT: James and I are hungry.

WHY IT IS RIGHT: The pronoun *I* is a subject pronoun. In this sentence, *I* is one of the subjects. (The other is *James.*)

WRONG: Are you and him ready for the grammar test?

WHY IT IS WRONG: The pronoun *him* cannot act as a subject. In this sentence, *him* is a subject.

RIGHT: Are you and he ready for the grammar test?

WHY IT IS RIGHT: Now the subject pronoun *he* is correctly acting as a subject, along with the pronoun *you.* (The pronoun *you,* by the way, has the same form as a subject or an object. Very convenient.)

WRONG: Us young people will lead the way into that dangerous area.

WHY IT IS WRONG: *Us* is an object pronoun, but in this sentence it is acting as a subject.

RIGHT: We young people will lead the way into that dangerous area.

WHY IT IS RIGHT: The subject pronoun *we* now acts as a subject.

You cannot use a subject pronoun as an object, either. Take a look at these examples:

WRONG: The waiter brought food to James and I.

WHY IT IS WRONG: The pronoun *I* is a subject pronoun. In this sentence, you need an object pronoun after the preposition *to.*

RIGHT: The waiter brought food to James and me.

WHY IT IS RIGHT: The pronoun *me* is an object pronoun. In this sentence, *me* is one of the objects of the preposition *to.* (The other is *James.*)

WRONG: For help with her project, Rosie asked he.

WHY IT IS WRONG: You need an object pronoun to "receive" the action from the verb *asked. He* is a subject pronoun.

RIGHT: For help with her project, Rosie asked him.

WHY IT IS RIGHT: The object pronoun *him* is now correctly placed to receive the action of the verb *asked*.

WRONG: This conversation is secret and must remain between you and I.

WHY IT IS WRONG: The preposition *between* needs objects. *I* is a subject pronoun.

RIGHT: This conversation is secret and must remain between you and me.

WHY IT IS RIGHT: Now the object pronoun *me* follows the preposition *between*. (The pronoun *you* has the same form for both subject and object situations.)

In many of the examples, the mistakes appear when you are using two pronouns or a noun and a pronoun together. Be extra careful in this type of sentence. Sometimes you may discover the right pronoun more easily if you pretend for a moment that the pronoun is all by itself. For instance, suppose you are not sure which pronoun to select for this sentence:

Charlie gave Bobby and (I? me?) a book.

Cross out "Bobby and." Reread the sentence with the pronouns inserted:

Charlie gave I a book.

Charlie gave me a book.

The second sentence is correct, because the object pronoun *me* receives the action of the verb *gave*.

See whether you can sort these pronouns into *subject, object, and either subject or object* columns: *him, us, you, they, I, me, we, he, her, she, it, them.*

Subject   **Object**   **Either Subject or Object**

In the subject column you should have *they, I, we, he,* and *she*. In the object column you should have *him, us, me, her,* and *them*. In the "either subject or object column," you should have *you* and *it*.

Pronoun "selfies"

Have you ever snapped a *selfie* (a photo of yourself, taken with your smartphone)? If so, you know you have to get everything just right. Otherwise, the photo will be too light, too dark, or out of focus. When you select a pronoun that has *–self* or *–selves* tacked on the end, you also have to be careful. Pronouns that end in *self* are special. They may act as objects in sentences like these:

Gina told <u>herself</u> not to worry. (*herself* receives the action from the verb *told*)

I washed <u>myself</u> carefully after tending to the sick child. (*myself* receives the action from the verb *washed*)

Mommy, I tied my shoes all by <u>myself</u>! (*myself* follows the preposition *by*)

In these sentences, the action flows from the subject (the one doing the action) back to the same person. Do not use a *–self* or *–selves* pronoun as an object in other situations.

Sometimes, a *self* pronoun appears with a subject to add emphasis. In this sort of sentence, the *self* pronoun may be a subject pronoun. Here are some examples:

Gina <u>herself</u> led the yoga class and was very proud of the result.

Do not get up. I <u>myself</u> will answer the door.

Do not use a *self* pronoun, all alone, as a subject:

WRONG: Myself cleaned the house.

WHY IT IS WRONG: *Myself* cannot act as a subject, unless it is next to *I,* for emphasis.

RIGHT: I cleaned the house.

ALSO RIGHT: I myself cleaned the house.

WHY THEY ARE RIGHT: *I* may act alone as a subject. *I myself* may act as a subject, when special emphasis is what you want.

Sometimes people say *meself.* In proper English, that word doesn't exist. Use *myself, I,* or *me,* depending upon the job the pronoun performs in the sentence.

Now place a subject or object pronoun in each blank. The word the pronoun replaces appears in parentheses.

1. The nurse injected _____ (medicine) into _____ (Benjamin).

2. _____ (Benjamin) cried for five minutes.

3. _____ (Benjamin's mother) comforted _____ (Benjamin).

4. _____ (The doctors) laughed and said, "_____ (the people speaking) have never seen _____ (Benjamin) cry for such a long time."

5. _____ (Sally) did much better.

6. _____ (Sally) surprised _____ (the people speaking) by crying for less than a minute.

7. _____ (Sally and Benjamin) are both babies.

8. The nurses like _____ (Sally and Benjamin) and do not care how long _____ (Sally and Benjamin) cry.

Here are the answers: 1. *it* (object pronoun, receives the action of the verb *injected*), *him* (object pronoun after the preposition *into*). 2. *He* (subject of the verb *cried*). 3. *She* (subject of the verb *comforted*), *him* (object pronoun, receives the action of the verb *comforted*). 4. *They* (subject of the verbs *laughed and said*), *We* (subject of the verb *have seen*), *him* (object pronoun, receives the action of the verb *have seen*). 5. *She* (subject of the verb *did*). 6. *She* (subject of the verb *surprised*), *us* (receives the action of the verb *surprised*). 7. *They* (subject of the verb *are*). 8. *them* (object pronoun, receives the action of the verb *like*), *they* (subject of the verb *cry*).

For more explanations and practice with subjects and objects, read Chapters 11 (subjects) and 13 (objects).

Forming Possessive Pronouns

What do you own? A house, a car, a computer? Everyone owns something! Pronouns that express ownership are called *possessive,* because "to possess" means "to own." Here is a table showing some common possessive pronouns:

Singular Possessive Pronouns	*Plural Possessive Pronouns*
my, mine	our, ours
your, yours	your, yours
his (for males), her and hers (for females), its (for things)	their, theirs
whose	whose

Isn't it great that most of these pronouns do not change form when the owner is a male or a female? Most of the time, one form works for males, females, and objects. (Yes, an object can possess something: the pen has a tip, so *its* tip is a possessive situation.)

You probably noticed that none of the words in the table have an apostrophe (a punctuation mark shaped like a hook and placed above the line). Apostrophes create possessive nouns: *Mary's book, Greg's foot, students' notes.* Possessive pronouns never carry an apostrophe.

Who owns what? Write a possessive pronoun in the second column that can take the place of the underlined word in the first column. ***Note:*** When a question refers to "the speaker" or "the speaker and a group," imagine that you are speaking. When a question refers to "the listener" or to "the listener and a group," imagine that you are addressing someone else.

Owner	*Possessive Pronoun*

1. <u>Nancy's</u> foot
2. <u>Billy's and Betty's</u> pajamas
3. <u>the door's</u> frame
4. <u>Jack's</u> punch
5. <u>Eliza's</u> favorite show
6. the <u>speaker's</u> cousin
7. the <u>speaker's and a group's</u> houses
8. the <u>listener's</u> furniture

Here are the answers: 1. *Her* 2. *Their* 3. *its* 4. *His* 5. *Her* 6. *My* 7. *Our* 8. *Your*.

Many people confuse the possessive pronoun *whose* with *who's,* a short form of *who is.* Check out these examples:

WRONG: Who's coat is on the floor?

WHY IT IS WRONG: *Who's* means *who is,* so the sentence reads, "Who is coat is on the floor?" This makes no sense.

RIGHT: Whose coat is on the floor?

WHY IT IS RIGHT: Now the possessive pronoun *whose* is attached to *coat,* where it makes sense.

WRONG: I know whose responsible for the mess.

WHY IT IS WRONG: *Whose* is a possessive pronoun, but nothing is possessed in this sentence.

RIGHT: I know who's responsible for the mess.

WHY IT IS RIGHT: *Who's* means *who is.* The correct sentence means "I know who is responsible for the mess."

Chapter 5

Doing and Being Words: Verbs

I like to think of a sentence as a shopping cart. You pile things into a cart when you shop; you pile meaning into a sentence when you speak or write. The cart takes things to the cashier, and the sentence takes meaning to your listener or reader. The most important part of a shopping cart is the wheels. If one is missing, you can't easily move your purchases to the checkout line. The "wheels" of a sentence are its verbs. Without a verb, you don't have a sentence, and you have a tough time carrying meaning to your audience.

In this chapter, you take a close look at verbs. You see how verbs work to talk about the past, the present, and the future. You review various verb forms, including some important irregular verbs: *be, have,* and *do.* You also learn how to form questions and negative statements with helping verbs. You see how adding a helping verb such as *may* or *should* changes meaning. When you are finished, you will have a smooth ride with all kinds of verbs.

Searching Out Verbs

I am a curious person. I always want to know what everyone is doing. I also care about how people are feeling. Plus, I love to learn new facts. Here are some statements that satisfy my curiosity. Take a good look at the underlined words:

> Sam <u>is</u> extremely tired.

> He <u>climbed</u> Mount Everest yesterday.

Sam and Elizabeth <u>will run</u> many marathons.

A marathon <u>is</u> a race.

You <u>train</u> for long races also.

I <u>sit</u> when you <u>train</u>.

<u>Are</u> you jealous?

<u>Stop</u> and <u>relax</u>!

The underlined words all tell about actions or states of being. Words that express "doing" or "being" are verbs. Without verbs, you discover very little. Pull the underlined words out of the preceding sentences. Can you understand the meaning? Probably not! Even when you do grasp the meaning, you have to try harder to understand what's going on if a verb is missing.

Asking Questions to Find the Verb

To do almost anything with a sentence, you have to find the verb. If the verb is wrong, the sentence will not work. How can you find a verb? Look for "doing" or "being" words. Read each sentence. Ask these questions:

- ✔ Which word tells you what is happening?
- ✔ Which word tells you what happened?
- ✔ Which word tells you what will happen?
- ✔ Which word makes a statement about being?

Most likely, you will get an answer to one of these questions. The words that answer these questions are verbs.

Sometimes, you get a one-word answer (*twist, are, sings,* and so on). Other times, two words answer your question (*have done, do go, might be, is appearing,* and many others). In special cases, three words create one verb (*will have written, should have painted, could have been,* and so on). It doesn't matter how many separate words you find, as long as you find the "doing" or "being" words — the verbs.

Here are more sentences. The verbs are underlined. After each sentence, I explain how the verbs answer the questions on the list:

Yesterday Martha <u>changed</u> a flat tire. (Which word tells you what happened? *changed*)

Her car <u>is</u> old. (Which word makes a statement about being? *is*)

She <u>will</u> probably <u>buy</u> a new car soon. (Which words tell you what will happen? *will buy*)

Her car dealer <u>has</u> always <u>given</u> her a good price. (Which words tell you what happened? *has given*)

He <u>could charge</u> more. (Which words tell you what is happening? *could charge*)

Martha <u>should be</u> grateful, but she <u>is</u> not. (Which words make a statement about being? *should be, is*)

Martha <u>does</u> not even <u>thank</u> the car dealer! (Which words tell you what is happening? *does thank*)

I admit that you have to stretch some of the questions a little, because sometimes the question is really "What is *not* happening?" or "What *should or could* happen?" However, the basic method works well. Look for "doing" or "being" words, and you will find verbs.

See whether you can identify the verbs in these sentences. Every sentence has at least one. Some sentences have verbs that contain more than one word.

1. John limped home.

2. He had fallen over a toy.

3. John's mother was quite upset.

4. She cleaned the cut on John's knee.

5. The bandage was too tight.

6. Walk home before nightfall!

7. You may hurt yourself.

8. Does John obey his mother?

9. I guess he will obey because his knee is really sore.

10. No, he will not obey.

Here are the answers: 1. *limped* 2. *had fallen* 3. *was* 4. *cleaned* 5. *was* 6. *Walk* 7. *may hurt* 8. *Does obey* 9. *guess, will obey, is* 10. *will obey*. All these words or expressions are verbs.

The word *not* is not part of the verb. The word *not* creates a negative, but it does not express action or state of being.

As you see, verbs come in different shapes and sizes. Some create statements, some ask questions, and some issue commands. Verbs can do all these things and more.

Telling Time with Verbs

Historians like timelines, listing events in order. So do verbs! By changing form, verbs talk about things that have already happened, are happening now, or will happen in the future. In fact, sorting out events according to time is one of the most important jobs that verbs do. This quality of verbs is called *tense*. You should not become tense about verb tense, though. You can make sense of tense easily.

In Chapter 10, I go into detail about verb tense, including what English teachers call the "perfect tenses." (I doubt that you will find these tenses "perfect," but you do have to use them!) Here I explain the basics.

Present tense

Present tense tells what is happening now, at the present time. Read these examples and pay close attention to the underlined, present-tense verbs:

Maria <u>studies</u> history.

John <u>likes</u> Maria, so John <u>goes</u> to history class with her.

The class <u>is</u> very interesting.

Several children <u>are</u> in the science class.

They <u>study</u> both science and history.

My favorite subjects <u>are</u> lunch, playtime, and gym.

I <u>am</u> not a good student.

Most present-tense verbs change form only when you are writing about one person or one thing. When you speak or write as yourself with the word *I* or to another with the word *you,* the form stays the same. To show you this pattern, here is a table of a regular verb, *dance:*

Singular (for one person or thing)	Plural (for more than one person or thing)
I dance	we dance
you dance	you dance
he dances	they dance
she dances	
it dances	

In this table, the last box of the first column is where you see the verb change. The letter *S* creates a singular verb, which is the form you want when one person or thing *dances*. I listed only the masculine (male) pronoun *he,* the feminine (female) pronoun *she,* and the pronoun for things, *it*. If I listed every possible word that can pair with the verb *dances,* though, that box would be even more crowded. Do you know why? I could have listed any masculine noun, any feminine noun, and a noun naming any and every thing in the entire world! I could have placed *Henry dances, the girl dances,* or *the doll dances* (and many more examples). In the same way, the last box of the second column could also grow. *They,* a plural pronoun, stands in for any plural noun. I might have included *boys dance, girls dance,* or *flowers dance,* and so on.

Do not confuse nouns and verbs. To create a plural noun (the name of more than one person, place, or thing), you often add the letter *S: boys, rivers, bats.* To create a singular verb that talks about one person or thing, you add the letter *S.* English is strange, isn't it?

You can also talk about the present time with another form, as you see in these sentences:

> George <u>is dancing</u>.
>
> I <u>am watching</u>.
>
> You <u>are groaning</u> because George is a terrible dancer.

I discuss this form — which English teachers call the *present progressive* — in Chapter 10.

See whether you can find the present-tense verbs in this paragraph:

> Jack needs a candle. The lights are out! The house is dark. Jacks searches his closet and finds three candles. He now looks for a match. Unfortunately, Jack has no matches. Jack sits in the dark and cries. I hear him and give him a match. He thanks me.

Here are the answers: *needs, are, is, searches, finds, looks, has, sits, cries, hear, give, thanks.*

Past tense

You can talk about the past, in English, with several different verb forms. Take a look at these sentences, in which the past-tense verb forms are underlined:

> Three lambs <u>walked</u> around the field.
>
> You <u>jumped</u> when I <u>screamed</u> at them.

The lambs <u>have walked</u> through my garden every day since last May!

Mary <u>had finished</u> her painting of the lambs before I <u>started</u> mine.

I <u>was</u> pleased with Mary's paintings.

The lambs <u>loved</u> Mary's work.

They <u>were chewing</u> on the painting.

I <u>chased</u> the lambs away.

All these verbs tell about the past. In this section, I focus on the simple past tense. To find out more about the other past-tense verb forms, turn to Chapter 10.

Lucky for you, regular verbs in the simple past tense do not change form. Here is a table of the past-tense forms of the verb *count:*

Singular (for one person or thing)	*Plural (for more than one person or thing)*
I counted	we counted
you counted	you counted
he counted	they counted
she counted	
it counted	

To save space, I wrote the pronouns *he, she,* and *it* in the last box in the first column, and the pronoun *they* in the last box of the second column. Any singular, masculine (male) noun — *Peter, man, Paul, fisherman* — uses the form for *he.* Any singular, feminine (female) noun — *Lorna, woman, Angela, mermaid* — uses the form for *she.* The noun for any single thing — *bed, shoe, lion* — uses the form for *it.* Every plural noun — *children, dishes, shoes* — uses the form for *they.*

The past tense has other forms, which I explain in detail in Chapter 10.

See whether you can find the past-tense verbs in this paragraph:

Jack hired an electrician. The electrician told Jack that the wires in the house were old. Jack paid the electrician, who replaced all the wires. Jack was not afraid of the dark. He never worried about his wires again. He returned the candles and matches.

Here are the answers: *hired, told, were, paid, replaced, was, worried, returned.*

Future tense

You cannot know what will happen next week or next year, but you can learn the forms of future-tense verbs. Here I show you the basic forms. Turn to Chapter 10 for what English teachers call the "future perfect."

Take a look at the simple future-tense verbs I underlined in these sentences:

I <u>will write</u> a letter every day.

My letters <u>will be</u> boring.

Nothing exciting <u>will happen</u>!

You <u>will do</u> great things.

Helen <u>will throw</u> my letters away.

She <u>will save</u> yours.

These forms for the future tense do not change, as you see in this table of the future-tense forms of the verb *slap:*

Singular (for one person or thing)	*Plural (for more than one person or thing)*
I will slap	we will slap
you will slap	you will slap
he will slap	they will slap
she will slap	
it will slap	

I wrote only the pronouns *he, she,* and *it* in the last box in the first column, and the pronoun *they* in the last box of the second column. These pronouns represent all the nouns in the dictionary. Every noun! No matter who or what you are talking about, the future-tense verb is the same.

In older writing, *shall* sometimes substitutes for *will*. The meaning stays the same.

The future tense has other forms. Turn to Chapter 10 to learn more.

See whether you can find the future-tense verbs in this paragraph.

Elizabeth will make a sandcastle. We will help her by giving her a bucket and a spoon. The sand will be damp, so it will hold its shape easily. She will finish the castle, and we will take a picture of it. Then she will stomp on the castle. The castle will be ruined!

Here are the answers: *will make, will help, will be, will hold, will finish, will take, will stomp, will be ruined.*

Recognizing Forms of Some Important Verbs

Listen to your friends talk. If you kept a scorecard listing every word they say, chances are the words you hear most often are forms of three important verbs, *be, do,* and *have.* (By the way, I do not recommend keeping track of your friends' words. If you do, no one will talk to you!)

In this section, you see how these verbs change form depending upon who is *being, doing,* or *having.* These verbs also change forms in different time periods. Here I cover the basic present, past, and future forms. To learn more about verb tense (time), check out "Telling Time with Verbs" earlier in this chapter.

The verb "be"

The most important and basic part of life is *being* alive. That makes *be,* in all its forms, the most important verb. This verb, though, is a strange creature. It follows no rules. When you match this verb with a different subject (the person or thing that is "being"), the form often changes. Here are three tables to help you figure out *be.* The first places *be* forms in the present, the second moves to the past, and the third goes into the future. Get ready for some time travel.

Present: Singular Forms
I am
you are
he is
she is
it is

Present: Plural Forms
we are
you are
they are

Past: Singular Forms
I was
you were
he was
she was
it was

Past: Plural Forms
we were
you were
they were

Future: Singular Forms
I will be
you will be
he will be
she will be
it will be

Future: Plural Forms
we will be
you will be
they will be

In each of the preceding tables, the last box of the first column contains the masculine (male) pronoun *he,* the feminine (female) pronoun *she,* and the pronoun for things, *it.* These pronouns represent any masculine noun, any feminine noun, and a noun naming any and every thing in the entire world. I could have placed *Henry is, the actress was, the secretary will be . . .* and many more examples. In the same way, the last box of the second column could also grow. *They,* a plural pronoun, stands in for any plural noun. I might have included *trees are, flowers were, the children will be,* and so forth.

In the following table, the first column contains a subject. In the second column is a time period — past, present, or future. Your job is to write the correct form of the verb *be* in the third column.

Subject	*Time*	*Be Verb*
Ellen	present	
horses	past	
I	future	
the box	present	
you (singular, for one person)	past	
puppies	future	
you (plural, for more than one person)	present	

Here are the answers: *is, were, will be, is, were, will be, are.* **Note:** I told you that *you* referred to one person in the fifth box and more than one person in the last box. I did not have to bother explaining how many people were included in that pronoun, though, because the pronoun, *you,* and the verb forms that pair with *you,* are the same for both singular and plural. (To discover more about the pronoun *you,* check out Chapter 4.)

The verb "do"

"Don't just sit there! *Do* something!" Have you heard these lines from an actor in a film, perhaps as a car's brakes fail and it heads toward a cliff? The command to "do something" seems to be a basic fact of human life. All day long, people *do* things. For these reasons, *do* is an important verb. (This verb also creates questions and negative statements. To learn more about questions and negatives, read "Getting Assistance from Helping Verbs" later in this chapter.)

The verb *do* is an important verb. Luckily, it is not as strange as the verb *be.* You should know its irregular forms. Take a close look at the following three tables, which cover the verb *do* in the present, past, and future time.

Present: Singular Forms
I do
you do
he does
she does
it does

Present: Plural Forms
we do
you do
they do

Past: Singular Forms
I did
you did
he did
she did
it did

Past: Plural Forms
we did
you did
they did

Future: Singular Forms
I will do
you will do
he will do
she will do
it will do

Future: Plural Forms
we will do
you will do
they will do

You probably noticed that *do* changes only in the present tense, when you are talking about someone or something doing an action. How nice that this verb is easier!

I listed the masculine pronoun *he,* the feminine pronoun *she,* and the pronoun for things, *it,* in the last box of the first column of each table. If you want to pair the verb *do* with a noun that names one male, use the form for *he.* For the name of one female, use the form for *she.* The name of one thing pairs with the form of the verb listed for *it.* If you have a plural noun, use the form for *they.*

Try your hand at pairing a form of the verb *do* with each subject in the first column, selecting a verb for the time period in the second column.

Subject	Time	Do Verb
the snake	present	
I	past	
you (referring to many people)	future	
awards	present	
boxer	past	
we	future	
a bird	present	

Here are the answers: *does, did, will do, do, did, will do, does.* I gave you more information than you need here. I told you that *you* referred to many people. Whether *you* refers to one person or to many people, the form is the same.

The verb "have"

You may *have* lots of things — friends, a cold, books, fun — and many, many other things. You therefore need to know the correct forms of the verb *have.* (This verb also helps to create some tenses, or time periods. See Chapter 10 to find out more.)

Present: Singular Forms	***Present: Plural Forms***
I have	we have
you have	you have
he has	they have
she has	
it has	
Past: Singular Forms	***Past: Plural Forms***
I had	we had
you had	you had
he had	they had
she had	
it had	
Future: Singular Forms	***Future: Plural Forms***
I will have	we will have
you will have	you will have
he will have	they will have
she will have	
it will have	

Did you notice that the verb *have* changes form only in the present tense, when you are talking about one person or thing? The other forms stay the same. Take care not to confuse *has* and *have.*

If you are reading this chapter in order (and you do not have to do so), by now you know that the pronouns in the last box of the first column are the masculine (male) pronoun *he,* the feminine (female) pronoun *she,* and the pronoun for things, *it.* The verb form that matches the masculine pronoun works for any masculine noun. The verb form that matches the feminine pronoun works for any female noun. The form that pairs with *it* is the form you use for any noun that names one thing. The verb form paired with the plural pronoun *they,* which represents a group, works for all plural nouns.

Do you want to see whether you *have* a good grasp of the verb *have?* In the following table, the first column contains a subject, and the second column contains a time. Fill in the third column with a form of the verb *have.*

Subject	Time	Have Verb
firefighter	present	
tigers	past	
artist	future	
I	present	
you	past	
everyone	future	
Michael	present	

Here are the answers: *has, had, will have, have, had, will have, has.*

Getting Assistance from Helping Verbs

English sentences rely on a main verb and, at times, some *helping verbs. Helping verbs* link up with the main verb to create questions, make negative statements, and express duty, probability, and other meanings. In this section I put helping verbs in the spotlight, so you can use them properly in your writing.

Asking questions with helping verbs

In some languages, you ask a question simply by changing your tone of voice or punctuation. You may declare, "We eat now" or ask, "We eat now?" with the same words. In English questions, the order of the words changes, and sometimes you must insert a helping verb such as *do, does,* or *did.* Read these sentences. Notice how they change. Examine the underlined verbs.

STATEMENT: John <u>shops</u> in his hometown.

QUESTION: <u>Does</u> John <u>shop</u> in his hometown?

STATEMENT: John and his friends <u>support</u> local businesses.

QUESTION: <u>Do</u> John and his friends <u>support</u> local businesses?

STATEMENT: Mary <u>used</u> a coupon to reduce the price.

QUESTION: <u>Did</u> Mary <u>use</u> a coupon to reduce the price?

STATEMENT: The store owner <u>gave</u> Mary the reduced price anyway.

QUESTION: <u>Did</u> the store owner <u>give</u> Mary the reduced price anyway?

As you can see, adding the helping verb creates a question in the preceding sentences. When a helping verb appears in the statement, you don't need to add another one to make a question. All you have to do is rearrange the words.

STATEMENT: The coupon <u>had expired</u>.

QUESTION: <u>Had</u> the coupon <u>expired</u>?

STATEMENT: Mary <u>has forgotten</u> her checkbook.

QUESTION: <u>Has</u> Mary <u>forgotten</u> her checkbook?

You don't have to add any words to create a question about the future, either. Just move the word *will:*

STATEMENT: The soup <u>will be</u> on sale next week.

QUESTION: <u>Will</u> the soup <u>be</u> on sale next week?

STATEMENT: Mark <u>will skip</u> class today.

QUESTION: <u>Will</u> Mark <u>skip</u> class today?

For statements with a form of the verb *be,* you can ask a question without adding an extra helping verb. Changing the order of the words is all you have to do.

STATEMENT: I <u>am</u> too busy.

QUESTION: <u>Am</u> I too busy?

STATEMENT: Spot <u>has been</u> a good dog.

QUESTION: <u>Has</u> Spot <u>been</u> a good dog?

STATEMENT: Ellie and Bill <u>were</u> the first guests.

QUESTION: <u>Were</u> Ellie and Bill the first guests?

In the following table, change the statement in the first column to a question. Write the question in the second column. Underline the verbs in the question.

Statement   *Question*

1. Arthur reads every advertisement.

2. They ride the train every day.

3. The baseballs have fallen out of the basket.

4. I will walk four miles tomorrow.

5. The mystery is solved.

Statement	*Question*

6. The brave soldiers fight for their country.
7. All teachers have read that book.
8. The principal likes the book.

Here are the answers: 1. <u>Does</u> *Arthur* <u>read</u> *every advertisement?* 2. <u>Do</u> *they* <u>ride</u> *the train every day?* 3. <u>Have</u> *the baseballs* <u>fallen</u> *out of the basket?* 4. <u>Will</u> *I* <u>walk</u> *four miles tomorrow?* 5. <u>Is</u> *the mystery solved?* 6. <u>Do</u> *the brave soldiers* <u>fight</u> *for their country?* 7. <u>Have</u> *all teachers* <u>read</u> *that book?* 8. <u>Does</u> *the principal* <u>like</u> *the book?*

As you see, you needed no extra helping verbs in 3, 4, 5, and 7. Those statements have forms of *be, do, have,* and *will* in them. Simply rearranging the words is enough to create a question. The other statements do not have one of those words, so you must insert a helping verb.

Creating negative statements with helping verbs

A positive outlook is a good thing, except when you want to say "no" or make some other negative statement. In that situation, you generally need a helping verb and the word *not.* Take a look at these pairs:

POSITIVE STATEMENT: I <u>go</u> to a concert every Friday.

NEGATIVE STATEMENT: I <u>do</u> not <u>go</u> to a concert every Friday.

POSITIVE STATEMENT: The musicians <u>tuned</u> their instruments.

NEGATIVE STATEMENT: The musicians <u>did</u> not <u>tune</u> their instruments.

POSITIVE STATEMENT: The violin <u>has</u> a broken string.

NEGATIVE STATEMENT: The violin <u>does</u> not <u>have</u> a broken string.

POSITIVE STATEMENT: The conductor <u>raised</u> his hands.

NEGATIVE STATEMENT: The conductor <u>did</u> not <u>raise</u> his hands.

POSITIVE STATEMENT: The audience <u>quieted</u> down.

NEGATIVE STATEMENT: The audience <u>did</u> not <u>quiet</u> down.

Do you see the pattern? In these examples, you add a helping verb and the word *not* to make a negative statement.

Sometimes, to turn negative, all you need is the word *not.* When? In these situations:

✔ If the only verb in the sentence is a form of *be,* you do not need a helping verb.

✔ If another helping verb, such as *has* or *have,* is already in the sentence, you do not need to add a new one.

✔ If you are speaking of the future, you do not need any extra helping verbs.

In all these situations, just insert *not:*

POSITIVE STATEMENT: The conductor <u>is</u> upset.

NEGATIVE STATEMENT: The conductor <u>is</u> not upset.

POSITIVE STATEMENT: The conductor <u>has led</u> the orchestra well.

NEGATIVE STATEMENT: The conductor <u>has</u> not <u>led</u> the orchestra well.

POSITIVE STATEMENT: She <u>will go</u> to the dance performance tomorrow.

NEGATIVE STATEMENT: She <u>will</u> not <u>go</u> to the dance performance tomorrow.

POSITIVE STATEMENT: Al <u>has been snoring</u> all night.

NEGATIVE STATEMENT: Al <u>has not been snoring</u> all night.

You may see a *contraction* — a shortened form — in a negative statement. The word *not* is very often part of the contraction. Whether the whole word is present or not, the meaning is still negative:

he is not — he isn't

we are not — we aren't

Allie did not swim — Allie didn't swim

In Chapter 14, you can find out more about contractions.

In the following table, see whether you can change the positive statement in the first column into a negative statement. Write the negative statement in the second column. Identify the verbs in the negative statement.

Positive   *Negative*
1. The chair has a broken leg.
2. Ellie is very happy with her part in the play.
3. Gene sneaks some gum into class.
4. The executives raised the salaries of their employees.

Positive   *Negative*

5. Every driver beeps the horn often.

6. The princess costume was very popular this year.

7. The janitor has cleaned the halls recently.

Here are the answers: 1. *The chair <u>does</u> not <u>have</u> a broken leg.* 2. *Ellie <u>is</u> not very happy with her part in the play.* 3. *Gene <u>did</u> not <u>sneak</u> some gum into class.* 4. *The executives <u>did</u> not <u>raise</u> the salaries of their employees.* 5. *Every driver <u>does</u> not <u>beep</u> the horn often.* 6. *The princess costume <u>was</u> not very popular this year.* 7. *The janitor <u>has</u> not <u>cleaned</u> the halls recently.*

Notice that you did not have to add a helping verb to statements 2, 6, and 7. Statements 2 and 6 have forms of the verb *be* in them. Statement 7 already includes a helping verb, *has*. To change statements 2, 6, and 7 into negatives, you simply add *not*.

Expressing duty, ability, and possibility with helping verbs

<u>Should</u> you <u>study</u> English grammar? You <u>can learn</u> the rules easily. With strong English skills, you <u>may earn</u> higher grades and a better salary.

What do you see in the preceding paragraph? Yes, I know you see a reason to buy this book! Apart from that, you also see helping verbs that add a sense of duty *(should)*, ability *(can)*, and possibility *(may)*. Here are some other helping verbs that add meaning to your sentences:

> *must* — duty: I <u>must mail</u> my tax return today.

> *could* — ability: Helen said she was so tired that she <u>could sleep</u> for days.

> *might* — possibility: Norman <u>might be</u> hungry, so cook a lot of food.

> *will* — willingness: The conductor <u>will help</u> with your baggage, if you wish.

> *would* — willingness, with conditions: Jean said she <u>would wash</u> the dishes if you <u>would dry</u> them.

These helpers are very powerful. Add them to a sentence to improve your expression of ideas.

Three pairs of "twins" are in the helping-verb family:

> ✔ *Can* and *could* both express ability. Strict grammarians usually insert *can* in present or future situations and *could* in past situations.

> ✔ *Will* and *would* are another pair that express the same meaning: willingness. *Will* may be better for the present or future, and *would* for the past.

> ✔ *May* and *might* express possibility. *May* is generally used for present or future situations, and *might* for the past.

Don't worry too much about these pairs. Most people pick one or the other at random, and the meaning still comes across clearly.

Try your hand at adding *should, can, may, must, could, might,* or *would* to each sentence using the following table. To help you decide, I placed some choices in the second column and the intended meaning in the third column.

Sentence	*Possible Helping Verbs*	*Intended Meaning*
1. Henry said that he _____ paint the room for you.	could, should, would	willingness
2. _____ we help you with that suitcase?	May, Will, Must	possibility
3. You _____ take care of the children while I am away.	may, must, would	duty
4. The first grader proudly said, "I _____ read!"	can, should, might	ability
5. Jane _____ dance, if her legs were not sore.	could, would, must	conditions
6. Take an aspirin; it _____ help.	should, must, may	possibility
7. This new tape _____ seal the hole in the roof.	would, should, could	ability
8. She placed apples in the children's rooms because she knew they _____ be hungry.	would, can, might	possibility

Here are the answers: 1. *would* 2. *May* 3. *must* 4. *can* 5. *would* 6. *may* 7. *could* 8. *might.*

Never close?

A sign in the window of a restaurant in my neighborhood proudly states that it is "never close." I like living in New York City, and I know that space is expensive. I peeked in and saw that the tables were very close together. The restaurant is open 24 hours a day, 7 days a week. In other words, it is "never closed." The person who made the sign forgot the letter *D*. These two words sound almost, but not exactly, alike. They have different meanings:

close As a description, the last sound is a strong *s,* like a whistle. It means "near, not far away." (Example: Because Linda lives <u>close</u> to me, I visit her often.)

close As a present-tense verb form, the last sound is a strong *z.* The verb *close* means "to shut." (Example: Please <u>close</u> the door on your way out.)

closed This word may be a past-tense verb form. The last *S* sound in a strong *z.* (Example: Linda <u>closed</u> the book and put it on the shelf.) This word may also be a description, which you apply to something that is not open. (Example: I knocked on the <u>closed</u> door.)

Chapter 6

Describing with Adjectives and Adverbs

- -

In This Chapter

▶ Describing people, places, and things with adjectives

▶ Telling *how*, *where*, and *why* with adverbs

▶ Placing *a* and *an* correctly

▶ Creating comparisons with adjectives and adverbs

- -

*J*ohn paints. Workers build houses. Children play games. These sentences give information, but only a little. Most people want to know more. These sentences tell more: *John paints <u>carefully</u>. <u>Skilled</u> workers build <u>fancy</u>, <u>expensive</u> houses. <u>Noisy</u> children play <u>video</u> games <u>frequently</u>.*

The underlined words are adjectives and adverbs. They add meaning and interest to your sentences. These two parts of speech are the same in one way: They both describe. Adjectives and adverbs are not the same in other ways: They describe different parts of speech and give different information.

In this chapter, you find everything you need to know about adjectives and adverbs — how to tell one from another, when to use them, and how to create comparisons with them. You also sort out the proper use of two tiny but important words, *a* and *an*.

Adding Detail with Adjectives

Adjectives give information about people, places, and things. In English-teacher terms, adjectives describe nouns and pronouns. (For more information on nouns, see Chapter 3. Chapter 4 tells you about pronouns.)

Take a look at the way adjectives add meaning. You ask little Mike what he wants for his third birthday. Mike replies, "Snake!" What do you buy?

a <u>poisonous</u> snake

a <u>hungry</u> snake

a <u>giant</u> snake

a <u>rubber</u> snake

The police may want to know which of the underlined words is correct before little Mike opens his present. The underlined words are all adjectives, and they all describe the noun *snake.* As you see, adjectives can give very important information.

Even in less serious situations (those not involving poison!), adjectives add helpful details. Read the sentences in the following table. Notice what the underlined words in the second column add to the sentence. The adjectives are underlined. In the third column, the words the adjectives describe are identified.

Original	*Original Plus Adjectives*	*Explanation*
The waiter brings our soup.	The <u>overworked</u> waiter brings our <u>cold</u> soup.	*overworked* describes *waiter* *cold* describes *soup*
Diners complain about the soup.	<u>Annoyed</u> diners complain about the <u>tasteless</u> soup.	*Annoyed* describes *diners* *tasteless* describes *soup*
The owner apologizes to the customers.	The <u>embarrassed</u> owner apologizes to the <u>disappointed</u> customers.	*embarrassed* describes *owner* *disappointed* describes *customers*
Owners hire waiters.	<u>Wise</u> owners hire <u>extra</u> waiters.	*Wise* describes *owners* *extra* describes *waiters*
Owners pay salaries.	<u>Generous</u> owners pay <u>high</u> salaries.	*Generous* describes *owners* *high* describes *salaries*
Applicants compete for jobs.	<u>Many good</u> applicants compete for <u>desirable</u> jobs.	*Many* and *good* describe *applicants* *desirable* describes *jobs*
Restaurants have customers.	<u>Efficient</u> restaurants have <u>happy</u> customers.	*Efficient* describes *restaurants* *happy* describes *customers*

In this table, every adjective gives information about the nouns in the sentence.

Occasionally, adjectives can also describe pronouns. Pronouns take the place of nouns. The pronoun *everything,* for example, substitutes for the name of every single thing in the group. Look at this sentence:

> Everyone <u>available</u> should report to duty.

In this sentence, *available* is an adjective describing the pronoun *everyone.*

How to find adjectives

Adjectives give information about nouns and pronouns (see Figure 6-1). To find adjectives, look at a noun and ask three questions:

- ✔ How many?
- ✔ Which one?
- ✔ What kind?

Figure 6-1: How to identify adjectives.

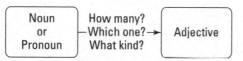

You may get an answer to one question or to more than one question. The word that answers the question is an adjective. Watch these questions in action, based on this sentence:

> Three soft pillows were on the lumpy bed.

First, notice the nouns — *pillows* and *bed.* Focus on one noun at a time:

- ✔ How many *pillows? Three. Three* is an adjective. It describes the noun *pillows.*
- ✔ Which *pillows?* No answer.
- ✔ What kind of *pillows? Soft pillows. Soft* is an adjective. It describes the noun *pillows.*

Now look at the second noun, *bed.* Ask the questions:

✔ How many *bed?* No answer.

✔ Which *bed?* No answer.

✔ What kind of *bed? Lumpy bed. Lumpy* is an adjective. It describes the noun *bed.*

You probably noticed that the first question (*How many bed?*) is odd. Normally, you would ask, "How many *beds?*" Do not focus on how the questions sound. Just ask each question and search the sentence for an answer.

Do you have enough energy for another example? Take a look at this sentence:

Every bill is unpaid and overdue.

The noun in this sentence is *bill.* Apply the questions:

✔ How many *bills?* No answer.

✔ Which *bills? Every bill. Every* is an adjective. It describes the noun *bill.*

✔ What kind of *bill? Unpaid* and *overdue. Unpaid* and *overdue* are adjectives. They describe the noun *bill.*

Do not rest now. Try one more:

Nothing bad will happen!

This sentence has one pronoun, *nothing.* Ask the questions:

✔ How many *nothing?* No answer.

✔ Which *nothing?* No answer.

✔ What kind? *Bad. Bad* is an adjective. It describes the pronoun *nothing.*

Sometimes, when you ask questions to find adjectives, the answer contains many words. English teachers call these longer answers *phrases* and *clauses.* Do not worry about labels. They are not important! For now, focus on single-word answers.

Where to find adjectives

Finding adjectives is easier if you know where to look. So where can you find adjectives? In the Adjective Department of your local store. Just kidding! Adjectives usually show up in front of the words they describe:

> <u>pretty</u> flower
>
> <u>smelly</u> cheese
>
> <u>rotten</u> tomatoes
>
> <u>grouchy</u> lady
>
> <u>uncomfortable</u> chair
>
> <u>eager</u> fans

Sometimes adjectives appear in different places. They may follow a verb that expresses a state of being. A verb that expresses a state of being is like an equal sign in math. Two ideas, one before and one after the verb, are linked. (For more information on verbs, turn to Chapter 5.)

Take a look at this sentence:

> Scott is <u>tired</u> and <u>cranky</u>.

Here is another way to think about this sentence:

> Scott = <u>tired</u> and <u>cranky</u>

The adjectives *tired* and *cranky* describe the noun *Scott*. The verb *is* expresses a state of being and acts as an equal sign.

Here is another example of a sentence that follows the same pattern. The adjectives are underlined.

> Lola has been <u>cheerful</u>, but I know that she is <u>tense</u>.
>
> Lola = <u>cheerful</u>   she = <u>tense</u>

In the first part of the sentence, the adjective *cheerful* describes the noun *Lola*. The verb *has been* expresses a state of being. In the second part of the sentence, the adjective *tense* describes the pronoun *she*. The verb *is* expresses a state of being.

Take a look at this example, which follows the same pattern.

> That box seems <u>mysterious</u>.
>
> box = mysterious

The adjective *mysterious* describes the noun *box*. The verb *seems* expresses a state of being.

Here is one more example:

I am <u>unhappy</u> because the cake looks <u>disgusting</u>.

I = <u>unhappy</u>   cake = <u>disgusting</u>

The adjective *unhappy* describes the pronoun *I*. The verb *am* expresses a state of being. In the second part of the sentence, the adjective *disgusting* describes the noun *cake*. The verb *looks* expresses a state of being.

Verbs that express a state of being are usually forms of the verb *be*. Sometimes, verbs that explain how you take in information through your senses also express a state of being. *Look, appear, seem, smell, taste,* and *feel* are examples of these verbs. These verbs may link a description to a noun or pronoun.

An adjective may also follow the noun or pronoun it describes:

Something <u>sticky</u> was inside. (The adjective *sticky* describes the pronoun *something*.)

Peter, <u>funny</u> and <u>confident</u>, easily won the election. (The adjectives *funny* and *confident* describe the noun *Peter*.)

Everything <u>scary</u> and <u>silly</u> appears on Halloween. (The adjectives *scary* and *silly* describe the pronoun *everything*.)

Now it is time for you to search for adjectives. Write the adjectives in the middle column. In the last column, write the word the adjectives describe.

Sentence	*Adjectives*	*Words the Adjectives Describe*
1. My cat, hungry and tired, scratched me.		
2. The sauce smells terrible.		
3. Happy children are running over there.		
4. Bright sunlight hurts my eyes.		
5. Fatty food may damage your health.		
6. Hamburgers taste delicious.		
7. Everything ready should be in the car now.		

Here are the answers: 1. The adjectives *hungry* and *tired* describe *cat*. 2. The adjective *terrible* describes *sauce*. 3. The adjective *happy* describes *children*. 4. The adjective *bright* describes *sunlight*. 5. The adjective *fatty* describes *food*. 6. The adjective *delicious* describes *hamburgers*. 7. The adjective *ready* describes *everything*.

Adjectives add useful information to your sentences. They describe nouns and pronouns and answer the questions *how many? which one?* or *what kind?*

Writing Well with Adverbs

Every English sentence contains at least one "doing" or "being" word (a verb). Many verbs come with descriptions attached — words that tell you *how, when, where,* or *under what conditions* the "doing" or "being" occurs. Words that describe verbs are *adverbs.* The relationship between verbs and adverbs is very close. In fact, one word (adverb) contains the other (verb)! Adverbs have another job, too. Adverbs such as *very* or *less* change the intensity of a description. In this section, you see how adverbs perform both of these roles.

Adding information to verbs

A film director speaks to four actors. The director says, "Go to the door." The actors go to the door — but not in the same way:

> Mary goes <u>slowly</u>.
>
> Mark goes <u>quickly</u>.
>
> Jenny goes <u>immediately</u>.
>
> Arthur goes <u>later</u>.

The underlined words are adverbs. Each one changes the way the action occurs. The adverbs add meaning to the verb *goes.* In other words, the adverbs describe the verb *goes.*

Here is the film director again, in an outdoor scene. This time, the director yells, "Go!" Once more, the actors react differently:

> Mary goes <u>here</u>.
>
> Mark goes <u>there</u>.
>
> Jenny goes <u>reluctantly</u>.
>
> Arthur goes <u>eagerly</u>.

The adverbs add information about the action expressed by the word *goes.* Words that explain what someone or something is doing are verbs. Adverbs may describe these verbs.

Adverbs may also describe verbs that express a state of being — what someone or something *is, was,* or *will be.* Look at these examples:

> The director was <u>home</u>.
>
> Mary <u>originally</u> seemed smart.
>
> Mark <u>definitely</u> is smarter than Mary.

Do not worry about what kind of verb an adverb describes. Just remember that adverbs give important information about action or state of being.

Using the example of a film director, the director gets better results by adding adverbs. In the table below, you find the director's statements and then the same statements with adverbs. Can you see how the underlined adverbs help the actors understand what the director wants?

Director's Original Comment	Original Plus Adverbs	Explanation
Mary says her line.	Mary says her line <u>sadly</u>.	*sadly* describes *says*
Arthur falls.	Arthur <u>now</u> falls.	*now* describes *falls*
Mark helps Arthur.	Mark <u>promptly</u> helps Arthur.	*promptly* describes *helps*
Jenny speaks.	<u>Then</u>, Jenny speaks <u>angrily</u>.	*Then* and *angrily* describe *speaks*
Jenny's character is upset.	Jenny's character is <u>always</u> upset.	*always* describes *is*
Mary, Mark, and Arthur pay attention to Jenny.	Mary, Mark, and Arthur <u>never</u> pay attention to Jenny.	*never* describes *pay*
Jenny walks.	Jenny walks <u>out</u>.	*out* describes *walks*

To locate an adverb, first pay attention to verbs (doing or being words). Ask these questions:

- ✔ How?
- ✔ When?
- ✔ Where?
- ✔ Under what conditions?

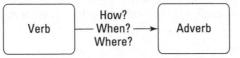

Figure 6-2: Questions to find adverbs.

Verb — How? When? Where? → Adverb

Figure 6-2 shows you the questions. Take a look at them, applied to this sentence:

> Later, alone, Bert completely understood the reason for Ellen's impolite comment.

This sentence contains one verb, *understood.* Apply the questions:

> *Understood* how? *Completely understood. Completely* is an adverb. It describes the verb *understood.*
>
> *Understood* when? *Understood later. Later* is an adverb. It describes the verb *understood.*
>
> *Understood* where? No answer.
>
> *Understood* under what conditions? *Understood alone. Alone* is an adverb. It describes the verb *understood.*

Here is another sentence, so you can see the questions in action again:

> Peter recently moved away.

The sentence contains one verb, *moved.* Apply the questions:

> *Moved* how? No answer. *Moved* when? *Recently. Recently* is an adverb. It describes the verb *moved.*
>
> *Moved* where? *Away. Away* is an adverb. It describes the verb *moved.*
>
> *Moved* under what conditions? No answer.

Adverbs that describe verbs like to travel — not around the world, but around a sentence. They may appear at the beginning, middle, or end of a sentence. As long as the meaning is clear, you may place an adverb anywhere you like.

Adding meaning to descriptions

How stubborn are you? <u>Very</u> stubborn? <u>Rather</u> stubborn? <u>Only slightly</u> stubborn? The answer to this question may matter a lot to a parent, a teacher, or an employer who has to tell you what to do! Each underlined word adds to the meaning of the descriptive word *stubborn.* Each underlined word is an adverb. In these examples, the adverbs describe another description, *stubborn,* adding or taking away intensity.

Here are more examples of adverbs that give information about other descriptive words:

<u>very</u> pretty

<u>less</u> friendly

<u>extremely</u> hard

<u>too</u> easy

<u>fairly</u> simple

<u>overly</u> complicated

Where do you find an adverb doing this job? Right in front of the word the adverb describes. Besides location, you can find an adverb that describes a description by asking one question: How?

Figure 6-3:
Adjective or
adverb.

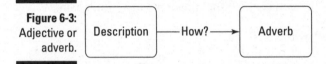

Would you like to see this question in action? Here is an example sentence. Pay close attention to the descriptions:

Much earlier, Bert had made a very rude comment to Ellen.

Examine the descriptions and ask the question. The sentence includes two descriptive words. One is an adverb. The other is an adjective. (Look at the section "Adding Detail with Adjectives" earlier in this chapter for more information on adjectives.) Start with the description *earlier:*

Earlier how? *Much earlier. Much* is an adverb. It describes another adverb, *earlier.*

Now look at the descriptive word *rude:*

Rude how? *Very rude. Very* is an adverb. It describes the adjective *rude.*

Adverbs can change the intensity of a description. Sometimes the description becomes more intense:

<u>extremely</u> talented

<u>totally</u> secure

<u>very</u> silly

Sometimes the description becomes less intense:

<u>slightly</u> confusing

<u>least</u> boring

<u>less</u> greedy

When you ask questions to find adverbs, the answer may contain many words. English teachers call these longer answers *phrases* and *clauses*. Do not worry about labels. They are not important! For now, focus on single-word answers. If you want to know more about phrases, turn to Chapter 7.

It is time for you to search for adverbs. Write the adverbs in the middle column. In the last column, write the word, or words, the adverb describes.

Sentence	*Adverbs*	*Words the Adverbs Describe*

1. Johnny often lost his temper.
2. The teacher was quite skilled.
3. Sophie is really hungry.
4. Andrew never tells very long stories.
5. The mayor's extremely late budget has now created problems.
6. Yesterday, you strongly favored that decision.
7. Ed prefers a more modern style of furniture.

Here are the answers: 1. The adverb *often* describes the verb *lost.* 2. The adverb *quite* describes another description, *skilled.* 3. The adverb *really* describes another description, *hungry.* 4. The adverb *never* describes the verb *tells.* The adverb *very* describes another description, *long.* 5. The adverb *extremely* describes another description, *late.* The adverb *now* describes the verb *has created.* 6. The adverbs *yesterday* and *strongly* describe the verb *favored.* 7. The adverb *more* describes another description, *modern.*

Adverbs add useful information about actions and states of being. They also change the intensity of other descriptions.

Choosing between Adjectives and Adverbs

Builders need the right tools for every kind of job. They cannot hammer a nail with a screwdriver. They cannot turn a screw with a hammer, either! When you build a sentence, you must also choose the right tool — the part of speech that can do the job you have in mind.

Adjectives and adverbs are like hammers and screwdrivers. They work differently. When you select a descriptive word, follow these guidelines:

- ✔ **When you are describing a person, place, or thing, use an adjective.** Adjectives tell you how many, which one, or what kind of person or thing you are talking about. (For more information on nouns, refer to Chapter 3. Turn to Chapter 4 to learn more about pronouns.)

- ✔ **When you are describing an action or state of being, select an adverb.** Adverbs tell you how, when, where, why, or under what conditions in reference to words that express action or states of being.

- ✔ **When you increase or decrease the intensity of another description, use an adverb.** Words such as *very, too, extremely,* and *less* are adverbs. They attach to other descriptions.

- ✔ **Many descriptive words have two forms — one an adjective and the other an adverb.** For example, *frequent* is an adjective and *frequently* is an adverb. Be sure to use the right one!

- ✔ **Adverbs often end with the letters *ly*.** Be careful! Not every adverb has this ending. Some words that end with *ly,* such as *lovely,* are not adverbs.

- ✔ **The dictionary identifies the part of speech.** If you are not sure whether a word is an adjective or an adverb, the dictionary will tell you.

Here are some adjectives and adverbs. In each pair, the first word is an adjective, and the second is an adverb. Look carefully at the examples, so you see how these words are properly used.

Adjective	Example	Adverb	Example
real	Nancy buys real butter.	really	David is really funny.
sure	Harriet thinks this is a sure bet.	surely	He surely knew the name of the murderer.
good	We write good books.	well	I feel well.
bad	I felt bad when I saw the damage.	badly	They danced so badly that they were told not to go on stage again.
hungry	Martha is hungry, so she is cooking now.	hungrily	Martha hungrily gobbled up the stew.
beautiful	A beautiful flower sits on my desk.	beautifully	Henry danced beautifully.
ordinary	On an ordinary day, I get up early.	ordinarily	Max ordinarily shops on Main Street.

Adjective	Example	Adverb	Example
usual	An apple is his usual snack.	usually	Do you usually go to the theater, or is today a special event?
quick	A quick move to the left saved her from the speeding truck.	quickly	Come quickly!
secret	Shall I tell you the secret password?	secretly	Mary secretly loves Tim, but she will never tell him.
sweet	Everyone in my family loves sweet desserts.	sweetly	She asked so sweetly that he had to say yes.

For each sentence, choose the correct word from the parentheses.

1. My dog barks _____ (loyal, loyally) when he sees me.

2. The neighbors are _____ (real, really) annoyed by his barking.

3. I think he is a _____ (good, well) pet, but they disagree _____ (strong, strongly).

4. Do you _____ (true, truly) want me to send my _____ (poor, poorly) dog away?

5. You need earplugs _____ (bad, badly).

Here are the answers: 1. *loyally* (an adverb describing the verb *barks*) 2. *really* (an adverb describing the description *annoyed*) 3. *good* (an adjective describing the noun *pet*); *strongly* (an adverb describing the verb *disagree*) 4. *truly* (an adverb describing the verb *do want*); *poor* (an adjective describing the noun *dog*) 5. *badly* (an adverb describing the verb *need*).

Do you feel bad? Or badly?

How should you answer this question? Probably with the word *bad*, because *bad* is an adjective. When you say that you feel *bad*, you are describing yourself — your mood, your feelings, or your physical condition. The word *badly* is an adverb. Adverbs attach to verbs. If you say that you feel *badly*, you are making a statement about your ability to feel. Maybe you have gloves on and cannot feel anything with your fingertips. Perhaps you have a medical condition that deadens your nerves. In those situations, you feel *badly*. Most of the time, though, the right word is *bad*.

Placing "a" and "an" in the Proper Place

Do you have <u>an</u> apple? How about <u>a</u> pear? I love to find <u>a</u> bargain when I shop for <u>an</u> automobile. Do you have <u>an</u> accountant? <u>An</u> expert helps me fill out <u>a</u> tax form quickly and easily. <u>A</u> tax attorney is also useful.

As you probably noticed, I underlined two little words — *a* and *an* — in the preceding sentences. *A* and *an* attach to nouns. (Nouns are words that name people, places, and things. For more information, read Chapter 3.) These words do the same job. Each tells you that you are speaking of one person, place, or thing — but in a general way. If I offer you <u>a</u> piece of fruit, I can pick anything from the fruit basket. If I refer to <u>an</u> orange, I don't have one particular orange in mind.

The word *the* is sometimes mentioned when people talk about *a* and *an,* because *the* does more or less the same job. *The* works for both singular (one) and plural (more than one) nouns. *The* is more specific, though. If I say, "I ate <u>the</u> pear," I have one particular pear in mind.

To decide between *a* and *an,* follow these steps:

- ✔ **Check the beginning of the word that follows.** What sound does the word begin with?

- ✔ **Generally, use *an* if the word begins with a vowel sound.** The letters *a, e, i, o,* and *u* are vowels. ***Note:*** The letter *u* is complicated. If it is long (you can hear the name of the letter), as in *university,* use *a.* If it is a short vowel, as in *uncle,* use *an.*

- ✔ **Use *a* if the word does not begin with a vowel sound.** If you can rule out *a, e, i, o,* and a short *u,* use *a.*

Notice that your decision between *a* and *an* is based on sound, not spelling. Most of the time, the actual vowel appears at the beginning of the word. Sometimes, the vowel has a silent letter in front: *hour,* for example, has a silent letter *h.* You study for *an hour,* not for *a hour.*

Place *a* or *an* in each blank:

1. _____ computer displays _____ image or words on _____ screen.
2. _____ addition problem is easy. You do not need _____ hour to find _____ answer.
3. _____ coat is _____ unnecessary item in _____ hot country.
4. Taking _____ walk to _____ park is _____ exercise you will enjoy.

Here are the answers: 1. *A, an, a* 2. *An, an, an* 3. *A, an, a* 4. *a, a, an.*

Making Comparisons with Adjectives and Adverbs

Do you like to compare yourself to others? Perhaps you wonder if you are happier than your friends. You may wish to know who is the smartest person in the class or who owns the least valuable car.

Most people do make comparisons. They do so with adjectives and adverbs. Take a look at some proper comparisons. The adjectives and adverbs are underlined.

> This piece of glass is sharp, but the other one is sharper.
>
> Out of 25 students, Gloria was the shortest.
>
> Arthur danced more gracefully than Alice.
>
> Alice's shoes were less comfortable than Arthur's.
>
> Of all the mathematicians, Gina solved the problems most efficiently.
>
> The least confident test-taker often scores the lowest grade.

Did you notice that some comparisons are created with one word, and others with more than one word? In the following sections, you see how to create both types of comparisons.

Single-word comparisons

Many comparisons have very simple forms. To compare one person or thing to one other person or thing, you add *er* to the description. To compare one person or thing to a group of two or more others, you add *est* to the description.

If the description already ends with the letter *e,* you just add *r* or *st.* You do not double the *e.*

Take a look at these comparisons. The description is in the first column. The second column contains the form for comparing two things. The third is the form for a group of three or more.

Description	Comparing Two	Comparing Three or More
simple	simpler	simplest
old	older	oldest
plain	plainer	plainest

Description	Comparing Two	Comparing Three or More
high	higher	highest
strange	stranger	strangest
narrow	narrower	narrowest
slow	slower	slowest
deep	deeper	deepest

Sometimes the spelling of the description changes when you add *er* or *est* to the end. Look at these examples:

Description	Comparing Two	Comparing Three or More
tasty	tastier	tastiest
pretty	prettier	prettiest
friendly	friendlier	friendliest
fat	fatter	fattest
lively	livelier	liveliest
lonely	lonelier	loneliest
noisy	noisier	noisiest

If you are not sure how to spell a single-word comparison, check the dictionary.

Two-word comparisons

Most single-word comparisons start with a simple description — a fairly short word. Comparisons that begin with longer words rely on an extra word. You add *more* or *most* to the basic description. *More* creates a comparison between one person or thing and one other person or thing. *Most* creates a comparison between one person or thing and a group of two or more others. Take a look at these examples:

Description	Comparing Two	Comparing Three or More
beautiful	more beautiful	most beautiful
expensive	more expensive	most expensive
experienced	more experienced	most experienced
recently	more recently	most recently
quickly	more quickly	most quickly
happily	more happily	most happily
generous	more generous	most generous

If you are not sure how to create a comparison, check your dictionary. Usually, a dictionary definition includes the word form for a comparison if that form is a single word. If you do not see a comparison, you probably need to add *more* or *most*.

Not every comparison is positive. Some are negative. Take a look at these examples:

> In singing, Alex is <u>less talented</u> than Oliver.
>
> Oliver is the <u>least talented</u> piano player in the class.
>
> This violin sounds <u>less beautiful</u> than the other one.
>
> My pony competes with ten others, and he is the <u>least afraid</u> of jumping.
>
> The corn muffin is <u>less sweet</u> than the blueberry muffin.
>
> Mary hates all the shoes, and she selects the <u>least ugly</u> pair.

As you see, *less* compares one person or thing to one other person or thing. *Least* compares one person or thing to a group of at least two others.

Irregular comparisons

English has many rules. English also breaks many rules! Some words do not depend on *er, est,* or *more, most, less,* or *least* to form comparisons. These rule-breakers are irregular, but important. Here they are:

Description	Comparing Two	Comparing Three or More
good	better	best
bad	worse	worst
well	better	best
little	less	least
many	more	most
much	more	most

You probably noticed that some words in the second and third columns repeat. The forms for comparing are the same. Why? I have no idea!

 To test your knowledge of comparisons, fill in the missing columns in this table. In the first column, you see the description, plus the word *positive* or *negative*. A *positive* comparison adds *er, est, more,* or *most* (plus some irregular forms). A *negative* comparison relies on *less* or *least* (plus some irregular forms). Good luck!

Description	Comparing Two	Comparing Three or More
1. ignorant (positive)		
2. tough (negative)		
3. modern (positive)		
4. valuable (negative)		
5. good (positive)		
6. bad (negative)		
7. spicy (positive)		

Here are the answers: 1. *more ignorant, most ignorant* 2. *less tough, least tough* 3. *more modern, most modern* 4. *less valuable, least valuable* 5. *better, best* 6. *worse, worst* 7. *spicier, spiciest.*

Going against the tide: *Anti*

You may have an old *auntie* in your family, the sister of your father or mother, who loves to protest. She hates the food you cook, she can't stand the way you decorated the guest bedroom, and she says that your friends are the most annoying people in the world. This type of auntie loves a word part, *anti*. Why? The word part, *anti*, means "against." When you attach *anti* to the beginning of a word, you state opposition. Take a look at these examples:

antiwar against war (Tens of thousands of people attended the antiwar protest.)

anticommunist against communism (The anticommunist forces won the battle after many years of struggle.)

antisocial against society, including individual private gatherings, and large communities (Because Jeff is antisocial, he seldom goes to parties. Spraying paint on the Town Hall is an antisocial act.)

antibiotic against germs (He took an antibiotic for ten days and recovered completely.)

antiabortion against abortion (Antiabortion groups criticized the judge's decision.)

antifreeze a liquid that doesn't freeze at normal temperatures because it works "against freezing" (Helen adds antifreeze during the winter.)

antiaircraft defenses that protect against attacks from the air (The antiaircraft defense station is near the border.)

antipoverty against poverty (The antipoverty program built housing for the poor.)

You can attach *anti* to many other words. Sometimes a small line called a *hyphen* appears between *anti* and the word it connects to, especially if that word is a name that is usually capitalized. For example, anti-Obama protesters are against, or oppose, the beliefs or actions of President Obama.

Warning: Sometimes a word begins with *anti*, but the meaning has nothing to do with being against something. *Antique,* for example, means "something very old." It does not mean "against que," because *que* is not a word in English.

Chapter 7

Little Things Mean a Lot: Prepositions

- -

In This Chapter

▶ Identifying prepositions and the phrases they appear in

▶ Locating the object of a preposition

▶ Selecting pronouns to follow prepositions

▶ Placing prepositional phrases in the correct spot

- -

Do you want to know more about a relationship? You can look at a dating site on the Internet. You can ask your friends. You can watch a talk-show on television. Or, you can check for prepositions. Yes, a part of speech actually helps to explain relationships!

In this chapter, you discover how to find the right preposition to express your intended meaning. You also identify the preposition's *object* — an important word — and see how to place prepositions and objects properly.

Recognizing Prepositions

Prepositions are usually little words. Some are only two-letters long. These little words, though, mean a lot when you add them to your sentences. Take a look at these examples:

> Where are you now? Sitting <u>on</u> a chair? <u>Under</u> the sofa?

> When do you study grammar? <u>After</u> lunch? <u>Until</u> May?

> What are you holding? A book <u>by</u> a famous writer? A gift <u>for</u> your mom?

The underlined words are prepositions. These words establish relationships in various ways. In the first set of examples, the preposition links *you* to a *chair* and *sofa*. In the second set, a preposition links *you* to *lunch* and *May*. Prepositions in the last set of examples link *book* and *writer* and *gift* and *mom*.

In this section, you learn to identify the most common prepositions and the relationships they create.

Locating items and actions with prepositions

One important job for prepositions is to act as a sort of grammatical compass, telling you where something is in relation to something else.

Here is a daisy. It is

> <u>in</u> the vase
>
> <u>behind</u> your ear
>
> <u>with</u> the roses
>
> <u>in front of</u> the classroom
>
> <u>next to</u> the other flowers
>
> <u>on</u> the counter
>
> <u>at</u> the center
>
> <u>under</u> your pillow

The underlined words are prepositions. They signal location by telling you where the daisy is in relation to the *vase, your ear, the roses, the classroom, the other flowers, the counter, the center,* and *your pillow.*

Here are other prepositions of location:

above	between	through
along	beyond	toward
among	down	underneath
around	into	up
behind	over	upon
below	past	within

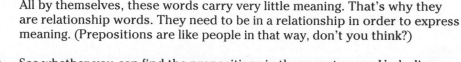

All by themselves, these words carry very little meaning. That's why they are relationship words. They need to be in a relationship in order to express meaning. (Prepositions are like people in that way, don't you think?)

See whether you can find the prepositions in these sentences. Underline them. Notice how these prepositions explain location.

1. The horse jumped over the fence and ran across the finish line.

2. Beyond the field, crowds gathered and watched the horse run past the farm.

3. He ran toward the mountains.

4. Everybody climbed up the mountain next to the farm.

5. The horse slid down the slope but did not go over the cliff.

Here are the answers: 1. *over, across* 2. *Beyond, past* 3. *toward* 4. *up, next to* 5. *down, over.*

Not every preposition is a single word. *Next to,* for example, is a two-word preposition.

Telling time with prepositions

When do you relax?

> Before bedtime? After lunch?

How long have you been studying?

> Since Tuesday? From nine until five?

The underlined words in the examples are prepositions. They give information about time. Other "time" prepositions include

> at
>
> before
>
> between
>
> beyond
>
> during
>
> for
>
> until

These prepositions are sometimes better than a clock. They do not always tell you a specific time, but they give you information about when an action is taking place.

Look for time expressions in these sentences. Underline the prepositions:

1. She slept until nine o'clock, and her class starts at eight!

2. Since September, she has been late on Tuesdays, but not on Fridays.

3. Her teacher believes she will not last beyond January.

4. If she works during her lunch hour, or between dinner and bedtime, she may pass.

5. Before tomorrow, she will buy an alarm clock.

Here are the answers: 1. *until, at* 2. *Since, on, on* 3. *beyond* 4. *during, between* 5. *Before.*

Discussing other relationships with prepositions

Time and space are important. So are other ideas that prepositions express. Read this message, sent from a supervisor to an employee:

> Without your help, Joan, I can complete the task. I can do that job by myself and the rest of the work with a group. I voted against you when you asked to be on the team. Everyone except you has skills we need. We need someone like Helen for our team.

What a cruel boss! The ideas may not be very helpful to Joan, but the underlined prepositions *are* helpful. They make the comment crystal clear. These prepositions explain other relationships. In the first sentence in this example, *without* shows the relationship between completing the task and Joan; you know that completing the task can happen without Joan, in her supervisor's opinion. Other prepositions not related to time and place include:

according to

besides

by

depending on

of

off

These prepositions give significant details to your reader or listener. Watch for them!

People who are learning English as a second language sometimes have trouble with prepositions. Often, a preposition that is proper in one language does not translate directly into English. If you are not sure which preposition to select, check the dictionary. Choosing the wrong one can create problems! For example:

> Mary: May I sit <u>with</u> you at the concert?
>
> James: Yes, of course.

> Mary: May I sit <u>on</u> you at the concert?
>
> James: No! Buy your own ticket!

Underline the prepositions in these sentences:

1. Among friends, the famous actor relaxed.
2. According to the photographer, the actor danced with many partners.
3. He knew everyone except me, but he was friendly to me anyway.
4. A film of the party will be on the Internet soon.
5. I received a large payment for it.

Here are the answers: 1. *Among* 2. *According to, with* 3. *except, to* 4. *of, on* 5. *for.*

Identifying Objects of Prepositions

Every so often, a story appears in the news about an unidentified flying object. People love to think that something they saw in the sky — an object — is a spaceship from Mars. Finding an object like that would make you rich and famous. Unfortunately, finding the object of a preposition will not make you rich and famous. However, you still need to look for these objects. You have to know what they are so you can use them properly.

One strange reason why you have to identify an object of a preposition is to ignore it! When you are matching subjects and verbs (a topic explained in Chapter 11), prepositions and their objects may confuse you and lead you to the wrong choice. If you know what they are, you can mentally cross them out and pair up the real subject and verb.

Finding objects through meaning

Every preposition begins a unit of thought. Take a look at these phrases:

around the full <u>moon</u>

by this <u>manufacturer</u>

into the <u>roof</u>

to <u>them</u>

on the same <u>topic</u>

to a large <u>audience</u>

about <u>Lola</u>

In each phrase, the underlined word is an object. It completes the meaning of the link the preposition creates. For example, suppose you say that:

The baseball crashed into the tiled roof.

The preposition *into* links an action, *crashed,* to a place, *roof.* Without *roof,* the link is incomplete.

An *object* is always a noun or a pronoun. (For more information on nouns, turn to Chapter 3. Chapter 4 provides more detail about pronouns.)

The object may have descriptions attached to it. In the example list at the beginning of this section, *full* describes the object *moon, same* describes the object *topic,* and *large* describes the object *audience.* Do not confuse the description with the object. Descriptions are usually adjectives. (Chapter 6 provides more information on adjectives.)

Sometimes, a preposition may have two or more objects. Read these sentences:

Mom yelled <u>at Bobby and me</u> this morning.

The package sent <u>by George and Will</u> arrived already.

Dust fell <u>on the chairs, tables, and floor.</u>

In the first example, the preposition, *at,* has two objects — *Bobby* and *me.* In the second sentence, the preposition *by* has two objects also — *George* and *Will.* In the last sentence, three nouns (*chairs, tables,* and *floor*) act as objects of the preposition *on.*

Locating objects with questions

You can also locate the object by saying the preposition and then asking two questions, *whom?* and *what?* Take a look at Figure 7-1:

The answer to these questions may include several words — the object plus descriptions. Focus on the object, which is always a noun or pronoun.

Here is this technique in action, based on this sample sentence:

> The top of the old tower was damaged in a recent attack.

In this sentence, you see two prepositions, *of* and *in.* Start with *of:*

> *of* whom? No answer.
>
> *of* what? *of the old tower*

The object of the preposition *of* is the noun *tower. Old* is a description, not an object. Now look at the second preposition, *in:*

> *in* whom? No answer.
>
> *in* what? *in a recent attack*

The object of the preposition *in* is the noun *attack. Recent* is a description, not an object.

A word may look the same as a preposition, but it is not a true preposition unless it has an object. Note how these two sentences differ:

> Mike climbed <u>up</u>.
>
> Mike climbed <u>up the ladder</u>.

In the first sentence, *up* is all by itself. *Up* is an adverb in this sentence. (For more information on adverbs, check out Chapter 6.) In the second sentence, *up* is a preposition because it has an object, *ladder.*

Check out the following sentences (column one). Write the prepositions in column two and the objects in column three.

Sentence	Prepositions	Objects
1. During the hurricane, the wind blew steadily.		
2. Water from the ocean flooded my basement.		
3. In a huge pile of dirty sand, I found my sneakers.		
4. A wet line on the basement wall marked the water's high point.		
5. My family and I carried sand out of the house.		
6. Mom made sandwiches for me and my helpers.		

Here are the answers: 1. *During* — preposition, *hurricane* — object 2. *from* — preposition, *ocean* — object 3. *In* — preposition, *pile* — object; *of* — preposition, *sand* — object 4. *on* — preposition, *wall* — object 5. *out of* — preposition, *house* — object 6. *for* — preposition, *me* and *helpers* — objects.

The easiest way to find the object is to look after the preposition. The object always follows the preposition.

Between: A misunderstood preposition

Pretend for a moment that *between* is a person, not a word. *Between* would be a popular guest on talk shows. Why? Because *between* is often misunderstood. On television, *between* would cry and talk about how often it is placed with *I* — not *me,* as it should be. *Between* would also complain that it does not belong in large groups.

Here is a guide to using *between* properly:

WRONG: Between you and I, I think this talk-show host is quite boring.

WHY IT IS WRONG: *Between* is a preposition. The object of a preposition must be an object pronoun. The pronoun *I* is a subject pronoun.

RIGHT: Between you and me, I think this talk-show host is quite boring.

WHY IT IS RIGHT: Now the object pronoun *me* acts as an object of the preposition *between.*

WRONG: Penny shared the profits between Alan and he.

WHY IT IS WRONG: *Between* is a preposition. The object of a preposition must be an object pronoun. The pronoun *he* is a subject pronoun.

RIGHT: Penny shared the profits between Alan and him.

WHY IT IS RIGHT: Now the object pronoun *him* acts as an object of the preposition *between.*

The preposition *between* is often used improperly in another type of situation. *Between* is the preposition you want when you are talking about two people or things. If the group is larger than two, the preposition you need is *among.* Check out these examples:

WRONG: Lola could not decide between the three motorcycles.

WHY IT IS WRONG: For a group of three, use the preposition *among.*

RIGHT: Lola could not decide between the two motorcycles.

ALSO RIGHT: Lola could not decide among the three motorcycles.

WHY THEY ARE RIGHT: *Between* is the proper preposition for a pair; *among* is the preposition you want for three or more.

WRONG: The contract was negotiated between all eight suppliers.

WHY IT IS WRONG: When you have *eight suppliers,* you need the preposition *among.* *Between* works only for pairs.

RIGHT: The contract was negotiated among all eight suppliers.

WHY IT IS RIGHT: *Among* is correct because the group of suppliers has more than two members.

Choosing Pronouns as Objects of Prepositions

When a noun — the name of a person, place, or thing — is the object of a preposition, everything is easy. Nouns work as subjects and objects without changing form. Pronouns — words that substitute for nouns — can cause a lot of trouble. Why? Pronouns are a divided family. Members of one branch of the family work as subjects. Members of another branch of the family are not allowed to do that job. They act as objects instead.

To serve as the object of a preposition, you need an object pronoun. Here are examples of correct and incorrect pronouns performing the "object of the preposition job":

WRONG: Take the pizza pie to <u>he</u>.

WHY IT IS WRONG: The pronoun *he* is for subjects, not objects.

RIGHT: Take the pizza pie to <u>him</u>.

WHY IT IS RIGHT: The pronoun *him* is for objects.

WRONG: She split the pie among Bill, Jenny, and I.

WHY IT IS WRONG: The pronoun *I* is for subjects, not objects.

RIGHT: She split the pie among Bill, Jenny, and me.

WHY IT IS RIGHT: The pronoun *me* is for objects.

WRONG: Bill threw his slice at she.

WHY IT IS WRONG: The pronoun *she* is for subjects, not objects.

RIGHT: Bill threw his slice at her.

WHY IT IS RIGHT: The pronoun *her* is for objects.

WRONG: Jenny was angry at Bill and we.

WHY IT IS WRONG: The pronoun *we* is for subjects, not objects.

RIGHT: Jenny was angry at Bill and us.

WHY IT IS RIGHT: The pronoun *us* is for objects.

The most common object pronouns are *me, us, you, him, her, it, them,* and *whom*. For more information on pronouns, turn to Chapter 4.

Select a pronoun to act as the object of a preposition from the choices in parentheses. Write the pronoun in the blank.

1. The robber told his story to _____ (they, them).

2. Then the robber escaped with _____ (she, her).

3. Police officers ran around _____ (we, us) to follow the criminal.

4. The newspaper article about the robber and _____ (he, him) is not true.

5. There were no romantic conversations between the robber and _____ (I, me).

Here are the answers: 1. *them* 2. *her* 3. *us* 4. *him* 5. *me*.

Placing Prepositional Phrases in the Proper Place

A preposition and its object form a description. Sometimes, you can place this description in several spots in the sentence without changing the meaning. Read these example sentences:

On the bed lay a bright blue quilt.

A bright blue quilt lay on the bed.

Over the fence sailed the baseball.

The baseball sailed over the fence.

Elena stepped into the mud puddle.

Into the mud puddle stepped Elena.

In every pair, the meaning is clear. Sometimes, though, the meaning changes when you move a descriptive phrase. Read these pairs:

He went by bicycle to the game, saw the winning goal, and returned afterwards.

He went by bicycle, saw the winning goal, and returned to the game afterwards.

Do you see the difference? In the first example sentence, *he* traveled *to the game* first. Then he *returned* to his starting point. In the second example sentence, *he* traveled somewhere else. Then he *returned to the game.* The meaning changes because one phrase, *to the game,* moves. Here is another example:

At the age of eight, Elizabeth drew a picture of her grandfather.

Elizabeth drew a picture of her grandfather at the age of eight.

In this first example sentence, *Elizabeth* is eight. In the second, the picture shows *her grandfather at the age of eight* — in other words, as a young boy.

When you place a description in a sentence, be sure it expresses the meaning you intend.

Are these sentences the same or different? You decide. The prepositional phrases are underlined.

1a. The letter to the governor has already been sent.

1b. The letter has already been sent to the governor.

2a. A performance by the dancers was poorly reviewed.

2b. A performance was poorly reviewed by the dancers.

3a. In the playground, children run and climb.

3b. Children run and climb in the playground.

4a. The jewelry <u>on her neck</u> is worth a fortune.

4b. The jewelry is worth a fortune <u>on her neck</u>.

Here are the answers: 1. Different: Sentence 1a clearly shows that the letter's intended reader is *the governor*. Sentence 1b could have a different meaning. The letter might be intended for the mayor, for example, with a copy sent to the governor. 2. Different: In 2a, *the dancers* performed. In 2b, someone else performed and received poor reviews from *the dancers*. 3. Same: In both sentences, the *children run and climb* in the same place. 4. Different: Sentence 4a implies that the jewelry has great value. Sentence 4b implies that the jewelry gains value because she is wearing it. (Perhaps she is a model or a star, and her jewelry becomes valuable because it is associated with her.)

Before and after

Three letters — *pre* — refer to earlier times, before something else. Four letters — *post* — go in the other direction, placing something after something else. Here are some examples:

prewar, postwar The first description describes the period before war breaks out. "The *prewar* planning assumed little resistance from the enemy." The second word refers to the period after the war ends. "*Postwar* efforts to rebuild the town were successful."

pregame, postgame The first description describes everything that happens before a game — a televised discussion of the team's chances, the players' practice, and so forth. "The coach's *pregame* speech inspired her team." The second description concerns what happens after the game — interviews with sports reporters, showers, and the like. "During the *postgame* show, the manager discussed his star player's performance."

preview To "view" or look at, beforehand. "Mr. Jones *previewed* the film and decided it was not appropriate for young children."

postpone To move to a later time, a time "after" the originally scheduled hour. "Charlotte *postponed* her trip because of the storm."

prevent To act beforehand so that something does not happen. "Because he checked the brakes and fixed the faulty part, he *prevented* a terrible accident."

prejudice Opinions formed before knowing the facts. "He had never met Ella, but his *prejudice* led him to believe that she was unreliable."

postscript Something added after the end of a piece of writing, the "P.S." of a letter. "In a *postscript*, Margaret gave the latest information about the accident."

Pay attention to *pre* and *post*. Then, when you watch a television show set in a hospital, you will understand why a patient is having *pre-op* or *post-op* tests! One checks for conditions the surgeon should know about before an operation. The other evaluates the patient's health after the operation. (These words, of course, are shortened forms of *pre-operative* and *post-operative*.)

Chapter 8

Joining and Commenting: Conjunctions and Interjections

In This Chapter

▶ Linking ideas of equal importance with *and, but, or, nor,* and similar words

▶ Joining ideas of unequal importance with *because, since, although,* and other words

▶ Inserting comments with interjections

Are you a matchmaker? Do you pair up your friends, hoping lonely individuals will find happiness when they are joined together? If so, you will love conjunctions, a part of speech that joins. In this chapter, you discover what you need to know about conjunctions. You also learn about interjections, a minor part of speech that adds spice to your writing.

Linking Ideas with Conjunctions

A survey of everything spoken in English yesterday reveals that *and* is the most frequently used word. I lied. No one did a survey. I do not know which word is most common. I suspect that it is *and,* though. How can anyone get through a day — or even just a few sentences — without *and?*

And joins ideas, as do many other words. Read this paragraph:

> I see your point, <u>but</u> I do not agree with you. <u>Because</u> you do not know all the people <u>and</u> circumstances, you came to the wrong conclusion. Look at the situation again, <u>or</u> ask for more information.

Four underlined words in the example paragraph — *but, because, and, or* — join ideas. English teachers call these "joining words" *conjunctions.* In this section, you see how useful conjunctions can be.

Adding meaning with conjunctions

When you tie two things together, you change each one just a little — or maybe a lot. Not all conjunctions are the same. When you combine two sentences with a conjunction, you must be careful to choose the correct word. Each one gives a different meaning to your new sentence. Consider these two statements:

> Sentence 1: Sarah wants to speak with her brother.

> Sentence 2: He is annoyed.

How should you combine these ideas? It depends on what you want to say. Look at this sentence:

> Sarah wants to speak with her brother, but he is annoyed.

This sentence hints that Sarah will wait until later, when her brother is in a better mood. Now check out this one:

> Sarah wants to speak with her brother because he is annoyed.

Now you know that Sarah is not going to wait for a smile from her brother. She is going to have a conversation about his mood or whatever caused his annoyance. How about this one:

> Sarah wants to speak with her brother although he is annoyed.

In this version, Sarah has something to say. Her brother's mood does not matter. She will speak with him whether he is in a good mood or a bad mood. Look at one more:

> Sarah wants to speak with her brother when he is annoyed.

Now Sarah comes across as a bossy sister. She calls her brother or drops in for a chat because she thinks she can calm him down.

Every conjunction has a slightly different meaning. Select carefully!

Connecting equals

Short sentences are boring. Short sentences are childish. Combining short sentences can be tricky.

Are you still awake? If so, you may want to edit the preceding paragraph. Here is a new version:

> Short sentences sound boring <u>and</u> childish, <u>but</u> combining them can be tricky.

The new version uses two *conjunctions (and, but)* to connect ideas of equal importance. The conjunction *and* joins two descriptions *(boring, childish)*. The conjunction *but* links one complete sentence *(Short sentences sound boring and childish)* with another complete sentence *(Combining them can be tricky)*. Other conjunctions that join equals are *or, nor,* and *yet.*

Watch conjunctions at work in these examples:

Sentence	*Conjunction*	*Ideas Connected*	*Identity of Connected Elements*
Peter or Rebecca will cook the turkey.	or	Peter Rebecca	nouns
Peter was no chef, nor was Rebecca a good cook.	nor	Peter was no chef was Rebecca a good cook	sentences
The turkey was dry yet tasty.	yet	dry tasty	adjectives
We will eat a lot of turkey, and we will not complain.	and	We will eat a lot of turkey we will not complain	sentences
The meal is not great, but it is free.	but	The meal is not great it is free	sentences
The leftovers will go to the dog, the cat, or the piglet.	or	dog cat piglet	nouns
These pets eat rapidly and hungrily.	and	rapidly hungrily	adverbs

In this table, you see that conjunctions may link single words or groups of words. Take a good look at the last column. The grammatical identity is the same for each of the connected ideas. (For example, *Peter* and *Rebecca* are both nouns, and *dry* and *tasty* are both adjectives. *The meal is not great* and *it*

is free are both sentences.) You should be sure that the grammatical identity of everything you connect matches.

How good are you at spotting conjunctions? Can you identify what each conjunction connects? Fill in this table:

Sentence	*Conjunction*	*Ideas Connected*
1. Herbie played the piano sweetly but skillfully.		
2. Janet looked around the corner and over the hedge.		
3. Cars do not have wings, nor do their drivers.		
4. The complicated yet important report is required reading.		
5. Do your homework now, or you will not be allowed to go out.		
6. Ellen or Justin will help you.		
7. Reading, writing, and arithmetic are essential skills.		

Here are the answers: 1. conjunction — *but,* ideas connected — *sweetly, skillfully* 2. conjunction — *and,* ideas connected — *around the corner, over the hedge* 3. conjunction — *nor,* ideas connected — *Cars do not have wings, do their drivers* 4. conjunction — *yet,* ideas connected — *complicated, important* 5. conjunction — *or,* ideas connected — *Do your homework now, you will not be allowed to go out* 6. conjunction — *or,* ideas connected — *Ellen, Justin* 7. conjunction — *and,* ideas connected — *reading, writing, arithmetic.*

You probably noticed that when you connect something with *nor,* the second item (*do their drivers*) sounds a bit different from the first. Do not worry. *Nor* is a negative word. The first item includes another negative word, *not.* You do not need another negative in the second item, because *nor* already does that job.

Paired conjunctions

Sometimes conjunctions work in pairs. (Perhaps they are lonely all by themselves.) *Or* often appears with *either. Nor* partners with *neither. Both* may show up with *and. Not only* works with *but also.*

Observe these pairs in their natural setting, a sentence:

Sentence	Conjunction Pair	Ideas Connected	Grammatical Identity of Connected Elements
Neither George nor Helen went to Florida last winter.	Neither, nor	George Helen	nouns
We must act either now or never.	either, or	now never	adverbs
Hugh can both dance and sing.	both, and	dance sing	verbs
Either we will take a taxi or Isabel will drive us.	Either, or	we will take a taxi Isabel will drive us	sentences
Bobby not only washed but also dried the dishes.	not only, but also	washed dried	verbs

Did you notice that everything paired conjunctions connect has the same grammatical identity? You do not need to know the grammatical terms, but you should be sure that everything you connect with these conjunction pairs matches. How do you detect a match? Listen! For example, *washed* and *Bobby dried* are a mismatch. They are different not only in length, but also in ideas. *Washed* is simply an action word. *Bobby dried* is a complete sentence.

Now it is your turn to look for pairs and the ideas they connect. Fill in the spaces in each column:

Sentence	Conjunction Pair	Ideas Connected
1. Neither the red pen nor the green one has ink in it.		
2. A teacher may be both strict and kind.		
3. Either wash the dishes or dry them.		
4. Both Margie and Peggy have lived in Pennsylvania for many years.		
5. Peggy reported that the fire was either deliberate or accidental.		

Here are the answers: 1. conjunctions — *Neither/nor*, ideas connected — *the red pen, the green one* 2. conjunctions — *both/and*, ideas connected — *strict, kind* 3. conjunctions — *Either/or*, ideas connected — *wash the dishes, dry them* 4. conjunctions — *Both/and*, ideas connected — *Margie, Peggy* 5. conjunctions — *either/or*, ideas connected — *deliberate, accidental*.

Joining unequal ideas

If you go to work, you probably have a boss. Bosses and employees often work together, but they are not equals. The boss can make decisions alone. The boss is *independent*. The employees, on the other hand, are *dependent* on the boss for paychecks, supervision, and other things.

Some sentences have the same structure as a workplace. One part — the "boss" — is *independent* and can stand alone. The other part — the "employee" — is *dependent* and must be attached to a "boss." A special type of joining word (a *conjunction*) ties them together. Here are examples of this type of conjunction:

after

although

as

because

before

even though

how

if

since

than

though

unless

until

when

where

whether

while

why

Some of the words on the preceding list also appear in Chapter 7 on a list of prepositions — a part of speech that expresses relationships. Often, the same word may act as several different parts of speech, depending upon context. The words on this list act as conjunctions when they introduce a statement that includes a verb. (For more information on verbs, turn to Chapter 5.)

Now take a look at these examples. Notice that the conjunction is part of the *dependent* statement — the "employee" — in every sentence.

Sentence	Conjunction	Independent Statement (Boss)	Dependent Statement (Employee)
While he was stirring the sauce, a bomb exploded.	While	a bomb exploded	While he was stirring the sauce
You can win the race because you trained every day.	because	You can win the race	because you trained every day
Jack wrapped the present after he bought it.	after	Jack wrapped the present	after he bought it
I have been driving since I was seventeen.	since	I have been driving	since I was seventeen
Although the cup is cracked, I want to keep it.	Although	I want to keep it	Although the cup is cracked
Check your work before you hand it in.	before	Check your work	before you hand it in
She worked in her garden until the rain started.	until	She worked in her garden	until the rain started

The word *dependent* helps you remember that these statements cannot stand alone. They are *dependent* on something else. Look at any box in the last column. Those statements make no sense by themselves. That's why they are called *dependent!* Now look at the *independent* statements in the third column. Each makes sense without an addition. They can stand alone. That's why they are *independent.* Be sure that every sentence you write has at least one independent statement.

Can you find the boss and employees — the independent and dependent statements? Do you recognize the conjunctions? See whether you can fill in this table:

Sentence	Conjunction	Independent Statement (Boss)	Dependent Statement (Employee)
1. Mary canceled the parade because it is raining.			
2. While Roger was at the dentist, his sister called.			
3. The farmers worked until darkness fell.			
4. Although the current mayor is popular, many voters favor another candidate.			
5. Candice always sounds happy when she is talking with Tom.			

Here are the answers: 1. conjunction — *because,* independent statement — *Mary canceled the parade,* dependent statement — *because it is raining* 2. conjunction — *While,* independent statement — *his sister called,* dependent statement — *While Roger was at the dentist* 3. conjunction — *until,* independent statement — *The farmers worked,* dependent statement — *until darkness fell* 4. conjunction — *Although,* independent statement — *many voters favor another candidate,* dependent statement — *Although the current mayor is popular* 5. conjunction — *when,* independent statement — *Candice always sounds happy,* dependent statement — *when she is talking with Tom.*

Punctuating sentences with conjunctions

Commas are little curved hooks that tell you to pause in your reading. Where to place commas puzzles many writers. Really, though, the rules for commas are quite simple. In Chapter 15, you can find out how to use commas in many situations. Here, you see how to place commas when your sentence contains a conjunction.

Combining equals

When you join two complete, equally important sentences with a conjunction, place a comma before the conjunction.

Suppose that you want to unite these sentences:

> Sentence 1: Andrew unlocked the safe.

> Sentence 2: It was empty.

Unite the sentences with the conjunction *but,* and place a comma before the conjunction:

> Andrew unlocked the safe, but it was empty.

Here is another example:

> Sentence 1: The sneakers fit perfectly.

> Sentence 2: They were very comfortable.

Tie these two ideas together with the conjunction *and,* placing a comma before the conjunction:

> The sneakers fit perfectly, and they were very comfortable.

When you combine two equal elements that are *not* sentences, do not insert a comma. Look at this sentence:

> Baby Mark laughs and smiles all day long!

Notice that the conjunction *and* joins two actions *(laughs, smiles).* These are not complete sentences, so you do not need a comma before *and.* Here is another example:

> Ron was busy but happy.

Now the conjunction *but* links two descriptions *(busy, happy).* These are not complete sentences, so no comma is needed before the conjunction *but.*

Combining unequals

Many sentences contain statements of unequal importance. (See "Joining unequal ideas" earlier in this chapter for more information.) If the less important statement — the *dependent statement* — comes first, you must always place a comma to separate it from the more important statement — the *independent statement*. Look at this example:

> SENTENCE: Although Martha already knew the material, she studied for several hours.
>
> DEPENDENT STATEMENT: *Although Martha already knew the material*
>
> INDEPENDENT STATEMENT: *she studied for several hours*
>
> COMMA NEEDED? Yes. The dependent statement is first, so it is followed by a comma.

Here is another example:

> SENTENCE: Since he started medical school, Stan has not attended a single party.
>
> DEPENDENT STATEMENT: *Since he started medical school*
>
> INDEPENDENT STATEMENT: *Stan has not attended a single party*
>
> COMMA NEEDED? Yes. The dependent statement is first, so it is followed by a comma.

You may be wondering what happens when the important statement comes first. Usually, no comma appears. (Yes, exceptions to this rule exist. However, if you follow this rule you will be right most of the time.) Take a look at this sentence:

> SENTENCE: Stan bought 15 textbooks when he enrolled in medical school.
>
> INDEPENDENT STATEMENT: *Stan bought 15 textbooks*
>
> DEPENDENT STATEMENT: *when he enrolled in medical school*
>
> COMMA NEEDED? No. The independent statement is first, and no comma appears in this sentence.

Here is another example:

> SENTENCE: Stan plans to party every night after his exams end.
>
> INDEPENDENT STATEMENT: *Stan plans to party every night*
>
> DEPENDENT STATEMENT: *after his exams end*
>
> COMMA NEEDED? No. The independent statement is first, and no comma appears.

Do you have good "comma sense"? Place commas in these sentences if needed.

1. Though he was only 12 he was a great chess player.

2. Louis changes diapers but he does not wash them.

3. We will miss Max when he moves to France.

4. Because he is a valuable employee he received a large raise.

5. After I sign the paper the house belongs to you!

Here are the answers: 1. Place a comma after *12* because *Though he was only 12* is a dependent statement. 2. Place a comma before the conjunction *but*. The conjunction *but* unites equal statements. 3. No comma. The independent statement *We will miss Max* comes first. 4. Place a comma after *employee*. The dependent statement, *Because he is a valuable employee,* comes first. 5. Place a comma after *paper*. The dependent statement, *After I sign the paper,* comes first.

Identifying Interjections

<u>Yes</u>! You can identify interjections easily. <u>No</u>, an interjection is not always followed by an exclamation point. <u>Oh</u>, you are confused. <u>Sorry</u>!

The underlined words in the preceding paragraph are *interjections,* a part of speech that loves attention. An interjection is not part of the grammatical structure of the sentence. Interjections often express emotion. They sometimes attach themselves to the sentence, but occasionally they stand alone. Frequently, an exclamation point follows an interjection. Sometimes, instead of an exclamation point, the interjection is set off by one or two commas from the rest of the sentence.

Read the following examples. The interjections are underlined.

<u>Ah</u>, this vacation home is very peaceful.

<u>Oops</u>. I bumped into the beehive.

<u>Oh no</u>! Bees are inside the house.

<u>Yikes</u>! I must run away.

<u>Wow</u>, bees fly fast.

As you see, interjections add interest. Grammatically, though, they add nothing — not a single thing — to the sentence. In fact, the definition of *interjection* is a word or words not connected grammatically to any sentence.

Because they have no grammatical function, you will probably never make a mistake with an interjection. Just be careful not to use them too often. Overly emotional writing sometimes annoys readers.

Can you identify interjections? Underline any interjection you find in this paragraph.

Rats! Sylvia lost the tickets. Yes, the tickets for the best concert ever. Oh my goodness, I cannot believe that she lost them. No, this chance to see the band will never come again.

Here are the answers: *Rats, Yes, Oh my goodness, No.*

Get the "duct" tape!

I often hear that duct tape, the strong silver material, can fix anything. I do not know whether duct tape can fix a faulty vocabulary, but knowing the root word *duct,* as well as its cousin, *duc,* helps build a strong vocabulary. These root words mean "lead." Check out these words:

conduct to lead an orchestra or tour group. "The guide *conducted* the tourists through the palace."

educate to teach (to lead from ignorance to knowledge). "Mr. Samuels *educated* thousands of students before he retired from teaching."

reduction decrease (leading on a downward path). "The *reduction* in taxes was welcome."

duct a channel or tube (which leads from one place to another). "The air *duct* must be kept open at all times."

introduce to bring something or someone new into a situation (to "lead" a new element into another). "When you *introduce* me to strangers, be sure to use my royal title."

aqueduct a structure to carry water over long distances (to lead water from one place to another). "Roman aqueducts are still standing in many places."

Introduce new words, such as *aqueduct* or *duct,* into your conversation and you will *educate* others and *reduce* ignorance!

However is not a conjunction

However is an impressive word. It is long and sounds sophisticated. You may want to use *however* as a conjunction. People often try to do so! However, *however* is not a conjunction. It adds meaning to a sentence, but the rules of Standard English do not allow *however* to tie two sentences together.

> WRONG: Sam sipped my coffee, however, I forgave him.

> WHY IT IS WRONG: Two complete statements (*Sam sipped my coffee* and *I forgave him*) cannot be linked by *however*.

> RIGHT: Sam sipped my coffee. However, I forgave him.

> WHY IT IS RIGHT: Each complete statement is a separate sentence.

> WRONG: Sam immediately brought me another cup, however, the coffee was cold.

> WHY IT IS WRONG: Two complete statements (*Sam immediately brought me another cup* and *the coffee was cold*) cannot be linked by *however*.

> RIGHT: Sam immediately brought me another cup, but the coffee was cold.

> ALSO RIGHT: Sam immediately brought me another cup. However, the coffee was cold.

> WHY THEY ARE RIGHT: In the first correction, the conjunction *but* joins these statements properly. In the second, each complete statement is in a separate sentence.

However much you want to use *however* to unite sentences, do not do so. Use a real conjunction!

Part III
Creating Correct Sentences

Expressing your thoughts

When you want to express yourself, individual words are seldom enough. You need complete and clear sentences. This part tackles the important elements that must appear in every sentence:

- ✔ **Verbs:** Verbs, the "being" and "doing" words in a sentence, give information about time — past, present, and future. Chapter 9 shows you how to form the most basic, simple tenses. You also review progressive tenses, which include the *–ing* form of a verb. Chapter 10 helps you identify situations that call for the *perfect* tenses, which depend on *has, have,* or *had*.

- ✔ **Subjects:** Someone or something must "be" or "do" what the verb expresses. That's the subject, which is the focus of Chapter 11. That chapter also shows you how to pair subjects and verbs correctly.

- ✔ **Complements:** Choosing proper subjects and verbs starts you off, but you often need a *complement* to finish your idea — and the sentence. Chapter 12 explains different types of complements and shows you when to use each.

- ✔ **Complete sentences:** Finish what you start! That is good advice. It is also the topic of Chapter 13, which tells you how to check every sentence to ensure that it has the proper punctuation. In Chapter 13, you learn how to avoid improperly joined sentences and half-sentences, which English teachers call *fragments*.

web extras

For a bonus article on Parts of a Sentence, go online and take a look at www.dummies.com/extras/basicenglishgrammar.

In this part . . .

- ✔ Create verb forms in every tense.

- ✔ Examine the role of helping verbs such as *has* or *had, can, will, may,* and others.

- ✔ Identify the subject of every sentence and match the subject to the proper verb form.

- ✔ Punctuate every sentence correctly.

- ✔ Employ complements to add meaning to your sentences.

Chapter 9

Making Progress: Verbs Ending in –*ing*

How do you know what time it is? Do you look at your phone or at a clock? Perhaps you wear a watch. All these mechanical things tell you the time. So do verbs.

In Chapter 5, you find some information about verbs — how to recognize them, how they change form, and other basic facts. In this chapter, you explore verbs that express an action or state of being in progress — what English teachers call the *progressive tenses*. Relax! Soon you will know everything about past, present, and future progressive verb tenses.

Keeping Time with –*ing* Verb Forms

Look at this paragraph. Pay special attention to the underlined words.

> Last week my granddaughter <u>gave</u> me this cup. I <u>love</u> it. No one but me <u>will drink</u> from it at my dinner party tonight.

The underlined words are verbs. Verbs are the "doing" and "being" words in a sentence. Verbs tell whether you are talking about the past, the present, or the future. The quality of verbs that shows time is called *tense*. In the preceding example, verbs tell about the past (*gave*), the present (*love*), and the future (*will drink*). The time, or *tense*, is expressed by the form of the verb.

Grammarians call these forms *simple tenses.* To learn more about the simple tenses, turn to Chapter 5.

Now read this paragraph. Once again, notice the underlined words.

> Elizabeth <u>was playing</u> chess an hour ago. Now she <u>is riding</u> her bike. During my visit next week, we <u>will be working</u> on her new puzzle every day.

These underlined words are also verbs. They also tell about the past *(was playing),* the present *(is riding),* and the future *(will be working).* As you see, these verbs are a bit different from the verbs in the first example paragraph. These verb forms are not simple. English teachers call them *progressive.* Each includes a form of the verb *be* and another verb form ending with the letters *–ing.*

Be is a strange verb. It changes form depending upon the person or thing you pair it with. (In Chapter 5, you find more information about this verb, including all its forms in the simple present, past, and future tenses.)

You should know the present, past, and future progressive tense. You use them often when you are speaking, as well as when you are writing. (By the way, *are speaking* and *are writing* are both progressive verb forms.)

Present progressive

To make a present progressive tense verb, you add the *–ing* form of a verb to the proper present tense form of *be.* Here is a table showing the present progressive forms of the verb *pay:*

Singular (One)	**Plural (More than One)**
I am paying	we are paying
you are paying	you are paying
he is paying	they are paying
she is paying	
it is paying	

Did you notice that the pronoun *you* may be either singular (talking to one person) or plural (talking to more than one). How convenient!

In the last row of the first column, I listed *he, she,* and *it.* I could have listed every noun that names one person, place, or thing (what English teachers call *singular nouns*). In the last row of the second column, you see *they*. I could have added every noun that names more than one person, place, or thing (*plural nouns*, in other words). To talk about someone or something, just remember these two simple rules:

  ✔ Pair *is* plus an *–ing* form of a verb with any singular noun or pronoun.

  ✔ Pair *are* plus an *–ing* form of a verb with any plural noun or pronoun.

For more information on nouns, turn to Chapter 3. Everything you need to know about pronouns is in Chapter 4.

See whether you can form present progressive tense verb forms. In the third column, write the verb form that pairs with the nouns or pronouns in the first column. The second column tells you the verb you're working with.

Noun or Pronoun	Verb	Present Progressive Form
we	lift	
you	frown	
Bob	fall	
the astronauts	place	
Monica	iron	
the hose	drip	
I	ride	

Here are the answers: *are lifting, are frowning, is falling, are placing, is ironing, is dripping, am riding.*

Past progressive

To talk about the past with a progressive verb, you need a past tense form of the verb *be.* You also need to add the *–ing* form of the verb. Here is a table of the past progressive forms of the verb *mix:*

Singular	Plural
I was mixing	we were mixing
you were mixing	you were mixing
he was mixing	they were mixing
she was mixing	
it was mixing	

In the last row of the first column, you see *he, she,* and *it.* The verb form in that box works for *singular nouns.* In the last row of the second column, you see *they.* That form pairs with *plural nouns.*

(For more information on nouns, turn to Chapter 3. Everything you need to know about pronouns is in Chapter 4.)

See whether you can form past progressive tense verb forms. In the third column, write the verb form that pairs with the nouns or pronouns in the first column. The second column tells you the verb you're working with.

Noun or Pronoun	Verb	Past Progressive Form
the knight	tilt	
they	paint	
you	scream	
Jay	cry	
we	eat	
the cooks	bake	
it	bother	

Here are the answers: *was tilting, were painting, were screaming, was crying, were eating, were baking, was bothering.*

Future progressive

This form is easy. Why? The verb *be* doesn't change forms in the future. *Will be* pairs with every noun or pronoun, whether you are talking about one or more than one. All you have to do is attach the *–ing* form of the verb to *will be.* Take a look at this table of the future progressive forms of the verb *go:*

Singular	Plural
I will be going	we will be going
you will be going	you will be going
he will be going	they will be going
she will be going	
it will be going	

The last row lists only pronouns (*he, she, it,* and *they*). *He* represents all the singular nouns that name one male. *She* represents all the singular nouns that name one female. *It* represents the name of any single thing. *They* represents any noun that refers to more than one.

Check your future progressive verb forms by filling in this table:

Noun or Pronoun	Verb	Future Progressive Form
he	date	
glass	break	
Angela	mail	
Bob	catch	
children	read	
it	cover	
soldiers	protect	

Here are the answers: *will be dating, will be breaking, will be mailing, will be catching, will be reading, will be covering, will be protecting.*

Choosing between Simple and Progressive Tenses

Simple and progressive tenses are close in meaning. Often, you can select either one to say the same thing. Sometimes, though, choosing between simple and progressive tenses matters. In this section, you take a close look at progressive forms that talk about the present, past, and future. To show you the difference, I also provide examples of simple tenses.

Present

This book <u>discusses</u> grammar. You <u>are reading</u> about verbs now. You <u>are learning</u> a lot about present tense. I always <u>hope</u> that readers <u>enjoy</u> my books. <u>Are</u> you <u>having</u> fun?

Probably you are not having fun. Grammar is not as much fun as many other subjects, such as gossip about famous people. Grammar, however, is useful. Look at the underlined verbs in the first paragraph of this section. Do you see the simple present tense forms *(discusses, hope, enjoy)* and the progressive forms *(are reading, are learning, are having)*? Follow these guidelines to choose between simple present tense and present progressive tense:

> ✔ **The simple present tense talks about things that are generally true.** Check out these sentences. The simple present tense verbs are underlined. In the parentheses after each sentence, you learn more about the situation. Notice how the verb tense fits the meaning:
>
> > Mary <u>speaks</u> Dutch. (She knows the language and can communicate in Dutch whenever she wants to do so.)

Pete <u>teaches</u> math and science. (This is his job.)

Helen and Sarah <u>cook</u> delicious meals for us. (They are kind enough to prepare meals whenever we visit.)

You <u>need</u> a college degree for that job. (This is a general requirement for all applicants.)

✔ **Simple present tense expresses action that happens over and over again.** In other words, simple present tense is for habits. Read these sentences. The simple present tense verbs are underlined. In parentheses after each sentence, you see more information about the situation. See how the verb tense matches the meaning:

Tom <u>runs</u> in the park. (When he exercises, that's where he goes.)

Candice <u>votes</u> before work. (On election day, she is always first in line.)

Mr. Smith <u>talks</u> too much. (Whenever you meet him, be sure you are in a comfortable spot. You will be there for a long time!)

That dog <u>bites</u> everyone. (Stay away from the dog. He looks friendly. He is not!)

✔ **Often, the present progressive tense expresses what is true right now.** Read these sentences. Pay attention to the underlined, present progressive verbs. In the parentheses after each sentence, you learn more about the situation. Notice how the verb tense fits the meaning:

The company <u>is sifting</u> through a hundred applications. (An employee is sitting at a desk, reading many pieces of paper from job seekers.)

Mary and Matthew <u>are talking</u> in Russian. (They are talking right now.)

Pete <u>is traveling</u> in Africa this week. (Pete is on vacation.)

In the kitchen, Helen and Sarah <u>are preparing</u> steamed carrots. (Helen is chopping and Sarah is setting up the steamer right now.)

✔ **Present progressive may seem more dramatic than simple present.** In this way, a present-progressive verb is like the action in a film. Here are some present-progressive verb forms, all underlined. See how they fit the situation:

Tom <u>is running</u> away from a robber. (Call the police! He needs help now!)

Candice <u>is campaigning</u> for Roger, her favorite candidate. (There she is on the street corner, holding a sign praising Roger.)

Sally <u>is yawning</u> and <u>falling</u> asleep. (She is bored or tired. Time for a nap.)

The dog <u>is biting</u> Matt's toe! (Ouch. Matt has to find some hamburger quickly. Then the dog will leave his toe alone.)

Simple present is more general. Present progressive shows you something in progress. In many situations, both are correct.

See whether you can select a verb form from the pair in parentheses. Underline your choice. Be sure you have a reason for your selection.

> Please be quiet. The baby (sleeps, is sleeping). He (hates, is hating) noise. His mother (says, is saying) that the baby (wakes, is waking) up often. She (wants, is wanting) him to rest more. Fortunately, everyone (leaves, is leaving) now.

Here are the answers: *is sleeping* (action happening now), *hates* (something generally true about the baby), *says* (the mother has a habit of saying this), *wakes* (the baby's habit), *wants* (her constant desire — always true!), *is leaving* (action happening now).

Past

> Nancy and her friends <u>watched</u> television for five hours yesterday. While they <u>were watching</u>, the house <u>caught</u> fire. They <u>were arguing</u> about their favorite show, so they <u>noticed</u> nothing until the fire department <u>came</u>. The firefighters <u>were battling</u> the flames when I <u>arrived</u>.

All the underlined words are verbs, and all tell about something that happened in the past. Well, actually the verbs tell about two things that happened in the past: a television-watching marathon and a fire! Some of these verbs are simple past tense forms *(watched, caught, noticed, came, arrived)*. Others are past progressive forms *(were watching, were arguing, were battling)*.

The difference between simple past and past progressive is small. Most of the time, either works nicely. Occasionally, one form is better than the other. Here are some guidelines to help you:

> ✔ **To speak about something that happened at a particular moment in the past, use simple past tense.** Take a look at these sentences. In the parentheses after each sentence, you learn more about the situation. The simple past tense verbs are underlined.
>
>> Olivia <u>slipped</u> on the ice. (She placed her foot on the wrong spot and fell.)
>>
>> It <u>snowed</u> 17 times last winter! (At 17 specific points in time, the snow came down.)
>>
>> Skiers <u>went</u> to the mountain when the snow <u>stopped</u>. (This sentence talks about two specific moments in the past — when the skiers <u>went</u> to the mountain and when the snow <u>stopped</u>.)

✔ **To talk about something that occurred over a period of time in the past, try past progressive tense.** Check out these sentences. The past progressive tense verbs are underlined. In parentheses, you find an explanation of the meaning.

> She <u>was trying</u> to get home before the storm. (The journey took some time.)

> Everyone <u>was dreaming</u> about spring. (The *dreaming* started with the first flake of snow and continued for a while.)

> They <u>were hoping</u> for even more snow! (This action continued all winter.)

✔ **To make a past action more vivid, you may use past progressive tense.** This tense gives a "you are there" feeling. Read these examples. The past progressive verbs are underlined. The situation is explained in parentheses.

> Marge <u>was skiing</u> while Henry <u>was sitting</u> by the fire. (You are in the ski resort. You see the scene as if it were happening right in front of you.)

> Eleanor <u>was frowning</u> because her brother <u>was stealing</u> her toys. (Lots of drama here. You can almost see yourself grabbing Eleanor's brother and taking back her toys.)

> As the fireworks <u>were exploding</u>, everyone <u>was cheering</u>. (This sentence paints a picture of an exciting evening.)

Simple past tense is usually best for specific moments. Past progressive tense adds drama and covers situations that occur over a period of time.

Choose the correct verb form and underline it. If both forms work, underline both.

Belle (talked, was talking) on the phone while her little brother (ripped, was ripping) her homework in half. Belle (screamed, was screaming) at her brother when her mother (came, was coming) home. Their mother (patted, was patting) her son's shoulder because he (cried, was crying). Then Belle (sat, was sitting) down to do her homework again.

Here are the answers: *was talking* (an action that took place over a period of time), *ripped* (probably a short, specific moment in the past), *was screaming* (an action taking place over a period of time), *came* (a specific moment in the past), *patted* or *was patting* (either simple past or past progressive is okay here), *was crying* (action taking place over a period of time), *sat* (an action at a specific moment in the past).

Future

This evening heavy rain <u>will fall,</u> and the roads <u>will flood</u>. The traffic police <u>will be working</u> overtime to keep drivers safe. Schools <u>will close</u> early because of the storm. Teachers and students <u>will be celebrating</u> the extra free time.

The underlined verbs all talk about the future. English teachers say that these verbs are in future tense. (You are not surprised, right? The name makes sense.) Simple future tense is what you need when something has not happened yet. Future progressive tense, with the *–ing* form of the verb, also talks about something in the future. Which one should you select? Here are some guidelines:

✔ **To talk about the future, simple future tense is nearly always correct.** You do not have to complicate your life worrying about this tense. Go for the simple form, and most of the time you will be right. Look at these examples:

Henry <u>will pay</u> your bill. (This payment happens at a particular moment in the future.)

You <u>will write</u> him a check to repay the loan. (The writing takes place in a specific moment in the future.)

Henry thinks that you <u>will thank</u> him for his generosity. (The thanking takes place in a specific moment in the future.)

Henry's friends <u>will tell</u> him about your insulting remarks. (Uh oh. You are in trouble! The conversation happens at a specific moment. I bet Henry's anger will extend over a long period of time.)

✔ **For an action in the future that goes on for a period of time, you may use future progressive tense.** Notice that I wrote *may use,* not *must use.* Either form is usually correct. Here are some examples of future progressive tense.

When the plane lands, I <u>will be waiting</u> for you. (The plane touches the ground at a specific moment, so simple present tense works nicely there. *Waiting* extends over a period of time.)

While you <u>are claiming</u> your luggage, the taxi <u>will be circling</u> the airport. (*Claiming* the suitcases to be unloaded and *circling* in the taxi take some time.)

Martha <u>will be preparing</u> a welcome for you, but Paul <u>will be placing</u> spiders in your room. (These two actions occur over a period of time.)

Simple future tense and future progressive tense are very similar. Often, you may choose either and still be correct.

See whether you grasp the best use of future progressive verbs. Write the proper form of the future progressive tense in the blank. The verb you are working with appears in parentheses after the sentence.

1. The teachers_____ the board and probably will not see the students' bad behavior. (erase)

2. The frog _____ while the turtle is sleeping. (jump)

3. She _____ the plane because the pilot is sick. (land)

4. The horse _____ the wagon, not the ox. (pull)

5. You _____ the witness tomorrow for about three hours. (question)

6. Nancy and Peter _____ every weed when they walk through the garden tonight. (notice)

7. We _____ pumpkins this Halloween, so wear washable clothes. (smash)

Here are the answers: 1. *will be erasing* 2. *will be jumping* 3. *will be landing* 4. *will be pulling* 5. *will be questioning* 6. *will be noticing* 7. *will be smashing*.

Some Help with Spelling –ing Verb Forms

Most of the time, all you have to do is add –*ing* to the end of the verb when you want to create the progressive form. Sometimes, though, you have to change or add letters before tacking on the –*ing*.

Here is a good spelling rule to remember: When you write the –*ing* form of a verb that ends in the letter *e*, most of the time you must drop the *e* before adding –*ing*. Look at these examples:

smile — smiling

write — writing

hate — hating

continue — continuing

bake — baking

slice — slicing

illustrate — illustrating

rule — ruling

Some verbs double the last letter before adding *–ing*. Check out these examples:

cut — cutting

put — putting

drop — dropping

sip — sipping

hop — hopping

shed — shedding

spot — spotting

slam — slamming

Verbs that end in the letters *ie* exchange those letters for a *y* before adding *–ing:*

die — dying

tie — tying

If you are unsure about the proper spelling of any *–ing* verb form, check the dictionary.

Write the *–ing* form of the verb in the last column. Be careful! Sometimes you must add only *ing,* but you may have to change the spelling of others.

Verb	*–ing Form*
provide	
hit	
make	
see	
lie	
rate	
rub	

Here are the answers: *providing, hitting, making, seeing, lying, rating, rubbing.*

Setting up and sitting down

Two verbs that may puzzle you are *sit* and *set.* The first verb, *sit,* is what you do when you stop standing and *sit* in a chair or on the ground (or any other place!). Look at these examples:

> The cat was sitting on the sunny window sill.
>
> She often sits on my lap.
>
> Tomorrow, I will sit on the sofa and watch the basketball game.
>
> The cat will be sitting on my lap then, too.

The second verb, *set,* is what you do when you place an object somewhere or when you adjust or arrange something. Read these examples:

> Grandpa sets his book on the table every night before he goes to sleep.

> Uncle Bert is setting the temperature dial to "very cold."
>
> The principal sets the time and date of the final exam.
>
> The little boy was setting his toys on the shelf in neat rows.
>
> My cousin will set the timer so that it rings at exactly 9 p.m.

Did you notice one big difference between these two verbs? *Sit* is something you do by yourself. *Set* is almost always something you do to something else. Why "almost always"? Because the sun sets all by itself.

Going outside and staying inside with i*nter* and i*ntra*

Five letters tacked onto the beginning of a word can take you outside to a larger group or inside a group. *Inter* means "between or among." *Intra* means "within." Watch these letters in action:

> **International** means "between or among nations." "The *international* gathering of health experts took place at the United Nations headquarters."
>
> **Interstate** means "between states." "The *interstate* highway was the fastest route from New York to Pennsylvania."
>
> **Interview** refers to "a question-and-answer session between two or more people" or "to question one or more people." "Charlotte's job *interview* lasted three hours." "The

supervisor *interviewed* ten people before hiring Charlotte."

> **Intramural** refers to sports contests "within a group or organization." "The best part of the day was the *intramural* basketball tournament, when the ninth grade played the tenth grade."
>
> **Intravenous** describes medicine placed "within the blood or circulatory system." "The doctor ordered *intravenous* painkillers for the wounded soldier."

Note: Many medical words begin with *intra.* Listen to your doctor, and your vocabulary will improve!

Chapter 10

Revisiting the Past: The Perfect Tenses

*Y*ou should not live in the past, according to psychologists. I don't know much about psychology: Maybe their advice is good, or maybe it is bad. However, I do know grammar. In grammar, the past is important. It can also be very complicated. (The past is complicated in real life, too, don't you think?) You do not have to live in the past, but you do have to pay attention to verbs when you are speaking or writing about it.

Many English verb tenses (the "time" expressed by a verb) have connections to the past. Chapter 5 reviews simple past tense. Chapter 9 covers the past progressive tense, the one that adds *–ing* to a verb. In this chapter, you learn about the "perfect" tenses. Sadly, these tenses are not perfect. They can be complicated. Do not worry! Once you finish reading this chapter, you will know the most important uses of present perfect and past perfect tenses. You also take a brief look at a strange and rare tense, the future perfect.

Building a Bridge between the Present and the Past: Present Perfect Tense

Charlie <u>has studied</u> in Thailand for three years. He <u>has learned</u> much about Thai culture from his teachers and friends. Charlie and his sister Anna <u>have toured</u> many important places in Bangkok, the capital of Thailand. They <u>have taken</u> photos of the most interesting monuments.

The underlined words are all verbs in the *present perfect tense.* The name of this tense contains a clue to its meaning. Present perfect tense links the past to the present. Use this tense when an action started in the past and continues in the present time. In this section, you see how to form the present perfect tense. Then you watch this tense "in action."

I said "action" in the preceding paragraph, but a verb can also express a state of being. That type of verb also links the past and present in the present perfect tense. Look at the underlined verbs in these examples:

Kelly <u>has been</u> president of that club for six months. (She was president in the past and continues to hold that office.)

Club members <u>have been</u> happy with her work. (They were happy in the past, and they still have the same feelings now.)

Elizabeth <u>has been</u> in Seattle since she was born. (She was born there and lives there at the present time.)

Joshua and Elaine <u>have seemed</u> sad lately. (They seemed sad in the past and remain so now.)

When you connect the past to the present, you need present perfect tense.

Present perfect forms

Verbs in present perfect tense always contain two words: either *has* or *have* plus a form of the verb you are using. English teachers call this form a *participle.* For regular verbs, the verb form accompanying *has* or *have* ends with the letters *–ed.* Unfortunately, many irregular verbs exist. See "Breaking the Rules: Irregular Past Forms" later in this chapter for a list of the most common irregular participles.

Here is a table of the present perfect forms of the regular verb *sail:*

Singular (One)	*Plural (More than One)*
I have sailed	we have sailed
you have sailed	you have sailed
he has sailed	they have sailed
she has sailed	
it has sailed	

To make your life more interesting, present perfect tense also has a progressive form. This tense adds *has been* or *have been* to the *–ing* form of the verb.

(For more information on progressive forms, turn to Chapter 9.) Here is the verb *sail* again, this time in its present perfect progressive tense:

Singular (One)	**Plural (More than One)**
I have been sailing	we have been sailing
you have been sailing	you have been sailing
he has been sailing	they have been sailing
she has been sailing	
it has been sailing	

The last row of each column shows you the form to use when you talk about someone, something, or a group. I placed the pronouns *he, she, it,* and *they* in these boxes. To the first column, I could have added many nouns — all the nouns that name one person, place, or thing. To the second column, I could have added every plural noun in the dictionary. What a heavy book this would be! You would need a team just to carry it. I inserted only the pronouns in the last row. Remember to use these forms of the verb with singular and plural nouns.

To find out how well you know the forms of present perfect tense, fill in the following table. The first column tells you which verb you are working with. The second column explains whether you want the present perfect or the present perfect progressive. The third column contains the word that pairs with the verb.

Verb	*Present Perfect or Present Perfect Progressive?*	*Paired with?*	*Verb Form*
spill	present perfect	it	
chase	present perfect progressive	dogs	
purchase	present perfect	Oliver	
amaze	present perfect	you	
sleep	present perfect progressive	I	
discuss	present perfect	reporter	
meet	present perfect progressive	executives	

Here are the answers: *has spilled, have been chasing, has purchased, have amazed, have been sleeping, has discussed, have been meeting.*

In this section, I chose regular verbs to show you the present perfect tense. Unfortunately, many verbs are not regular. Read "Breaking the Rules: Irregular Past Forms" later in this chapter to learn some common irregular forms.

When to use present perfect tense

Take a look at these examples of present perfect tense. I placed additional information in parentheses after each example. This information makes the order of events clear.

> Alan <u>has climbed</u> many mountains. (Some of the climbing happened in the past, but Alan has not given up this hobby. He continues to climb mountains in the present.)

> Alan <u>has been</u> a good skier for many years. (He was a good skier in the past, and he is still a good skier.)

> Maria <u>has mailed</u> most of the packages. (Some went off already, but others are on her desk, waiting to be mailed.)

> I <u>have been giving</u> you too much attention already! (This statement is made in the present, talking about past actions that continue to the present moment.)

> The slippery floor <u>has caused</u> many accidents. (The accidents took place in the past, but the floor is still dangerous in the present.)

> Sylvia and her family <u>have been living</u> in Granada for twenty years. (They arrived in the past, but they are still there in the present.)

Did you notice that some present perfect verbs contain *has,* and some contain *have?* In general, *has* is the form you need when you pair *he, she,* and any singular noun with the verb. *Have* is the form you should select when you pair a plural noun or pronoun with the verb. However, *I* and *you* are special. These words pair with *have.*

Present perfect and present perfect progressive verbs express nearly the same meaning. The progressive form seems a little more immediate. It puts you in the center of the action. Here are some examples:

> The football player's toe <u>has been hurting</u> since the last game. (The pain started in the past and continues now.)

> The coaches <u>have been discussing</u> their game plan. (The discussion started in the past and continues now.)

> They <u>have been listing</u> the names of replacement players on the board. (They started listing in the past and continue to add names.)

Do not worry about the difference between the *–ing* form of the present perfect tense and the form without the *–ing.* Most of the time, either form works well.

Do you see a connection between the past and the present? If so, choose either the simple or the progressive present perfect tense. (For more information on the simple tenses, turn to Chapter 5.) Underline your choice.

1. For a long time, Douglas (plans, planned, has been planning, have been planning) to buy a new car.

2. He (researched, has researched, have researched) the advantages and disadvantages of each model.

3. Douglas (saved, has been saving, have been saving) for three years.

4. He and Anna (visited, has visited, have visited) four showrooms already and plan to go to two more tomorrow.

5. The sales people at the last showroom (helped, has helped, have helped) Doug a lot.

Here are the answers: 1. *has been planning* (Douglas is one person, so *has* is correct. The action started in the past and continues in the present.) 2. *has researched* (Douglas is one person, so *has* is correct. The action started in the past and continues in the present.) 3. *has been saving* (Douglas is one person, so *has* is correct. The action started in the past and continues in the present.) 4. *have visited* (*He and Anna* name more than one person, so *have* is correct. The action — visiting showrooms — started in the past and continues in the present.) 5. *helped* (No connection to the present exists because the sentence says *at the last showroom*. The action started in the past and ended there.)

Placing Events in Order with Past Perfect Tense

Sometimes when you speak or write about the past, you mention many actions. Take a look at this example:

> When I <u>was</u> little, I <u>played</u> baseball very well. I also <u>participated</u> in basketball games. Sometimes, I <u>competed</u> in tennis tournaments.

In the preceding paragraph, the order of events does not matter. You have a list — a summary of activities. No one cares whether baseball, basketball, or tennis came first. The underlined verbs are in simple past tense. (For more information on simple past tense, read Chapter 5.)

Occasionally, though, the order of events does matter. Then the *past perfect tense* shows up. This tense always includes at least two words (and sometimes three). One of those words is always *had*. Here are some examples of past perfect tense. The verbs are underlined.

> Kelly <u>had cleaned</u> the house before I arrived with my brooms and mops.

> I <u>had been planning</u> to work for an hour, but I changed my mind.

Mark <u>had</u> already <u>enrolled</u> in a science class when he realized that he was more interested in history.

In this section, you see how to form past perfect tense and how to use it correctly.

Past perfect forms

Today is your lucky day. Why? The regular forms of past perfect tense are extremely easy. Just add *had* to the regular past tense form of the verb. (Regular past tense forms end with the letters *–ed.*) No matter who or what did the action, the past perfect remains the same. Take a look at this table of the past perfect forms of the regular verb *kiss:*

Singular (One)	**Plural (More than One)**
I had kissed	we had kissed
you had kissed	you had kissed
he had kissed	they had kissed
she had kissed	
it had kissed	

The past perfect also has a progressive form, one that includes the letters *–ing* plus *had been.* Check out this table, still on the verb *kiss:*

Singular (One)	**Plural (More than One)**
I had been kissing	we had been kissing
you had been kissing	you had been kissing
he had been kissing	they had been kissing
she had been kissing	
it had been kissing	

Don't you feel lucky, now that you know all these forms are the same? However, today is also your unlucky day. Why? Many verbs are irregular. To find out which form should accompany *had* or *had been,* flip to "Breaking the Rules: Irregular Past Forms" later in this chapter.

In the last row of each table, you see the pronouns *he, she, it,* and *they.* I did not include any nouns, but I could have included every noun — yes, every single one! To save space, I left them out.

The verb tenses in the preceding two tables are very close in meaning. Do not worry about choosing between them. Most of the time, you can use either one.

Write the past perfect form of the verb in the fourth column. The first column tells you which verb you are working with. The second column explains whether you want the past perfect or the past perfect progressive. The third column contains the word that pairs with the verb.

Verb	Past Perfect or Past Perfect Progressive?	Paired with?	Verb Form
rain	past perfect progressive	it	
sniff	past perfect	cats	
return	past perfect	Wendy	
surprise	past perfect	you	
think	past perfect progressive	I	
refuse	past perfect	clerk	
end	past perfect	film	

Here are the answers: *had been raining, had sniffed, had returned, had surprised, had been thinking, had refused, had ended.*

In this section, I chose regular verbs to show you the past perfect tense. Life would be wonderful without irregular verbs. (Life would also be wonderful without many other things, too, such as taxes.) Unfortunately, many verbs are not regular. Read "Breaking the Rules: Irregular Past Forms" later in this chapter to discover some common irregular forms.

When to use past perfect tense

Has this situation ever happened to you? You wrote a report for a teacher or a boss. You clicked the Send button on the email. Then you realized that you forgot to attach the document. Here is one way to describe this situation:

> I <u>had clicked</u> the Send button before I <u>realized</u> my mistake.

Examine this timeline:

> —*had clicked—realized*—present moment

On the timeline, the earlier action is *had clicked.* The more recent action is *realized.* Both are in the past, but the *had* places one action before the other. The earlier action, *had clicked,* is in past perfect tense.

Here is another example:

> The teacher <u>had explained</u> everything, but when William <u>sat</u> down to take the test yesterday, his mind <u>was</u> blank.

This sentence explains that the teacher did the right thing, going over the material before the test, not after. If William fails the test, he cannot blame the teacher. Here are the events on a timeline:

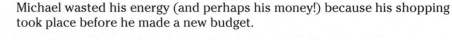

———— *had explained* ———— $\dfrac{sat}{was}$ ┤ present moment

The timeline shows you three things. The earliest is *had explained*. The next two take place more or less at the same time *(sat, was)*. Everything is in the past, but *had explained* is in the more distant past. The teacher's explanation happened before William *sat* and before William's mind *was* blank.

Read another example:

Jane <u>had worked</u> for an hour before the computer <u>froze</u>.

Now look at the timeline:

——*had worked*——*froze*——present moment

Poor Jane! I hope she saved her work. These two actions in the past occur in this order: *had worked* (earlier action), *froze* (more recent action).

Here is one more example for you:

Michael <u>made</u> a new budget, but all the money <u>had</u> already <u>been spent</u>.

Plot this example on a timeline:

——*had been spent*——*made*——present moment

Michael wasted his energy (and perhaps his money!) because his shopping took place before he made a new budget.

The most common mistake with past perfect tense is to use it too much. Read these examples:

WRONG: I had told him about the empty ketchup bottle.

WHY IT IS WRONG: Nothing in this sentence places past actions in order.

RIGHT: I told him about the empty ketchup bottle.

WHY IT IS RIGHT: Simple past tense *(told)* is fine because the sentence doesn't put past events in order.

WRONG: Every day the monkeys had climbed trees, had looked for food, and had played.

WHY IT IS WRONG: The timing of the events in the sentence does not matter. The sentence simply lists common monkey activities, which could occur at any time and in any order.

RIGHT: Every day the monkeys climbed trees, looked for food, and played.

WHY IT IS RIGHT: The simple past tense works best when the order of events does not matter.

WRONG: Vanessa had been born in 1977 and now lives in Rochester.

WHY IT IS WRONG: Two events are mentioned in the sentence, but one is in the present *(lives)*. Use the past perfect tense only when you are dealing with more than one past event, placing them in order.

RIGHT: Vanessa was born in 1977 and now lives in Rochester.

WHY IT IS RIGHT: Simple past tense *(was born)* places that action before the present time *(lives)*.

Use past perfect verbs to place more than one past event in order. The earlier event should be in past perfect tense (with a *had* attached). The more recent event should be in simple past tense. (For more information on simple past tense, turn to Chapter 5.)

See whether you know how to put past events in order by selecting the proper verb from the choices in parentheses. Underline your choice. Be careful! To be sure you are paying attention, I give you one or two sentences that do not need the past perfect tense.

1. Because the soup (stained, had stained) his shirt, Gene went home to change his clothes.

2. He (searched, had been searching) his closet for an hour before he gave up.

3. Gene realized that he (forgot, had forgotten) to do the laundry.

4. Gene (grumbled, had grumbled) and (decided, had decided) to take better care of his clothes.

5. When Gene finally arrived at the restaurant, his friends (ordered, had ordered) dinner already.

Here are the answers: 1. *had stained* (Two events are in the past. The earlier — the soup accident — is expressed in past perfect tense. The more recent — *went home* — is in simple past tense.) 2. *had been searching* (Two events are in the past. The earlier — the closet search — is expressed in past perfect progressive tense. The more recent — *gave up* — is in simple past tense.) 3. *had forgotten* (Two events are in the past. The earlier — Gene's forgetfulness — is expressed in past perfect tense. The more recent — *realized* — is in simple past tense.) 4. *grumbled, decided* (Did I fool you? These two actions take place at more or less the same time in the past. Simple past tense is fine here.) 5. *had ordered* (Two events are in the past. The earlier — ordering food — is expressed in past perfect tense. The more recent — *arrived* — is in simple past tense.)

Breaking the Rules: Irregular Past Forms

If you break the rules, you get in trouble. When English verbs break the rules, they get a special section in a grammar book. Do you think this is fair? I do not. However, you do need to know the verb forms that break the rules — the *irregular verbs*.

Rule-breakers are most common in simple past tense (refer to Chapter 5 for more information), and in present perfect and past perfect tenses. The *has, have,* or *had* portion of the perfect verbs does not cause problems. The *participle* — the form of the verb attached to *has, have,* or *had* — is the troublemaker.

Here is a table of the most common irregular forms. The verb appears in the first column. The irregular simple past form is in the second column. The participle, which attaches to *has, have,* or *had,* is in the third column.

Verb	*Past-Tense Form*	*Participle*
be	was or were	been
begin	began	begun
bite	bit	bitten
break	broke	broken
bring	brought	brought
build	built	built
catch	caught	caught
choose	chose	chosen
come	came	come
do	did	done
drink	drank	drunk
drive	drove	driven
eat	ate	eaten
fall	fell	fallen
feel	felt	felt
fly	flew	flown
freeze	froze	frozen
get	got	gotten *or* got
go	went	gone

Verb	*Past-Tense Form*	*Participle*
have	had	had
know	knew	known
lead	led	led
lend	lent	lent
lose	lost	lost
ride	rode	ridden
ring	rang	rung
rise	rose	risen
run	ran	run
say	said	said
see	saw	seen
shake	shook	shaken
sing	sang	sung
sit	sat	sat
sleep	slept	slept
speak	spoke	spoken
steal	stole	stolen
swim	swam	swum
take	took	taken
teach	taught	taught
throw	threw	thrown
wear	wore	worn
win	won	won
write	wrote	written

You probably noticed that sometimes the past and the participle are the same. Sometimes, though, they differ. When the participle is different, it never appears without a helping verb (*has, have, had,* or some others). Here are some common mistakes I hear:

> WRONG: Henry done some work for me.
>
> WHY IT IS WRONG: The participle *done* needs a helping verb.
>
> RIGHT: Henry has done some work for me.

> WRONG: The lamb gone.
>
> RIGHT: The lamb has gone.

Another common mistake is to attach a helping verb to the past-tense form. Here are more mistakes to avoid:

> WRONG: Sam had went to the store.
>
> WHY IT IS WRONG: The past-tense form *went* should not be attached to a helping verb.

RIGHT: Sam went to the store.

WRONG: He had wrote a shopping list.

WHY IT IS WRONG: The past-tense form *wrote* should not be attached to a helping verb.

RIGHT: He wrote a shopping list.

If you do not know the correct past-tense form or the participle, check the dictionary.

To check your knowledge of irregular verbs, write the past tense or the participle in each blank. In the parentheses, I tell you which verb you are working with and which form to insert.

1. Brad _____ (swim, past tense) in the pool every day.

2. Michelle had _____ (build, participle) the pool before she started on the house.

3. During the summer, the children _____ (go, past tense) to the pool every day.

4. They _____ (wear, past tense) brightly colored bathing suits.

5. Michelle and Brad had _____ (write, participle) safety rules, but the children ignored the sign.

6. The older kids _____ (know, past tense) that they were supposed to watch the younger ones.

7. No one _____ (see, past tense) the accident!

8. Before anyone _____ (catch, past tense) the little boy, he had already _____ (fall, participle) in the water.

Here are the answers: 1. *swam* 2. *built* 3. *went* 4. *wore* 5. *written* 6. *knew* 7. *saw* 8. *caught, fallen*.

Glancing at the Future Perfect Tense

I imagine that you often face deadlines. You have homework or a business project to complete before a certain time. Deadlines appear in verb tense, too. An odd verb tense, the future perfect, shows up when there is a deadline inside a sentence. This tense places one event before another. Although the tense is called *future perfect,* the earlier event may be taking place in the present or in the future.

Read this example. The future perfect verb is underlined.

Bert <u>will have eaten</u> all the cookies before Ernie arrives.

Imagine these timelines:

present moment ——*will have eaten—arrives*

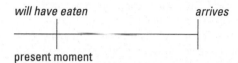

The earlier action, Bert's cookie eating, is expressed in future perfect tense. The action that occurs after is in present tense.

Here is another example, again with the future perfect verb underlined:

By the time the test ends, Max <u>will have answered</u> 150 questions.

Poor Max! That's a lot of questions. Here is the timeline for this sentence:

present moment——*will have answered—ends*

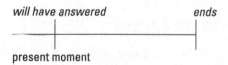

The earlier action, Max's answering, comes before the end of the test. As you see in both examples, the future perfect tense is created from *will have* plus the participle. Here are some other future perfect verbs:

will have run

will have typed

will have graduated

will have slept

will have won

will have aged

This sort of sentence does not appear often. However, if you see a deadline in the sentence, consider using future perfect tense.

You guys understand grammar, right?

You may have noticed that the word *you* is both singular and plural. Why? I have no idea! The same pronoun works when you are speaking to one person or to more than one. The verb forms that pair with the singular *you* also pair with the plural *you.* Great idea, right? Wrong. For some reason, many people like to show that a particular *you* is plural. That's why I hear these words:

y'all

you guys

you people

youse

These expressions are fun, and they may be fine when you are speaking with friends and family. However, they are not correct in formal, Standard English. If you truly wish to show that you are speaking or writing to just one person or to a group, try adding other clues. Here are two examples:

> You must all run the race today. We need everyone's help to win the trophy! (The *you* is plural.)

> Peter loves you and no one else, Margie. (The *you* is singular.)

The ex factor

Two letters, *ex,* add meaning to many words. *Ex* means "out of" or "used to be." Take a look at these words:

Ex-wife means "a woman who is out of the marriage." "Stan greeted his *ex-wife* in a friendly way."

Ex-president means "used to be president." "Although he was an *ex-president* of the association, no one paid attention to his suggestions."

Extract means "take out of." "Please *extract* the gun from your pocket and give it to the officer."

Expel means "to force out of." "The child cheated so often that he was *expelled* from the school."

Exclude means "to keep out of a group." "The players *excluded* Matt from their tournament because Matt did not understand enough about chess."

Sometimes, the letters *ex* have other meanings. Use the definitions here as clues, but check the dictionary if you do not know what a particular word means.

Chapter 11

Searching for Subjects

· ·

· ·

Human beings always want to know *who* or *what* everyone is talking about. In a sentence, that's the *subject*. Subjects are the subject of this chapter. Here you see how to locate the subject of a sentence and how to match every kind of subject to a proper verb.

Locating the Subject of a Sentence

You come home and find a broken window. What is the first thing you do? You probably ask one or two questions:

> *Who* broke the window?

> *What* broke the window?

These are basic questions. The answer depends on what happened. Here are two possibilities:

> A <u>robber</u> broke the window.

> A falling <u>tree</u> broke the window.

Grammarians call the answer to these questions the *subject*. (Okay, I admit that this may be unrealistic. If your window is broken, you may not bother with grammar. You may call the cops instead!) In the first example sentence, the subject of the verb *broke* is *robber*. In the second example sentence, the subject of the verb *broke* is *tree*.

Did you notice that I mentioned the verb *broke* in the questions? Every sentence has at least one verb, a "doing" or a "being" word. (For more information on verbs, turn to Chapter 5.) However, verbs cannot sit by themselves in your sentence. Someone or something must perform the action or exist in the state of being expressed by the verb. That someone or something is the subject.

The "someone" or "something" may be a person, place, or thing. In other words, the subject may be a noun. The subject may also be a pronoun — a word that represents a noun. For more information on nouns, read Chapter 3. To learn more about pronouns, check out Chapter 4.

Now you know the basic rules for subject-hunting. In the sections that follow, I show you how to apply those rules to statements, questions, and commands.

Statement subjects

Most sentences make statements. Before you try to locate a subject in a statement, identify the verb. Ask these questions:

> Which word tells you what is happening?
>
> Which word tells you what was happening?
>
> Which word tells you what will happen?
>
> Which word makes a statement about being?

Once you have the verb, go for the subject. Ask two questions:

> Who?
>
> What?

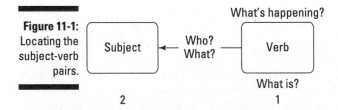

Figure 11-1: Locating the subject-verb pairs.

Attach these questions to the verb. Here is an example of a sentence that makes a statement so that you can see how these questions work:

> Martha lit the candles for her romantic dinner party.

First, find the verb:

> Which word tells you what is happening? No answer.
>
> Which word tells you what was happening? *lit*
>
> Which word tells you what will happen? No answer.
>
> Which word makes a statement about being? No answer.

Okay, now you know that the verb is *lit*. Ask your subject questions:

> Who *lit? Martha lit.*
>
> What *lit?* No answer.

Mission accomplished! The subject of the verb *lit* is *Martha*.

Look at one more example sentence:

> The new printer will run out of paper soon.

Find the verb first:

> Which word tells you what is happening? No answer.
>
> Which word tells you what was happening? No answer.
>
> Which word tells you what will happen? *will run*
>
> Which word makes a statement about being? No answer.

The verb is *will run*. Now ask your subject questions:

> Who *will run?* No answer.
>
> What will run? *printer*

The subject of the verb *will run* is *printer*.

Did you answer *the new printer* instead of *printer?* No problem! The subject is actually *printer,* but the longer version still tells you what you need to know.

Sometimes, when you ask the questions to find the subject, you get more than one answer. Take a look at this example:

> Sam and Anna visited their friends.

As always, find the verb first. Ask the verb questions:

> Which word tells you what is happening? No answer.

Which word tells you what was happening? *visited*

Which word tells you what will happen? No answer.

Which word makes a statement about being? No answer.

The verb is *visited.* Move on to the subject questions:

Who *visited? Sam, Anna*

What *visited?* No answer.

Sam and *Anna* are both subjects of the verb *visited.*

Try another sentence:

Either the computer or the printer is not working.

Find the verb:

Which word tells you what is happening? *is working*

Which word tells you what was happening? No answer.

Which word tells you what will happen? No answer.

Which word makes a statement about being? No answer.

You found your verb: *is working.* Are you wondering about the word *not? Not* is *not* a verb. It adds meaning to the verb, but it is not a "doing" or "being" word.

Now locate the subject:

Who *is working?* No answer.

What *is working? computer, printer*

The subjects of this sentence are *computer* and *printer.*

Are you wondering whether a sentence can have two verbs? Yes, it can! Here is one:

Nancy skipped class and went to the movies.

The words *skipped* and *went* answer this question: "Which word tells you what was happening?" Therefore, *skipped* and *went* are both verbs. In case you are curious, *Nancy* answers the subject question "Who *skipped* and went?" *Nancy* is the subject.

In most statements, the subject comes before the verb. In some unusual sentences, the subject is in a different place. Read these statements:

> Carl stepped into the basement.

> Into the basement stepped Carl.

These two sentences mean the same thing. In both sentences, the verb is *stepped.* When you ask the usual subject questions (Who *stepped?* What *stepped?*), you get the same answer: *Carl. Carl* is the subject of the verb *stepped.*

In statements beginning with *here* or *there,* you also find subjects after the verb. For more information, read "Dealing with Tricky Subjects," later in this chapter.

No matter how the words are arranged, use the same method for locating subjects. Find the verb, ask the *who?* and *what?* subject questions, and the real subject will pop up.

Look at each statement in the following table. Ask the questions to identify the verb. Write the verb in the second column. Then ask the questions to identify the subject. Write the subject in the third column.

Sentence	*Verb*	*Subject*
1. Everyone is very happy about the show.		
2. Simon will be here in about an hour.		
3. Nora and her brother played their guitars at the concert.		
4. That drawer does not stick.		
5. Stacy and Justin are in the school play.		
6. They have received many requests for help after the earthquake.		
7. The secretary will prepare the report and will send it to the boss.		
8. Up the hill climbed Marion.		

Here are the answers: 1. *is* (verb), *Everyone* (subject) 2. *will be* (verb), *Simon* (subject) 3. *played* (verb), *Nora, brother* (subjects) 4. *does stick* (verb), *drawer* (subject) 5. *are* (verb), *Stacy, Justin* (subjects) 6. *have received* (verb), *They* (subject) 7. *will prepare, will send* (verbs), *secretary* (subject) 8. *climbed* (verb), *Marion* (subject).

Question subjects

Do you like grammar? I am not asking that question to discover your feelings about my best subject. I am asking because I want you to locate the subject in that question. Here is the method for finding subjects that appear in questions.

First, find the verb by asking the verb questions. You may find it helpful to rearrange the question (keeping all the words) into statement form:

> you Do like grammar

Now ask the verb questions:

> Which word tells you what is happening? *Do like*
>
> Which word tells you what was happening? No answer.
>
> Which word tells you what will happen? No answer.
>
> Which word makes a statement about being? No answer.

Next, ask the subject questions:

> Who *do like? you*
>
> What *do like?* No answer.

The subject is *you.*

The questions may sound strange. No one says, "Who do like?" Do not worry about the sound of the questions. Just ask them and you will find the subject!

Here is another question:

> Did Cindy eat dinner already?

Follow the same steps. Start by rearranging the question's words into statement form:

> Cindy Did eat dinner already

Ask the verb questions:

> Which word tells you what is happening? No answer.
>
> Which word tells you what was happening? *Did eat*
>
> Which word tells you what will happen? No answer.
>
> Which word makes a statement about being? No answer.

Ask the subject questions:

> Who *Did eat? Cindy*

> What *Did eat?* No answer.

Cindy is the subject.

Like statements, questions may have more than one subject or more than one verb. (See the previous section on statements for more information.) Do not worry about whether you have one or more than one subject or verb. Just ask your questions and record the answers to find the subjects and verbs with no trouble.

Hunt for subjects and verbs in these questions. Ask the questions to identify the verb. Write the verb in the second column. Then ask the questions to identify the subject. Write the subject in the third column.

Question	Verb	Subject
1. Are we there yet?		
2. Will Sarah repair the car?		
3. Have Allen and Steve chosen the band?		
4. Is the company hiring or firing workers?		
5. Does everyone have a fork?		
6. Can Ben drive to school?		
7. Why is Andrew angry?		

Here are the answers: 1. *Are* (verb), *we* (subject) 2. *will repair* (verb), *Sarah* (subject) 3. *have chosen* (verb), *Allen, Steve* (subjects) 4. *is hiring, firing* (verbs), *company* (subject) 5. *Does have* (verbs), *everyone* (subject). 6. *Can drive* (verb), *Ben* (subject) 7. *is* (verb), *Andrew* (subject).

Note: The second verb in Question 4 of this quiz, *firing,* is actually *is firing.* The first *is* attaches to both *hiring* and *firing.*

Command subjects

When you hear the word *command,* you probably think of an army general, or a queen — or maybe your mom. (I am a mom, and I love to give commands!) Sentences make commands, too. Look at these commands:

> <u>Stop</u> that noise.

> <u>Eat</u> your vegetables.

> Please <u>be</u> nice to your little sister.

> <u>Vote</u> in the next election.

The usual verb questions do not work as well with commands. Finding the verb in these sentences is easy, though. Just look for the word that tells you what to do. In the preceding command sentences, the verbs are underlined.

Where are the subjects? They do not appear in the command sentence. They are implied — understood without actually appearing. The subject of a command is always the same: *you*. Because the *you* does not appear in the command, English teachers call this subject "you understood."

In a command, the verb is the word that tells you what to do. The subject is always the same: *you*.

Matching Subjects and Verbs Properly

English teachers make a fuss about finding subjects and verbs. Why? The subjects and verbs must match. Here are two important rules for matching subjects and verbs:

- **If the subject is singular, the verb must also be singular.** A singular subject is *one* person, place, or thing. Here are some examples of singular subjects:

  - person
  - pen
  - Gina
  - he
  - driver
  - I
  - dog
  - this

- **If the subject is plural, the verb must also be plural.** A plural subject is *more than one* person, place, or thing. Here are some examples of plural subjects:

  - people
  - they
  - officers
  - both

- daisies

- these

- we

- men

Most of the time, figuring out what is singular and what is plural is easy. Occasionally, some unusual words may puzzle you. In this section, you find both types of sentences.

Once you have located a subject, of course, you have to decide which form of the verb is singular and which is plural. I am happy to say that nearly always, the verb forms are the same for both. The singular and plural forms are different in the present tense, when you are talking about someone, something, or a group. The forms are also different for a few verbs — *be, have,* and *do* — whether they appear alone or attached to another verb. You can find the forms of these verbs in Chapter 5.

Sorting out subjects and verbs in common situations

Imagine that you have two baskets. One is labeled "singular," and the other "plural." You can probably place nearly every subject of a statement into the *singular* (one) or *plural* (more than one) category without hesitating.

Take a look at these statement sentences. In parentheses, you see the matches.

> The monster pops out of the closet. (*monster* = singular subject, *pops* = singular verb)

> Seven monsters are still inside. (*monsters* = plural subject, *are* = plural verb)

> Clara has taught Spanish for five years. (*Clara* = singular subject, *has taught* = singular verb)

> They often eat in restaurants. (*They* = plural subject, *eat* = plural verb)

Statements are easy, but questions are a little harder. (Do not worry. Questions are not much harder!) The verbs in questions often contain two words. These words may be separated by the subject.

Look at some questions. In parentheses, you find the subject–verb matches.

Does Bobby have a new address? (*Bobby* = singular subject, *Does have* = singular verb)

Do the children need more crayons? (*children* = plural subject, *Do need* = plural verb)

Has Karen agreed with your plan? (*Karen* = singular subject, *Has agreed* = singular verb)

Have the birds flown away? (*birds* = plural subject, *Have flown* = plural verb)

Are they having trouble with this lesson? (*they* = plural subject, *Are having* = plural verb)

Was Ellen nervous about the test? (*Ellen* = singular subject, *was* = singular verb)

In the world of grammar, singular matches singular, and plural matches plural. No mixing is allowed. For more help identifying singular and plural words, turn to Chapter 3 (nouns), Chapter 4 (pronouns), and Chapter 5 (verbs).

Can you match the correct verb to the subject of these sentences? First, underline the subject of the sentence. Then look at the verbs in parentheses. Underline your choice.

1. My cousin (organizes, organize) his files by date.

2. Many bears (lives, live) in that wilderness area.

3. (Is, Are) the women in the pool?

4. (Has, have) Mary finished her chores?

5. Oliver (wants, want) a pony for his birthday.

Here are the answers: 1. *cousin* (singular subject), *organizes* (singular verb) 2. *Bears* (plural subject), *live* (plural verb) 3. *Women* (plural subject), *are* (plural verb) 4. *Mary* (singular subject), *has* (singular verb) 5. *Oliver* (singular subject), *wants* (singular verb).

Tackling tougher sentences

Life is beautiful because it offers so much variety. The English language, in my opinion, is beautiful for the same reason. However, unusual sentences sometimes make choosing the proper subject–verb match a little harder.

Not too hard! Do not worry. In this section, you tackle a few different types of sentences, matching subjects and verbs.

These sentences do not follow the common pattern, but the rule is exactly the same: Singular subjects pair with singular verbs, and plural subjects pair with plural verbs.

First, look at sentences with two subjects connected by one of these two words: *and, or.* Here are some guidelines for sentences with subjects connected by *and* or *or:*

 ✔ **Two singular subjects joined by *and* become a plural subject.** The word *and* is like a plus sign in math. You add when you see *and.* One singular subject plus one other singular subject equals a plural subject. Therefore, you need a plural verb. Look at these examples:

   • Paul and Harry like Chinese food. (*Paul* and *Harry* = plural subject, *like* = plural verb)

   • The bee and its hive are in that field. (*bee* and *hive* = plural subject, *are* = plural verb)

   • Math and science have always been my best subjects. (*Math* and *science* = plural subject, *have been* = plural verb)

   • Do Elaine and George like spaghetti? (*Elaine* and *George* = plural subject, *Do like* = plural verb)

   • Windows and mirrors break easily. (*Windows* and *mirrors* = plural subject, *break* = plural verb)

 ✔ **Two singular subjects joined by *or* stay separate, remaining as singular subjects.** The logic here is that you have one *or* the other, not both. You need a singular verb in this situation. Read these examples:

   • Johnny or Jean has the key. (*Johnny* or *Jean* = singular subject, *has* = singular verb)

   • The driver or the passenger has been ill. (*driver* or *passenger* = singular subject, *has been* = singular verb)

   • Spanish or French is spoken in that country. (*Spanish* or *French* = singular subject, *is spoken* = singular verb)

   • Has Steve or Sally set the table? (*Steve* or *Sally* = singular subject, *Has set* = singular verb)

   • Smoking or drinking was not allowed. (*Smoking* or *drinking* = singular subject, *was* = singular verb)

Check your understanding of sentences with subjects connected by *and* or *or.* First, underline the subjects of the sentence. Then look at the verbs in parentheses. Underline your choice.

1. Betty and Veronica (runs, run) to the door.

2. The butcher or the baker (answers, answer) the phone.

3. In the evening, a mosquito and a wasp (buzzes, buzz) around the campfire.

4. Shelly or her sister (swats, swat) the bugs.

5. (Is, Are) the tent and the sleeping bag comfortable?

Here are the answers: 1. *Betty* and *Veronica* (plural subject), *run* (plural verb) 2. *butcher* or *baker* (singular subject), *answers* (singular verb) 3. *Mosquito* and *wasp* (plural subject), *buzz* (plural verb) 4. *Shelly* or *sister* (singular subject), *swats* (singular verb) 5. *tent* and *bag* (plural subject), *Are* (plural verb).

Dealing with Tricky Subjects

Do you like everyone? Probably, in real life, you do not like everyone. In grammar, you may not like the pronoun *everyone* either. Why? *Everyone* is a tricky subject. In this section, you learn about *everyone* and other odd subjects.

Singular subjects that look like plurals

Everyone sounds like more than one. In other words, *everyone* appears to be a plural word. However, *everyone* is actually a singular word. Look at these example sentences:

WRONG: Everyone are here.

WHY IT IS WRONG: *Everyone* is singular, and *are* is a plural verb.

RIGHT: Everyone is here.

WHY IT IS RIGHT: Now the singular verb *is* matches the singular subject *everyone*.

Another tricky word is *everything*. This pronoun sounds big, as if all the things in the world were tucked inside. *Everything,* though, is actually singular. Read these sentences:

WRONG: Everything in the closet were mine.

WHY IT IS WRONG: *Everything* is singular, and *were* is a plural verb.

RIGHT: Everything in the closet was mine.

WHY IT IS RIGHT: Now the singular verb *was* matches the singular subject *everything*.

Everybody is another word that may fool you. It is also singular. Look at these sentences:

WRONG: Everybody in the swimming pool have splashed me!

WHY IT IS WRONG: *Everybody* is singular, and *have splashed* is a plural verb.

RIGHT: Everybody in the swimming pool has splashed me.

WHY IT IS RIGHT: Now the singular verb *has splashed* matches the singular subject *everybody*.

A few other words falsely appear to be plurals. These subjects, however, are also singular:

someone	anyone	no one
something	anything	nothing
somebody	anybody	nobody

Be careful with subjects that contain *–one, –thing,* and *–body.* They may seem to include a group, but actually, these words are singular. They must pair with singular verbs.

The preceding list shows you words that are always singular. The following words are always plural: *both, few, many,* and *several.*

Everyone should check singular and plural subjects. Read these sentences. Underline the correct verb form.

1. No one (has, have) taken out the garbage today.

2. Anything (was, were) possible when Henry helped.

3. Everybody (needs, need) a dictionary.

4. Both (includes, include) misspelled words.

5. Sally said that someone (is, are) poisoning the soup.

6. Nobody (is, are) to blame for that accident.

Here are the answers: 1. *has* 2. *was* 3. *needs* 4. *include* 5. *is* 6. *is.*

Again and again

Two letters, *re,* may mean "again" or "over again" when they appear at the beginning of a word. Read these examples:

Reconnect means "connect again." "I used social media to *reconnect* with some old friends."

Redo means "do again." "Your report is sloppy. Please *redo* it."

Redecorate means "decorate again." "Sheila and Sam hated the purple paint once they saw it in the room, so they decided to *redecorate* immediately."

Reconsider means "consider, or think about, again." "Jamie turned down the union's latest offer, but when they threatened to strike, he *reconsidered.*"

Usually, when you add *re* to the front of a word, you do not need a hyphen. (A hyphen is a short, horizontal line.) However, in one case you do need a hyphen. Read this sentence, written in a note I received from a student:

I resent the paper you assigned.

When I read that note, I was upset. *Resent* may mean "be offended by." I thought the student was angry about my assignment! Actually, the student *rewrote* the paper to make it better. Then he *re-sent* it (sent it again). By the way, did you notice that *rewrote* means "wrote again"?

Subjects in sentences with "here" and "there"

Tricky subjects also show up in sentences beginning with *here* or *there.* In these sentences, the subject is not *here* or *there.* The subject appears after the verb. Check these out:

Here is the path to the river. (*path* = singular subject, *is* = singular verb)

There are three socks in the dryer. (*socks* = plural subject, *are* = plural verb)

Here was a huge mountain! (*mountain* = singular subject, *was* = singular verb)

There were seven sisters in that family. (*sisters* = plural subject, *were* = plural verb)

Be careful when you see a *here* or *there* sentence. Choose a verb that matches the real subject.

Can you find the subject in a *here* or *there* sentence? Circle the subject and choose a matching verb from the parentheses. Underline your choice.

1. Here (is, are) a dozen roses for your birthday.

2. There (was, were) a gift on the table for you also.

3. Here (is, are) something you will enjoy.

4. There (is, are) everyone, ready to sing "Happy Birthday to You!"

5. There (is, are) many cards for you also.

Here are the answers: 1. *are* (*roses* = plural subject) 2. *was* (*gift* = singular subject) 3. *is* (*something* = singular subject) 4. *is* (*everyone* = singular subject) 5. *are* (*cards* = plural subject).

Changeable subjects

Some things never change. You let go of a rock, and it falls down. Gravity (unless you are in space!) is always the same. A few pronouns, though, do change. At times they are singular. At times they are plural. Two important pronouns in this category are *all* and *some.* Here are guidelines for proper handling of these subjects:

1. **Look at the words following the pronoun.** Generally, you see *of.* The word *of* begins a phrase, naming one thing or a group of things or people.

2. **If the phrase talks about one thing, the subject is singular.** When you see *of the air, of the earth, of the work,* and similar phrases, your subject is singular. Take a peek at these examples:

    - All of the smoke is blowing away. (After the subject *all,* you find *of the smoke. Smoke* is a singular word. *All* in this sentence is singular and pairs with the singular verb *is blowing.*)

    - Some of the soil is red. (After the subject *some,* you see *of the soil. Soil* is a singular word. *Some* in this sentence is singular and pairs with the singular verb *is.*)

3. **If the phrase talks about more than one thing or person, the subject is plural.** When you see *of the girls, of the pens, of the bears,* and similar phrases, your subject is plural. Look at these examples:

    - All of the papers are blowing away. (After the subject *all,* you find *of the papers. Papers* is a plural word. *All* in this sentence is plural and pairs with the plural verb, *are blowing.*)

    - Some of the balloons are pink. (After the subject *some,* you see *of the balloons. Balloons* is a plural word. *Some* in this sentence is plural and pairs with the plural verb *are.*)

Matchmaking is fun. Choose a verb from the parentheses that matches the subject. Remember to look at the phrase before you select a verb.

1. All of the windows (needs, need) to be washed.

2. Some of the kids (is wearing, are wearing) uniforms.

3. All of the food (has spoiled, have spoiled).

4. Some of the carpet (was, were) smelly.

5. All of the skaters (has fallen, have fallen) at least twice.

6. Some of the ice (is melting, are melting).

Here are the answers: 1. *need* 2. *are wearing* 3. *has spoiled* 4. *was* 5. *have fallen* 6. *is melting.*

Do it yourself!

Do you like to talk about yourself? Most of us do. The *—self* pronouns are very popular words. However, they usually are not allowed to be subjects. Look at these examples:

WRONG: Vicky and myself will collect money for charity.

WHY IT IS WRONG: The subjects of this sentence are *Vicky* and *myself. Myself* cannot be a subject.

RIGHT: Vicky and I will collect money for charity.

WHY IT IS RIGHT: Now the sentence has proper subjects: *Vicky* and *I.*

WRONG: *Herself* thinks she is as important as the president.

WHY IT IS WRONG: *Herself* cannot be a subject.

RIGHT: She thinks she is as important as the president.

WHY IT IS RIGHT: *She* is a proper subject.

The only time you can place a *—self* word in a subject spot is to emphasize a subject that is already present:

Angela herself will call you.

In this sentence, *Angela* is probably an important person — too important to make her own phone calls. The writer adds *herself* to show that a call from Angela is unusual.

Chapter 12

Adding Meaning with Complements

· ·

In This Chapter

▶ Locating objects

▶ Checking for subject and object complements

▶ Selecting pronouns to act as complements

· ·

Complements do not appear in every sentence. When they do show up, however, they are important. They add to the ideas expressed by the subject–verb pair. (You can read about subject–verb pairs in Chapter 11.)

In this chapter, you learn everything you ever wanted to know about the most common types of *complements* — what they are, how to insert them into your sentence, and how to choose the proper pronoun to act as a complement. At the end of the chapter, be ready to receive *compliments* (words of praise) for your knowledge of *complements* (parts of a sentence).

Surveying Complements

"Barney hits." When you read that sentence, I bet you are wondering *what* Barney hits. A home run? The lottery jackpot? Perhaps you wonder *whom* Barney hits. His little sister? A mugger? The answer to these questions (*what?* or *whom?*) is what English teachers call a *complement*.

A good general tries to see the big picture before going into battle. Before you battle to find complements, you should meet them. In this section, I introduce you to *objects* and *subject complements*.

Taking action: Objects

Action verbs express action. (I imagine you are not surprised to hear this fact!) Proper English sentences do not need complements. Without complements, though, an action-verb sentence gives less information.

Read these examples. The objects are underlined. Information on other parts of the sentence appears in parentheses.

> Joe drank <u>coffee</u> every morning. (*Joe* = subject, *drank* = action verb)
>
> The referee blew the <u>whistle</u>. (*referee* = subject, *blew* = action verb)
>
> Carmen filled the <u>tank</u> with gas. (*Carmen* = subject, *filled* = action verb)
>
> Everyone greeted <u>Philip</u> warmly. (*Everyone* = subject, *greeted* = action verb)
>
> He knew <u>someone</u> in the government. (*He* = subject, *knew* = action verb)

As you see, the action flows from the *subject* (who or what performs the action) to the *object* (whom or what receives the action). In every example sentence, the flow of action is direct, with no detours. Therefore, these complements are called *direct objects.*

A sentence may have more than one direct object. Look at these examples:

> Bert played <u>guitar</u> and <u>banjo</u> in the show. (*Bert* = subject, *played* = action verb)
>
> Simon read <u>stories</u> and <u>poems</u>. (*Simon* = subject, *read* = action verb)
>
> Hannah is chewing <u>steak</u> and <u>broccoli</u>. (*Hannah* = subject, *is chewing* = action verb)
>
> Somebody should use more <u>soap</u> and <u>deodorant</u>! (*Somebody* = subject, *should use* = action verb)

A sentence may have even more objects. In this example, you see three:

> The author wrote <u>poems</u>, <u>stories</u>, and <u>plays</u>. (*author* = subject, *wrote* = action verb)

Sometimes, the flow of action makes a little detour before arriving at the direct object. Read the following sentences. Notice the underlined word in each one. The underlined word is also an object, but a different kind:

Mark gave <u>Maria</u> some water. (*Mark* = subject, *gave* = verb, *water* = direct object)

Brad wrote <u>me</u> a letter. (*Brad* = subject, *wrote* = verb, *letter* = direct object)

Chris will buy <u>everyone</u> a present. (*Chris* = subject, *will buy* = verb, *present* = direct object)

Gardeners gave the <u>plants</u> extra water. (*Gardeners* = subject, *gave* = verb, *water* = direct object)

Gus told <u>her</u> a secret. (*Gus* = subject, *told* = verb, *secret* = direct object)

The underlined words in the preceding sentences are connected to the action, but these words do not receive the action directly. For this reason, the underlined words are called *indirect objects.*

You don't need to waste space in your brain remembering these grammar terms. All you need to remember is that objects come after action verbs and receive action from the verb directly or indirectly. Why? Good question! You need to identify objects so that when a pronoun takes that role in your sentence, it's easy to select the proper form. For more information, see "Choosing the Proper Complement Pronoun," later in this chapter.

How good are you at finding objects? See whether you can underline the objects in these sentences.

1. Edna milked the cow.

2. Charlie painted the fence and the house.

3. The horse ate 15 carrots.

4. I dusted the furniture in the living room.

5. Sylvia wrote me a note.

6. The host shouted welcoming words.

Here are the answers: 1. *cow* 2. *fence, house* 3. *carrots* 4. *furniture* 5. *me* (indirect object), *note* (direct object) 6. *words.*

Did you answer *15 carrots* for question three or *welcoming words* for question six? If so, count your answers as correct. The extra descriptions do not matter.

Finishing the thought: Subject complements

Not all sentences include action. Some express a state of being. Usually, the word doing this job is a form of the verb *be*. (Turn to Chapter 5 to see these forms.) Here are a few sentences with forms of *be* underlined:

The traffic <u>is</u> terrible.

We <u>will be</u> late.

John <u>was</u> anxious about the exam.

Annie <u>has been</u> helpful.

Occasionally, verbs that relate to your senses (sight, hearing, and so forth) also express a state of being. Take a look at these sentences. Notice how the underlined verb expresses a state of being:

The music <u>sounds</u> loud.

The cake <u>looked</u> disgusting.

The baby blanket <u>feels</u> soft.

English teachers love to create grammar terms. I know at least three different ways to name a *being* verb. Do not worry about terms. They are not important. All you need to do is recognize a verb that expresses a state of being.

Sentences with subjects and *being* verbs are unfinished. Wouldn't you wait for more information when you hear these?

The train is

Molly seems

The dinner will be

Our house has been

The stew tastes

You want to know more about *The train, Molly, The dinner, Our house,* and *The stew.* Now read this list, with the thoughts completed:

The train is my favorite <u>toy</u>. (*train* = subject, *is* = linking verb)

Molly seems <u>cheerful</u>. (*Molly* = subject, *seems* = linking verb)

The dinner will be <u>delicious</u>. (*dinner* = subject, *will be* = linking verb)

Our house has been a beloved <u>home</u>. (*house* = subject, *has been* = linking verb)

The stew tastes <u>salty</u>. (*stew* = subject, *tastes* = linking verb)

The underlined words relate to the *subject* of each sentence. For this reason, they are called *subject complements*. Subject complements complete the meaning of the sentence.

As always, you do not have to remember the grammar term. Just be sure that you can find a subject complement when one is present in your sentence. Why? If a pronoun does this job, you must use a *subject pronoun* (one that may properly be used as a subject). For more information, read "Choosing the Proper Complement Pronoun," later in this chapter.

Some sentences with linking verbs have one subject complement, and some have more than one. Read these examples:

Neil has been <u>sad</u> and <u>lonely</u> since his girlfriend left. (*Neil* = subject, *has been* = linking verb)

The secretaries are <u>Grace</u> and <u>Pete</u>. (*secretaries* = subject, *are* = linking verb)

The new rug is <u>soft</u> but <u>durable</u>. (*rug* = subject, *is* = linking verb)

At times, a linking-verb sentence has no subject complement. Instead, other words complete the meaning. The other words may refer to a location or a time. Look at these sentences:

He is <u>in the shower</u>. (*He* = subject, *is* = linking verb)

The game was <u>over</u>. (*game* = subject, *was* = linking verb)

The gift will be <u>here soon</u>. (*gift* = subject, *will be* = linking verb)

See whether you can underline the subject complements in these sentences. *Note:* To keep you on your toes, I placed one sentence without a complement in this quiz.

1. That coat is too long.

2. My dogs sound angry and tired.

3. The champion of the tournament is Ali.

4. The new senators were Mr. Smith and Ms. Jones.

5. Oak trees are in that forest.

6. The best player was Cameron.

Here are the answers: 1. *long* 2. *angry, tired* 3. *Ali* 4. *Mr. Smith, Ms. Jones* 5. no complement 6. *Cameron.*

Popping the Question to Identify Objects and Subject Complements

In romantic situations, you "pop the question" to find out whether marriage is in your future. In grammar, you "pop the question" to identify parts of a sentence, including complements. In this section, you see how to locate a complement by asking the right questions.

If the sentence contains an action verb, a few simple steps lead you to the object.

Direct objects

Here are the steps to find a direct object, a word that receives the action of the verb directly (no detours!). To help you understand, I explain these steps with an example. This is the sentence:

Stan painted my new kitchen.

1. **Identify the verb.**

   Ask these questions:

   What is happening? No answer.

   What was happening? *painted*

   What will happen? No answer.

   The answer, *painted,* is the action verb.

2. **Identify the subject.**

   Ask these questions, tacked onto the verb *painted.*

   Who painted? *Stan*

   What painted? No answer.

   The answer, *Stan,* is the subject.

3. **Identify the object.**

   Ask these questions, tacked onto the subject and verb:

   Stan painted whom? No answer.

   Stan painted what? *kitchen*

   The answer, *kitchen,* is the direct object.

Did you answer *my new kitchen* instead of *kitchen?* That is fine. The key word is *kitchen,* but including descriptive words will not cause any problems.

Figure 12-1 shows you the questions that help you find a direct object. The numbers indicate the order to follow.

Figure 12-1:
Locating the direct objects.

What's happening?

Subject ←—What?—— Verb ——What? Whom?→ Object

2   1   3

Here is another example of these questions in action, based on this sentence:

    Maria will glue tiles behind the stove.

First, find the verb:

    What is happening? No answer.

    What was happening? No answer.

    What will happen? *will glue*

The verb is *will glue.* Now ask the subject questions:

    Who *will glue? Maria*

    What *will glue?* No answer.

The subject is *Maria.* Ask the object questions, starting with the subject and verb you found:

    Maria will glue whom? No answer.

    Maria will glue what? *tiles*

The object is *tiles.*

Indirect objects

You may have more than one object — a *direct object* and an *indirect object* — in your sentence. (Refer to "Taking actions: Objects" earlier in this chapter for more information on these two types of objects.) The same questions work when you are looking for an indirect object, as long as you add one extra question. Look at this example sentence:

Barney gave Louisa a big kiss.

Here are the steps that lead you to the indirect object.

1. Identify the verb.

Ask these questions:

What is happening? No answer.

What was happening? *gave*

What will happen? No answer.

The answer, *gave,* is the action verb.

2. Identify the subject.

Ask these questions, tacked onto the verb *gave.*

Who *gave? Barney*

What *gave?* No answer.

The answer, *Barney,* is the subject.

3. Identify the direct object.

Ask these questions, tacked onto the subject and verb:

Barney gave whom? No answer.

Barney gave what? *kiss*

The answer, *kiss,* is the direct object.

Did you answer *a big kiss* instead of *kiss?* That is fine. The key word is *kiss,* but including descriptive words does not cause problems.

4. Identify the indirect object.

Ask these questions, tacked onto the subject, verb, and direct object:

Barney gave kiss to whom? *Louisa*

Barney gave kiss to what? No answer.

The indirect object is *Louisa.*

Sometimes the word *to* appears in the sentence. Look at this example:

Barney also wrote love letters to Louisa.

In this sentence, *Louisa* is not technically an indirect object. In case you are curious, *to Louisa* is a prepositional phrase. I am very happy to advise you that you do not have to worry about whether you have discovered an indirect object or a prepositional phrase. In either situation, you have an object, *Louisa.* That is all you need to know!

Figure 12-2 shows you the questions that help you find an indirect object. The numbers indicate the order to follow.

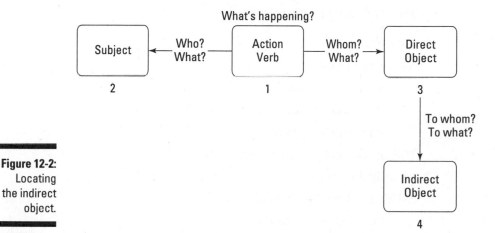

Figure 12-2:
Locating
the indirect
object.

See whether you can find the action verb, subject, and object(s) in the following sentences. *Note:* You may find one or more objects — or none at all!

Sentence	*Action Verb*	*Subject*	*Object(s)*
1. Shakespeare wrote many plays.			
2. Sonia accepted the award with a smile.			
3. The picture frame is tilting to the left.			
4. Hettie sang a beautiful song to me.			
5. Walter is sending him some money.			
6. Doctor Roberts injected the vaccine.			

Here are the answers:1. *wrote* (verb), *Shakespeare* (subject), *plays* (direct object) 2. *accepted* (verb), *Sonia* (subject), *award* (direct object) 3. *is tilting* (verb), *frame* (subject), no object 4. *sang* (verb), *Hettie* (subject), *song* (direct object) 5. *is sending* (verb), *Walter* (subject), *money* (direct object), *him* (indirect object) 6. *injected* (verb), *Doctor Roberts* (subject), *vaccine* (direct object).

Note: In Sentence 4, *me* is also an object, the object of the preposition *to.*

Locating subject complements

When a sentence has a *being* verb, not an action verb, you should look for the subject complement. The steps are very easy to follow. Take a look, working from this example sentence:

> The ocean will be calm tonight.

1. **Identify the verb.**

   Ask these questions:

   > What is? No answer.
   >
   > What was? No answer.
   >
   > What will be? *will be*

   The answer, *will be,* is the being verb.

2. **Identify the subject.**

   Ask these questions, tacked onto the verb *will be.*

   > Who *will be?* No answer.
   >
   > What *will be?* ocean

   The answer, *ocean,* is the subject.

3. **Identify the subject complement.**

   Ask these questions, tacked onto the subject and verb:

   > *Ocean will be* who? No answer.
   >
   > *Ocean will be* what? *calm*

   The answer, *calm,* is the subject complement.

Take a peek at one more example, based on this sentence:

> The dentist is a recent graduate of that university.

1. **Identify the verb.**

   Ask these questions:

   > What is? *is*
   >
   > What was? No answer.
   >
   > What will be? No answer.

   The answer, *is,* is the being verb.

2. Identify the subject.

Ask these questions, tacked onto the verb *is.*

Who is? *dentist*

What is? No answer.

The answer, *dentist,* is the subject.

3. Identify the subject complement.

Ask these questions, tacked onto the subject and verb:

dentist is who? No answer.

dentist is what? *graduate*

The answer, *graduate,* is the subject complement.

Figure 12-3 may help you follow the steps to the subject complement.

Figure 12-3:
Locating
the subject
complement.

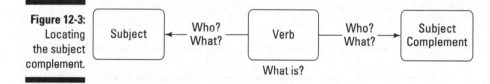

To find out how good you are at asking questions, follow the steps and fill in the columns to identify the *being* verb, the subject, and the subject complement. ***Note:*** You may find one or more subject complements or none at all.

Sentence	*Being Verb*	*Subject*	*Subject Complement*
1. Virginia Woolf was a fine writer.			
2. Her piano sounds strange.			
3. The rain will be heavy at times.			
4. My feet are on the pillow.			
5. Cough medicine tastes terrible.			
6. Mark is president of the student government.			

Here are the answers: 1. *was* (verb), *Virginia Woolf* (subject), *writer* (subject complement) 2. *sounds* (verb), *piano* (subject), *strange* (subject complement) 3. *will be* (verb), *rain* (subject), *heavy* (subject complement) 4. *are* (verb), *feet* (subject), no subject complement 5. *tastes* (verb), *medicine* or *cough medicine* (subject), *terrible* (subject complement) 6. *is* (verb), *Mark* (subject), *president* (subject complement).

Choosing the Proper Complement Pronoun

When you saw your brother, did you give *he* a hug? I hope not! Did you give *him* a hug? I hope so! *Him* is an object pronoun. *He* is a subject pronoun. When your sentence needs an object, turn to the object pronouns. Avoid the subject pronouns.

Suppose someone asks, "Who is there?" What is your answer — "It is me" or "It is I"? The correct response is "It is *I*." Why? The verb *is* expresses a state of being. A sentence with that type of verb has a subject complement, not an object. Therefore, the pronoun you need is a subject pronoun. Placing an object pronoun there is incorrect in Standard English.

In conversation, most people say, "It's me" or "It is me." In conversation with friends or relatives, these sentences are fine. In situations requiring your best, most proper grammar, though, these sentences are not fine. They are incorrect!

When you are selecting a pronoun as a complement, follow these guidelines:

- ✔ **Choose an object pronoun for sentences with action verbs.** Direct and indirect objects, if they are pronouns, are always object pronouns. Some common object pronouns are *me, us, him, her,* and *them.* (For more information about object pronouns, turn to Chapter 4.)

- ✔ **Choose a subject pronoun for sentences with being verbs.** Subject complements, when they are pronouns, are subject pronouns. Some common subject pronouns are *I, we, he, she,* and *they.* (For more information on subject pronouns, check out Chapter 4.)

Take a look at these examples. The complements, which are all pronouns, are underlined. More information about each sentence appears in parentheses.

The dog will bite <u>her</u>. (*will bite* = action verb, *dog* = subject)

Henry lost his gloves but found <u>them</u> quickly. (*lost, found* = action verbs, *Henry* = subject)

The best assistant is <u>she</u>. (*is* = being verb, *assistant* = subject)

It is <u>they</u> who are to blame for that mess. (*is* = being verb, *It* = subject)

The attorney always gives <u>us</u> his <u>attention</u>. (*gives* = action verb, *attorney* = subject)

In the last example sentence, *us* is an indirect object. The direct object is *attention*.

Select the proper pronoun from the parentheses. Remember that a sentence with an action verb needs an object pronoun. A sentence with a being verb needs a subject pronoun.

1. Marlene baked _____ (I, me) a cake.

2. My favorite musicians are _____ (they, them).

3. You must find _____ (she, her).

4. I predict that the champion will be _____ (he, him).

5. Max and Andy told _____ (they, themselves) to work harder.

6. The television show interested _____ (we, us).

Here are the answers: 1. *me* 2. *they* 3. *her* 4. *he* 5. *themselves* 6. *us*.

To, too, two = three confusing words

Three words sound exactly the same, just like the number 2. They are spelled differently, though, and they do not have the same meaning. Here they are:

To may be attached to a verb (*to like, to walk, to buy*). "Dan wanted *to* deal the cards." *To* may also show movement toward someone or something (*to the store, to me*). "Dan drove *to* the bank. He gave the money *to* Martha."

Too means "also" or "more than enough." "Are you going *too?*" "The suitcase is *too* heavy."

Two is the number 2. "I have *two* cousins in the navy."

Remember these *two* things: You are never *too* old *to* improve your understanding of proper grammar. You are never *too* young *to* begin learning!

Chapter 13

Finishing the Job: Writing Complete Sentences

In This Chapter

▶ Avoiding sentence fragments

▶ Surveying the elements of a complete sentence

▶ Adding proper punctuation to the end of the sentence

▶ Adjusting the rules for text messaging

Have you ever had a conversation like this one?

> Son: Why do I have to take out the garbage?
>
> Mother: Because.

In real life, the mother's reply is very annoying. The son deserves a better answer, such as "You have to take out the garbage because I will ground you for three weeks if you do not." This is a book about grammar, though, not parenting. In grammar, the mother's answer is not satisfactory for a different reason. It is not a complete sentence — an important requirement of Standard English. In this chapter, you see how to create complete sentences and punctuate them properly. This chapter also shows you how to change traditional rules when you send a text.

Halfway Is Not Enough: Expressing a Complete Thought

When you are writing, you must be clear. Clear meaning usually comes from complete sentences. A complete sentence must express a complete thought. Take a look at these examples. Do you know what they mean?

Since you left.

The job has been.

Knowing you.

The month of April was.

Because I need some time.

Over the rainbow and beyond the horizon, Henry.

Who does that

Although everyone believes you.

I bet you found these examples a little confusing. Each one gives you some information, but each one also leaves you wanting more information. Look at the first example again. You can expand it in several different ways:

I have been sad since you left.

Since you left, the office has been reorganized.

Since you left, John was promoted.

John has been happy since you left.

These are four meanings. You could probably add a million more! Each expresses a complete thought. Each, therefore, is a complete sentence, unlike the fragment *Since you left.*

Check out another example from the first list, expanded here:

Knowing you has been an honor.

Knowing you, the report will be perfect.

Is knowing you enough, or do I need work experience to get that job?

Knowing you, Amy, is simply impossible because you keep too many secrets.

These expanded sentences are not like the fragment *knowing you.* They express a complete thought. Turn your attention to one more example from the first list. See how the meaning may change with some simple additions:

Who does that?

Who does that!

I do not know who does that.

Sam said he knew a carpenter who does that.

In the first line of the preceding list, the punctuation mark completes the idea. Now you know that someone is asking a question about an action. In the second line of the list, the punctuation mark adds a bit of surprise and per-haps disapproval. The third and fourth lines fill out the meaning with words.

No matter how you complete these ideas, the point is the same. Fragments are unclear. More information or a punctuation mark must be added to change a fragment into a complete sentence, expressing a complete thought.

Length has nothing to do with whether your sentence expresses a complete thought or remains unclear. Some short sentences are complete:

> Allison dances.
>
> I am here.
>
> The flower blooms.
>
> Jean snores.
>
> Alex left.

Some long "sentences" are actually fragments, not expressing a com-plete thought:

> Although you bought me a car, sent me a basket of flowers, and hired a plane to write "I love you" in the sky.
>
> Robert, because he is so tall that he can touch the ceiling and reach the highest bookshelf in the library.
>
> If I am admitted to your school, which is near my house and which has an excellent reputation for academics and sports.
>
> Crying, screaming, running in circles, and generally behaving in a strange way.

No matter how long or short they are, all your sentences should be complete and clearly express your meaning.

Can you detect a complete thought? Try your hand by labeling these as "complete" or "fragment."

1. Although Sandy was standing on the beach.

2. The bucket leaked water onto the rug.

3. Finding a really good pen was impossible.

4. When it snows.

5. Who cheated.

6. Archie was going to the principal.

Here are the answers: 1. fragment 2. complete 3. complete 4. fragment 5. fragment 6. complete.

Cooking Up a Complete Sentence: The Essential Subject–Verb Pair

Every sentence is different, but the recipe for a complete sentence in Standard English always includes at least one matching subject–verb pair. When I say "matching," I do not mean the kind of match you make for a romantic evening. I mean that the verb form must pair properly with the subject. Keep these points in mind when you check for a proper match:

- **A verb expresses action or state of being.** Look for words that tell you what is happening or what is. (If you need more information about locating verbs, look at Chapter 5.)

- **The subject is whoever or whatever does the action or exists in the state of being.** Place the questions *who?* and *what?* in front of the verb. The answer is the subject. (Refer to Chapter 11 for help finding subjects.)

In this section, I show you some examples of subject–verb pairs that match and subject–verb pairs that do not match. Notice how the verb changes form when it pairs properly with each subject. Also examine the mismatches so that you can avoid them in your own writing.

Not flying solo: Verb forms ending in –ing

Often, you write or speak about an action that is in progress, or a state of being that is ongoing. The *–ing* form of a verb expresses these meanings, but you must use this form carefully.

Look at these pairs. The verb forms are underlined:

Matching Pair	*Nonmatching Pair*
bird is <u>flying</u>	bird <u>flying</u>
Henry <u>is going</u>	Henry <u>going</u>
I <u>am swimming</u>	I <u>swimming</u>
the prince and his wife <u>are being</u>	the prince and his wife <u>being</u>
mirrors <u>are reflecting</u>	mirrors <u>reflecting</u>
the river <u>is flowing</u>	the river <u>flowing</u>
musicians <u>are playing</u>	musicians <u>playing</u>

What did you notice about the matching pair? The *–ing* verb is always accompanied by a form of the verb *be. Flying, going, swimming,* and other *–ing* verb forms are fine, but not by themselves. To act as a proper verb in a subject–verb pair, the *–ing* form must be attached to *is, are, was, were, will be, had been,* or another form of the verb *be.* (For more information on forms of *be,* refer to Chapter 5.) For this reason, *I swimming* is wrong. *I am swimming* is right.

Remember that the guidelines in this section apply only to subject–verb pairs. The *–ing* form of a verb, all alone, may be correct in other roles. Read this example:

WRONG: Sam riding his bike.

WHY IT IS WRONG: *Sam riding* is not a proper subject–verb pair.

RIGHT: Sam, riding his bike, hit a tree.

WHY IT IS RIGHT: In this sentence, *riding* is not paired with *Sam. Riding* adds information about *Sam. Sam hit* is the real subject–verb pair in this sentence.

Here is one more example:

WRONG: Hitting a bump.

WHY IT IS WRONG: The "sentence" has no subject and no real verb.

RIGHT: Hitting a bump, Sam fell off his bike.

WHY IT IS RIGHT: In this sentence, *hitting a bump* gives more information about *Sam.* The subject–verb pair is *Sam fell.*

Check your understanding of *–ing* forms. Choose the correct verb from the parentheses.

1. You (are going, going) away tomorrow.

2. His sister (is waiting, waiting, are waiting) for a new credit card.

3. My toe (has been aching, aching) for three days.

4. Zina (telling, was telling) an amazing story to her friends.

5. The mansion (is standing, standing) on top of that hill.

6. I (am admiring, admiring) your new hairstyle.

Here are the answers: 1. *were going* 2. *is waiting* 3. *has been aching* 4. *was telling* 5. *is standing* 6. *am admiring.*

Help wanted: Past verb forms that cannot stand alone

Have you ever <u>spoken</u> to your friends about grammar? Probably not! Grammar has never <u>been</u> a topic to bring up at a party. When I discussed grammar at a party, I looked around and saw that everyone had <u>fallen</u> asleep!

The underlined words in the preceding paragraph are fine as part of a verb. However, they cannot stand alone. They cannot be a match for a subject unless they have a helper. In the preceding paragraph, these underlined verbs do have helpers:

> have <u>spoken</u>
>
> has <u>been</u>
>
> had <u>fallen</u>

With their helpers, the sentences are correct. Without them, you do not have a proper subject–verb pair.

Look at this set of matches and mismatches. The verb forms are underlined.

Matching Pair	*Nonmatching Pair*
Ross <u>has written</u>	Ross <u>written</u>
Anne <u>had gone</u>	Anne <u>gone</u>
ducks <u>have swum</u>	ducks <u>swum</u>
bricks <u>had fallen</u>	bricks <u>fallen</u>
he <u>was done</u>	he <u>done</u>
vases <u>were stolen</u>	vases <u>stolen</u>
president <u>has spoken</u>	president <u>spoken</u>

Do you see that the matching pair always includes *was, were, has, have,* or *had?* The verb forms here, and many others, do not work all by themselves as part of a subject–verb pair. These forms must have helpers attached. Because of this rule, *he was done* is proper English, but *he done* is incorrect.

In grammar terms, these forms are called *irregular past participles.* Do not waste brain cells remembering that term! Check Chapter 10 for a list of the most common irregular forms.

Sometimes a participle is not part of the verb in a sentence. Instead, the participle adds information. If the participle acts as a description, it is fine by itself. Here is an example:

WRONG: Elsa frozen on the iceberg.

WHY IT IS WRONG: *Elsa frozen* is not a proper subject–verb pair.

RIGHT: Elsa, frozen on the iceberg, called for help.

WHY IT IS RIGHT: In this sentence, *frozen* is not paired with *Elsa. Frozen* adds information about *Elsa. Elsa called* is the real subject–verb pair in this sentence.

Find out how well you understand past verb forms. Select the proper form from the parentheses.

1. The sky (was covered, covered) with clouds.

2. We (have done, done) the work.

3. Those ants (have gone, gone) away.

4. Sid (taken, has taken) the test twice.

5. The ball (was thrown, thrown) to the pitcher.

6. The horse (been ridden, has been ridden, ridden) in three races.

Here are the answers: 1. *was covered* 2. *have done* 3. *have gone* 4. *has taken* 5. *was thrown* 6. *has been ridden*.

Do not be alone

Another common type of subject–verb mismatch places the verb *be* all by itself. *Be* never works alone as part of a subject–verb pair. It always changes form or has a helping verb attached. Look at this table. The verb forms are underlined.

Matching Pair	*Nonmatching Pair*
Margie <u>will be</u>	Margie <u>be</u>
the polar bear <u>is</u>	the polar bear <u>be</u>
I <u>am</u>	I <u>be</u>
the teenagers on the train <u>are talking</u>	the teenagers on the train <u>be talking</u>
Ned <u>has been chopping</u>	Ned <u>be chopping</u>
the singers <u>will be performing</u>	the singers <u>be performing</u>

As you see in the table, sometimes *be* changes form when it is part of the matching pair *(is, am)*. Other times, *be* has a helping verb *(will, are, has)*. To see all the forms of *be*, check out Chapter 5.

Another error to avoid is to drop the *be* verb entirely. Take a look at this example:

WRONG: She happy.

WHY IT IS WRONG: The statement has no verb.

RIGHT: She is happy.

WHY IT IS RIGHT: The sentence now has a verb, *is*. Any other verb that pairs with *she* would also work: *She was happy. She will be happy. She seems happy. She sounds happy.*

WRONG: We right.

WHY IT IS WRONG: The statement has no verb.

RIGHT: We are right.

WHY IT IS RIGHT: The sentence now has a verb, *are*. Any other verb that pairs with *we* would also work well here: *We were right. We will be right. We have been right.*

See whether you can underline the correct form of the verb *be* from the choices in parentheses.

1. Jack (is, be) hungry.

2. Robin (be, will be) at school today.

3. (Are, Be) you pleased with the decorations?

4. Archers (been, be, have been) part of that competition since ancient times.

5. Everyone (should be, be) kind to animals.

6. The mountains (be, are, been) very snowy.

Here are the answers: 1. *is* 2. *will be* 3. *Are* 4. *have been* 5. *should be* 6. *are*.

Command performance

Complete sentences always have at least one subject–verb pair. Sometimes, the subject is hard to find. In fact, a subject may be implied, not stated, in the sentence.

In a sentence that gives a command, the subject, *you*, does not appear in the sentence. It is implied. These sentences are correct because they have a subject–verb pair. Look at this example:

Lock the door.

The verb is *lock*. It pairs with the subject *you*, even though the word *you* is not in the sentence. When you see a command, do not look for the subject. You will not find one on the paper or screen. The subject exists, though, in the readers' minds.

Ending Sentences with Proper Punctuation

Talk to me. Tell me about your life. As you speak, listen to yourself. You probably pause from time to time. If you ask a question, the tone of your voice changes. Maybe your voice becomes louder at important moments. The tone of your voice, the pauses, and perhaps even the expression on your face adds meaning to what you say. When you are writing, though, no one can hear or see you. For this reason, writing has punctuation marks. Every complete sentence needs an endmark — punctuation at the end of the sentence.

A *period* — a single dot — tells your reader that you are making a statement:

> I hate strawberry ice cream.
>
> The President announced his choice for the Supreme Court.
>
> Canberra is the capital of Australia.
>
> Everything you purchased is too expensive.
>
> Next year, the party will be at Alan's ranch.

A period also appears at the end of a sentence giving a command:

> Sit in the corner.
>
> Do not speak.
>
> Pet the dog gently.
>
> Bake the pie for an hour.
>
> Tell me everything.

A question mark (**?**) shows the reader that you are asking a question:

> Are you from Texas?
>
> Do you know how to drive?
>
> Have you taken the driving test?
>
> Will Caroline be on the team this year?
>
> May I come in?

An exclamation point (**!**) adds drama to a statement or command:

> You have grown tall since I last saw you!
>
> We have arrived!
>
> How nice you are!

Go away!

Stay here!

Your choice of punctuation mark matters. Whatever you choose, be sure to include one endmark. Otherwise, you do not have a complete sentence. Your meaning may not be clear if one sentence runs into another.

Read this example, which has no endmarks:

> Barbara fell she said the playground swing was broken before she sat down was she hurt

That line is very hard to understand. Place the endmarks, and the task is easier:

> Barbara fell. She said the playground swing was broken before she sat down. Was she hurt?

Here is the same example, with different endmarks and a different meaning:

> Barbara fell? She said the playground swing was broken before she sat down. Was she hurt?

Here is one more example. The words are the same, but the endmarks are different:

> Barbara fell, she said. The playground swing was broken before. She sat down. Was she hurt?

Do you see the difference the endmarks make? The breaks between one sentence and another change. The question mark tells you the writer doesn't know whether Barbara was hurt or not. The exclamation point reveals that the writer is upset by the extent of Barbara's injuries.

See whether you can add endmarks to each sentence.

1. Did you plant potatoes this year

2. The deer will stay away from that garden

3. Does he know much about geography

4. The spy stole information from the computer network

5. How happy I am

6. Are you thinking about your vacation

Here are the answers: 1. question mark 2. period 3. question mark 4. period 5. exclamation point 6. question mark.

Changing the Rules for Texting

One day, when I was little, I wanted to see my friend. I walked to her house. I knocked on the door. Then I yelled, "Cathy! Do you want to play?" These days, someone who wants to see a friend has other ways to communicate — phone calls and texts. Phone calls do not bring grammar problems. Your tone of voice and the reaction of the person you are speaking with help you express the right meaning. Texts, though, may cause some problems. Unless you are careful, your texts may be misunderstood.

Still, you can adapt grammar rules for complete sentences to suit texts. In this section, I give you some common-sense guidelines.

Dropping words

Because every character counts, you may at times break the "complete sentence" rules when you are texting. Many people cut the subject. Look at this statement:

> Left meeting early. Made no progress.

In some situations, this text is fine. Perhaps you and your co-worker spoke about the meeting. The two of you decided that you would stay if the meeting seemed worthwhile. You would leave if it was a waste of time. In this case, your text is clear.

Suppose, though, that the person you are texting does not know your intentions. Perhaps the person who receives the message has been wondering whether the other people at the meeting were willing to negotiate. In that case, will the reader know whether *you* left or whether *the others* left? The subject is important then. Read these:

> Smith left meeting early. I made no progress.

> I left meeting early. Smith made no progress.

In these examples, different people leave, for different reasons. The subjects matter!

Look at this text:

> We left meeting early. Made no progress.

The first sentence has a subject, but the second does not. In such a situation, readers usually assume that the same subject applies to both statements. Therefore, this text means:

> We left meeting early. We made no progress.

Most texters drop *the, a, an,* and similar words. These words are not important. The meaning comes across without them.

Sometimes, as part of an exchange, you may drop verbs. Look at these texts, sent by Bill and Bob to each other:

> Bill: Who attended?
>
> Bob: Mac
>
> Bill: Did you speak?
>
> Bob: No just Mac

Bob's texts have no verbs, so they are not complete sentences. However, the meaning is clear. By the way, you may notice that Bill's lines include punctuation, and Bob's do not. See the next section for more information on when you need punctuation in a text.

Skipping punctuation

When you are texting, you may be tempted to drop punctuation marks. Texting tires your thumbs! Sometimes, dropping the endmark doesn't matter. Check out this example:

> Come home early

This text cannot be misunderstood. The person texting does not want to wait. However, sometimes punctuation matters a lot. Look at this text, without endmarks:

> I left Barbara arrived safely the children are fine

You may think the text means divorce and a new living situation:

> I left Barbara. Arrived safely. The children are fine. (The second sentence implies that *I arrived safely.*)

The same text may simply report a babysitting change:

I left. Barbara arrived safely. The children are fine.

The rule for texting is simple. Use endmarks to make your meaning clear!

Pretend you have received these texts. Look at the expanded versions, labeled A and B. Decide which meaning fits — A, B, or both. Circle the letters of every possible meaning. *Note:* If more than one meaning is possible, the text is not written well.

1. Dinner at 8

A. Is dinner at 8?

B. Dinner is at 8.

2. Herb home now?

A. Herb is home now.

B. Is Herb home now?

3. Mike flew Phoenix

A. Mike flew to Phoenix.

B. Did Mike fly to Phoenix?

4. Terrible traffic in park!

A. There is terrible traffic in the park!

B. Is there terrible traffic in the park?

Here are the answers: 1. A and B (poorly written text) 2. B (well written text) 3. A and B (poorly written text) 4. A (well written text).

When you are texting friends, you may be less formal. I must confess that I hate abbreviations (*u* for *you,* for example). Between good friends, though, *u* may be acceptable. You must be careful when you write to someone who has more power than you do: a boss, a teacher, or an older relative. In these situations, be more formal. Follow the grammar rules for complete sentences. Do not abbreviate. Use punctuation. Include all or most words so that your meaning is clear.

A numbers game

Some letters act like numbers. Attached to a word, these letters tell you *how many*.

Bi means "two." Read these words:

Biannual means "every two years." "The *biannual* art exhibit will be held at the Metropolitan Museum in 2016."

A **bicycle** is a "vehicle with two wheels." "Selena rode a *bicycle* to work every day."

Bilateral means "having two sides." "The *bilateral* talks went well because both sides were willing to listen to each other."

Tri means "three." Look at these words:

Triannual or **triennial** means "every three years." "The *triannual* competition moves from city to city."

A **tricycle** is a "vehicle with three wheels." "The toddler rode his *tricycle* as fast as he could."

A **triangle** is "a figure that has three sides." "Draw a triangle to help you solve that math problem."

Quad means "four." Check these words:

A **quadrangle** is "a four-sided space." "The college students relaxed in the *quadrangle*."

Quadruple means "four times as much." "Earnings *quadrupled* in the last year."

Quadruplets are "four babies born from the same pregnancy." "The *quadruplets* weighed very little when they were born but were expected to grow rapidly."

These letters, attached to the beginning of a word, may help you figure out the definition. Be careful, though. Sometimes these letters do not signal that you have a number. For example, *tribe* is "a group," not a group of three.

Part IV
Punctuation and Capitalization

The Mechanics of Writing

Punctuation and capitalization — can you think of a more boring topic? Yet these skills, which English teachers call "mechanics," can only improve your writing. In this part, you examine several punctuation marks and see when capital letters are required. Specifically, you learn about these topics:

- ✔ **Apostrophes:** Small curves that sit above the line, apostrophes show ownership or shorten words. Chapter 14 explains when and where to insert this punctuation mark.

- ✔ **Commas:** Small curves that sit on and below the line, commas are frequently inserted where they do not belong and omitted where they are necessary. Chapter 15 shows you how to deal with commas in lists, introductions, and other situations.

- ✔ **Quotation marks and colons:** Quotation marks (a pair of short parallel marks sitting above the line) indicate that you are reporting someone's exact words or that the words inside the quotation marks represent a title. Colons (one dot atop another) introduce lists and long quotations. Chapter 16 tells you everything you need to know about these punctuation marks.

- ✔ **Capital letters:** Where should you use a capital letter, and where is lowercase (a non-capital) correct? Chapter 17 deals with capital letters in names, titles, abbreviations, and other situations.

For a bonus article on Capitalizing School Words, go online and take a look at www.dummies.com/extras/basicenglishgrammar.

In this part . . .

- ✔ Show possession and replace letters with apostrophes.
- ✔ Separate items in a list with commas.
- ✔ Insert commas to set off introductory material and the name of a person being addressed.
- ✔ Label quoted material and titles with quotation marks.
- ✔ Place colons before long lists or quotations.
- ✔ Employ capital letters where needed.

Chapter 14

Small Punctuation Mark, Big Trouble: Apostrophes

*I*f I were in charge of the world, I would make some changes: No more war! Ice cream for everyone, everyday! Freedom for all nations! After I finish those tasks, I would change some grammar rules, starting with getting rid of the apostrophe.

In my opinion, apostrophes cause more trouble than they are worth. Unfortunately, I am not in charge of the world. I am not even in charge of English punctuation rules. All I can do is explain the rules. In this chapter, I tell you how to use apostrophes correctly. I also show you how to avoid some common errors.

Possessed: Using Apostrophes to Show Ownership

Pretend you have a friend named Mary. She has a computer. You can express Mary's ownership of the computer in several different ways:

> the computer belonging to Mary
>
> the computer that Mary bought
>
> the computer Mary uses

Life would be simpler if these were the only ways to talk about ownership. However, the English language adds another, the apostrophe:

> Mary's computer

An apostrophe is a small, curved hook placed above the line. Apostrophes express ownership. In this section, you explore how an apostrophe works in singular situations (one owner) and plural situations (more than one owner).

Apostrophes and ownership

Ownership, or possession, is an important part of life. (Perhaps that's why there are so many lawyers. Someone has to sort out who owns what!) In Standard English, the apostrophe, along with the letter *s*, expresses ownership or possession. Therefore, if Mary buys a computer, an apostrophe and the letter *s* tell the reader that the computer belongs to Mary. When you see an apostrophe with a noun, you are probably reading a statement about ownership.

The term "ownership" includes temporary situations. Mary may work on a computer only when she is at school or in the office. For that period of time, though, she "owns" the computer. It is *Mary's computer* even though the school or the company purchased it.

Take a look at some other examples of apostrophes that show ownership:

> a boy's hat
>
> every team's goal
>
> Margaret's toe
>
> lawyers' files
>
> camels' humps
>
> Smith's job

Apostrophes may also show another kind of ownership — a relationship:

> Bob's uncle

The uncle does not actually belong to Bob the way a book or a pen may. However, Bob and his uncle are in a permanent uncle–nephew relationship. They may not like each other. They may not see each other. One of them may even be dead. Nevertheless, the apostrophe shows that the *uncle* belongs to *Bob*. Here are more examples of apostrophes showing "ownership" this way:

Barbara's mother

the president's son

a friend's cousin

Jane's first boyfriend

police officers' badges

In the preceding examples, the relationship is permanent. Of course, sometimes relationships change. Read these examples:

John's wife

Sally's best friend

Ellen's boss

Life happens! John may divorce. Sally may meet someone nicer. Ellen may change jobs. Still, the apostrophe shows a kind of "ownership," a relationship that is real while it lasts.

Think of an apostrophe as a little hand, holding on to, owning, or possessing whatever it is attached to.

Things or places can also be in an "ownership" role. Apostrophes work in this situation, too:

the book's cover

a store's roof

Brazil's coastline

the rug's pattern

Rome's ancient monuments

the rooms' decorations

the schools' principals

As you see, this type of "ownership" is expressed with an apostrophe and the letter *s*.

The "owner" — the person or thing that possesses — is the word with the apostrophe and the letter *s*.

How well can you spot ownership? Underline the words in which the apostrophe shows possession. Be careful! I have included words in which the apostrophe does a different job.

1. Sam's diploma hangs on the wall.

2. Did you bring Aunt Jane's umbrella?

3. Spain's trains are very fast.

4. The students' computers won't work.

5. Nobody's homework was finished.

6. The audience didn't laugh.

Here are the answers: 1. *Sam's* 2. *Aunt Jane's* 3. *Spain's* 4. *students*' 5. *Nobody's* 6. No possessive words are present.

Note: In quiz question 4, *won't* is not a possessive word.

Did you notice that the apostrophe moves around? Sometimes the apostrophe is followed by the letter *s*. In other expressions, the letter *s* comes before the apostrophe. The position change relates to the number of owners — one or more than one. In the following sections, you see how to write singular and plural possessives.

Forming singular possessives

In the world of grammar, sorting out singular (one) and plural (more than one) is important. When you place an apostrophe, you create what English teachers call a *possessive*. To write a possessive form properly, you must decide whether you are talking about one owner or more than one.

For one owner, a *singular possessive,* the apostrophe attaches to the end of the "owner" word. Then comes the letter *s*. Take a look at these examples. Notice where the apostrophe and the letter *s* appear:

Helen's skirt (the *skirt* belongs to one person, *Helen*)

Helen's sweaters (the *sweaters* belong to one person, *Helen*)

Peter's football (the *football* belongs to one person, *Peter*)

Peter's baseballs (the *baseballs* belong to one person, *Peter*)

Woods's chalk (the *chalk* belongs to one person, *Mr. Woods*)

Woods's assignments (the assignments belong to one person, *Mr. Woods*)

The book's introduction (the *introduction* belongs to one thing, the *book*)

The book's chapters (the *chapters* belong to one thing, the *book*)

The sun's brightness (the *brightness* belongs to one thing, the *sun*)

The sun's spots (the *spots* belong to one thing, the *sun*)

Hollywood's fame (the *fame* belongs to one place, *Hollywood*)

Hollywood's studios (the *studios* belong to one place, *Hollywood*)

The pattern never changes. You add an apostrophe and the letter *s* to a single owner. It does not matter how many things the owner has.

I use the term "owner" broadly. It includes people, places, and things. Look at the previous section, "Apostrophes and ownership," to see how the definition of "ownership" stretches to include these categories.

See whether you can use an apostrophe and the letter *s* to write the possessive form.

Owner	What Is Owned	Possessive
Jenny	tooth	
Tess	blankets	
chimney	smoke	
Argentina	people	
leg	scars	
painting	frame	
flame	heat	

Here are the answers: *Jenny's tooth, Tess's blankets, chimney's smoke, Argentina's people, leg's scars, painting's frame, flame's heat.*

To show ownership by one person, place, or thing, add an apostrophe and the letter *s*.

Forming regular plural possessives

The plural of nearly all English nouns (words that name people, places, things, and ideas) ends with the letter *s*. To make a possessive, all you have to do is add the apostrophe. Half the work (the letter *s*) is already done! Read these examples:

teenagers' music (the *music* belongs to *teenagers*)

teenagers' pimples (the *pimples* belong to *teenagers*)

whale<u>s'</u> route (the *route* belongs to *whales*)

whale<u>s'</u> fins (the *fins* belong to *whales*)

police officer<u>s'</u> union (the *union* belongs to *police officers*)

police officer<u>s'</u> uniforms (the *uniforms* belong to *police officers*)

classe<u>s'</u> final exam (the *final exam* belongs to a group of *classes*)

classe<u>s'</u> field trips (the *field trips* belong to a group of *classes*)

mountain<u>s'</u> beauty (the *beauty* belongs to *mountains*)

mountain<u>s'</u> slopes (the *slopes* belong to *mountains*)

librarie<u>s'</u> policy (the *policy* belongs to *libraries*)

librarie<u>s'</u> shelves (the *shelves* belong to *libraries*)

As you see, in every example the "owners" are identified by a plural word that ends with the letter *s*. The apostrophe follows the *s*. In some examples, one thing is owned *(music, route, union, exam, beauty, policy)*. In other examples, more than one thing is owned *(pimples, fins, uniforms, trips, slopes, shelves)*. In both situations, the apostrophe follows the letter *s*.

I stretched the definition of the terms "owner" and "thing" here. Read the earlier section, "Apostrophes and ownership," to see what these terms include.

When you are dealing with a regular plural noun in an ownership role, add the apostrophe after the letter *s*.

See whether you understand plural possessives by filling in the last column of this table.

Owner	What Is Owned	Possessive
mugs	design	
flowers	roots	
directors	meeting	
rivers	wildlife	
trees	leaves	
secretaries	announcement	
workers	rights	

Here are the answers: *mugs' design, flowers' roots, directors' meeting, rivers' wildlife, trees' leaves, secretaries' announcement, workers' rights.*

Forming irregular plural possessives

A small number of plural nouns, such as *children,* do not end with the letter *s.* To show ownership of an irregular plural, add an apostrophe and the letter *s* to the end of the noun. Take a look at these examples:

men'<u>s</u> department (the *department* for *men*)

men'<u>s</u> suits (*suits* that belong to or are intended for *men*)

children'<u>s</u> innocence (the *innocence* that *children* have)

children'<u>s</u> toys (the *toys* that belong to *children*)

people'<u>s</u> choice (the *choice* belonging to the *people*)

people'<u>s</u> voices (the *voices* belonging to the *people*)

mice'<u>s</u> nest (the *nest* belonging to the *mice*)

mice'<u>s</u> feet (the *feet* belonging to the *mice*)

teeth'<u>s</u> sharpness (the *sharpness* belonging to the *teeth*)

teeth'<u>s</u> tips (the *tips* belonging to the *teeth*)

women'<u>s</u> clothing (the *clothing* that *women* have)

women'<u>s</u> shoes (the *shoes* that *women* own or that are intended for *women*)

Can you create the possessive form of an irregular plural?

Owner	What Is Owned	Possessive
feet	blisters	
deer	noses	
fruit	sweetness	
fleet	guns	
aircraft	speed	
geese	wings	
bacteria	growth	

Here are the answers: *feet's blisters, deer's noses, fruit's sweetness, fleet's guns, aircraft's speed, geese's wings, bacteria's growth.*

Some irregular plurals look and sound exactly the same as the singular form. In other words, the word may be either singular or plural, depending on the context. Here is an example:

The pilot noticed a broken switch, so he ordered everyone off the aircraft.

Several other aircraft were idle, so passengers immediately boarded another plane.

For more information on irregular plural nouns, turn to Chapter 3.

Shortening Words with Apostrophes

Are you busy? Most people are. Everyone rushes from one task to another all day long. So it is not surprising that people rush through words, too. Instead of two sounds, "I am," you hear one sound, "I'm." Three letters, "he'd," take the place of seven: "he would."

As you probably noticed, in these examples an apostrophe appears where letters and sounds disappear. These shortened words are also known as *contractions*. They save you time when you are speaking and key strokes when you are typing. Read through these examples:

LONG FORM: <u>She is</u> happy to meet you at the office.

SHORT FORM: <u>She's</u> happy to meet you at the office.

LONG FORM: Henry asked if he <u>should have</u> returned the library book.

SHORT FORM: Henry asked if he <u>should've</u> returned the library book.

LONG FORM: The robin <u>did not</u> catch any worms.

SHORT FORM: The robin <u>didn't</u> catch any worms.

LONG FORM: <u>We have</u> no plans for dinner.

SHORT FORM: <u>We've</u> no plans for dinner.

LONG FORM: <u>They had</u> misunderstood.

SHORT FORM: <u>They'd</u> misunderstood.

In every example, you save time and space by inserting an apostrophe.

The apostrophe is small, but it is important. Without one, you may not get your meaning across. Also, you have a spelling error if you omit a needed apostrophe. Look at these examples:

WRONG: Theyll go on a date tonight.

WHY IT IS WRONG: *Theyll* is not a word in Standard English.

RIGHT: They'll go on a date tonight.

WHY IT IS RIGHT: The contraction *They'll* takes the place of *They will.*

WRONG: Whos there?

WHY IT IS WRONG: *Whos* is not a word in Standard English.

RIGHT: Who's there?

WHY IT IS RIGHT: The contraction *Who's* takes the place of *Who is.*

WRONG: Thats a beautiful painting.

WHY IT IS WRONG: *Thats* is not a word in Standard English.

RIGHT: That's a beautiful painting.

WHY IT IS RIGHT: The contraction *That's* takes the place of *That is.*

Table 14-1 shows the most common contractions.

Table 14-1	Common Contractions		
Original	*Shortened Form*	*Original*	*Shortened Form*
are not	aren't	she is	she's
cannot	can't	that is	that's
could not	couldn't	they are	they're
do not	don't	they will	they'll
does not	doesn't	they would	they'd
did not	didn't	we are	we're
he will	he'll	we will	we'll
he would	he'd	we would	we'd
he is	he's	we have	we've
is not	isn't	what is	what's
it is	it's	who is	who's
I am	I'm	will not	won't
I will	I'll	would not	wouldn't
I would	I'd	you are	you're
I have	I've	you have	you've
she will	she'll	you will	you'll
she would	she'd	you would	you'd

I hope that "won't" won't fool you. Most of the time, the substitution in a contraction is straightforward. One or two letters drop out, and an apostrophe drops in. Yet "will not" turns into "won't"! This is one of the strange details of the English language.

Apostrophes also shorten numbers. Look at these examples:

Martha graduated in '10, a year later than her brother.

Are you a member of the class of '99?

During the last battle, in '06, the king died.

The grape harvest in '55 produced delicious wine.

Do you know the full-length forms of these numbers? Here they are:

Martha graduated in 2010, a year later than her brother.

Are you a member of the class of 1999?

During the last battle, in 1206, the king died.

The grape harvest in 1955 produced delicious wine.

Do not drop numbers unless you are sure that your reader knows what is missing. A member of the class of 1910 is a lot older than a member of the class of 2010! Saving time is good. Being clear is better.

Over and under

Super and *sub* often appear at the beginning of a word. *Super* tells you that something is "over or above" average. *Sub* moves in the opposite direction, revealing that something is "under or below" the norm. Take a look at *super* and *sub* in context:

Superhuman means "better than a normal human being, resembling a comic book hero." "With <u>superhuman</u> strength, the firefighter lifted the burning beam and rescued the baby."

Supervise means "to oversee, to look over someone else's work." "As department head, Sandy <u>supervises</u> five writers and two artists."

A **superstar** is a celebrity with more than average fame. "<u>Superstars</u> earn many millions for film work."

A **superpower** is "a country with great influence and resources." "During the Cold War, the United States and the Soviet Union were <u>superpowers</u>."

Subpar means "below standard." "His <u>subpar</u> performance on that project drew much criticism."

A **submarine** is "a vessel (boat) that sails under water." "We toured the <u>submarine</u>, which was cramped and crowded."

Subconscious means "below the conscious level, unaware." "Dreams reveal <u>subconscious</u> needs and fears."

A **subordinate** is "someone under the authority of another, of less importance." "The boss treated her <u>subordinates</u> well, providing free coffee and sandwiches every day."

In each blank, write the correct, shortened form of the words or numbers in parentheses.

1. Debby _____ (did not) read the map before leaving.

2. Scott said, "_____ (What is) the name of the street?"

3. "I think _____ (we are) driving in the wrong direction," complained Ellen.

4. Debby _____ (will not) arrive on time.

5. _____ (They are) speeding now!

6. Officer Adams, who graduated in _____ (2012), gave Debby a ticket for speeding.

7. The host said that he _____ (would not) begin the party without Debby and her friends.

Here are the answers: 1. *didn't* 2. *What's* 3. *we're* 4. *won't* 5. *They're* 6. *'12* 7. *wouldn't.*

Avoiding Common Apostrophe Mistakes

I walk around New York City often. I see many signs. Some show good grammar, and many do not. An informal count reveals that apostrophes cause more grammar errors than any other punctuation mark.

The following sections describe the most frequent apostrophe mistakes, along with an explanation of how to avoid them.

Apostrophes in plurals

To make a noun plural, you add the letter *s*. A simple plural — not expressing ownership — does *not* need an apostrophe. Take a look at these examples:

WRONG: We sell muffin's.

WHY IT IS WRONG: The sentence has nothing to do with ownership or possession, and no word is shortened. No apostrophe should appear in the simple plural word, *muffins*.

RIGHT: We sell muffins.

WHY IT IS RIGHT: Plural nouns do not need apostrophes unless they express ownership or create a contraction.

WRONG: You should buy two new printer's.

WHY IT IS WRONG: The *printers* do not possess anything, and no letters are missing.

RIGHT: You should buy two new printers.

WHY IT IS RIGHT: The plural, *printers,* needs no apostrophe.

WRONG: Sally tied some ribbon's in her hair.

WHY IT IS WRONG: *Ribbon's* is not a statement of ownership, and no letters are left out.

RIGHT: Sally tied some ribbons in her hair.

WHY IT IS RIGHT: The plural, *ribbons,* should not include an apostrophe.

If all you need is a plural noun, skip the apostrophe.

Possessive pronouns

Some pronouns (*his, her, our, their, mine,* and many others) express ownership. The words themselves include the idea of possession. In fact, these pronouns are called *possessive pronouns.* (For a complete explanation of possessive pronouns, turn to Chapter 4.) Because possession is included in the word, an apostrophe is overkill. If you insert an apostrophe, the word is wrong. Look at these examples:

WRONG: I ate my sandwich, and she ate her's.

WHY IT IS WRONG: The possessive pronoun *hers* needs no apostrophe.

RIGHT: I ate my sandwich, and she ate hers.

WHY IT IS RIGHT: The possessive pronoun, *hers,* is now spelled correctly.

WRONG: The dog stepped on a nail and hurt it's paw.

WHY IT IS WRONG: The word *it's* is short for "it is." Here you do not need a contraction. You need the possessive pronoun *its.*

RIGHT: The dog stepped on a nail and hurt its paw.

WHY IT IS RIGHT: The possessive pronoun, *its,* shows that the paw belongs to the dog.

WRONG: Did you receive you're package?

WHY IT IS WRONG: The contraction *you're* is short for "you are." Here you want a possessive pronoun, *your.*

RIGHT: Did you receive your package?

WHY IT IS RIGHT: The possessive pronoun shows that the package belongs to you.

Do not confuse contractions (short forms) with possessive pronouns. No pronoun expresses ownership with an apostrophe.

Expanding contractions

Contractions shorten words. When you take out an apostrophe and re-expand the word, you must be sure to expand it properly. For example, the sound of the letter *v* is similar to the sound of the word *of*. However, these two sounds create very different words. Look at these examples:

ORIGINAL SENTENCE: Henry should've attended the meeting.

INCORRECT EXPANSION: Henry should of attended the meeting.

WHY IT IS WRONG: The contraction *should've* is short for "should have."

CORRECT EXPANSION: Henry should have attended the meeting.

WHY IT IS RIGHT: The expression *should of* does not exist in Standard English.

ORIGINAL SENTENCE: The children would've stayed outside, but their mother ordered them to stay indoors.

INCORRECT EXPANSION: The children would of stayed outside, but their mother ordered them to stay indoors.

WHY IT IS WRONG: The contraction *would've* is short for "would have."

CORRECT EXPANSION: The children would have stayed outside, but their mother ordered them to stay indoors.

WHY IT IS RIGHT: The expression *would of* does not exist in Standard English.

ORIGINAL SENTENCE: The boy could've ridden his bike all day.

INCORRECT EXPANSION: The boy could of ridden his bike all day.

WHY IT IS WRONG: The contraction *could've* is short for "could have."

CORRECT EXPANSION: The boy could have ridden his bike all day.

WHY IT IS RIGHT: The expression *could of* does not exist in Standard English.

In these sentences, you may find a missing apostrophe. If so, add one! You may also find an apostrophe that should not appear. If you do, cross out the incorrect apostrophe.

1. The chef added seven cup's of flour to the bowl.

2. The mens department has a good selection of new ties.

3. Richard doesnt want to spend too much money when he buys jean's.

4. Arthur's statue is larger than our's, but its not as heavy.

5. Whats the name of your dentist?

Here are the answers: 1. *cups* 2. *men's* 3. *doesn't, jeans* 4. *ours, it's* 5. *What's.*

Four pairs of trouble

When you are placing apostrophes, four pairs of words may give you trouble. They sound alike, but they are spelled differently. They have completely different meanings. Memorize these words, and your writing will improve.

who's and **whose** Both words sound like an owl making "hoo" sounds. The first, *who's,* is a contraction meaning "who is." The second is a possessive pronoun. Here they are in action:

"I know who's guilty," claimed the detective. (In this example, *who's* is short for "who is.")

The murderer, whose fingerprints were on the knife, soon confessed. (In this sentence, *whose* shows possession.)

you're and **your** I do not know any bird or other animal that makes this sound. I do know that the meaning of each is different. *You're* is the short form of "you are." *Your* shows possession. Read these sentences:

"You're making too much noise," complained the nurse. (In this sentence, *you're* means "you are.")

Cover your nose and mouth when you sneeze! (Here, *your* shows possession.)

they're and **there** and **their** These words are not twins. They are triplets! These triplets have very different meanings, though. Watch them in these sentences:

The general told his troops that they're returning home tomorrow. (The contraction *they're* is short for "they are.")

The troops will be very happy to arrive there. (The word *there* indicates a place.)

The soldiers will be welcomed by their families. (*Their* is a possessive pronoun.)

it's and **its** These little words have exactly the same letters, but the first includes an apostrophe. *It's* means "it is." The second, *its,* is a possessive pronoun.

Mary told me that it's too late to enroll in that course. (In this sentence, the contraction *it's* is short for "it is.")

I am not interested in the course, but I love its easy assignments. (Here you need the possessive pronoun *its.*)

Chapter 15

Pausing for a Rest: Commas

....

In This Chapter

▶ Understanding what commas do

▶ Placing commas in lists

▶ Separating parts of a sentence with commas

▶ Using commas after an introductory word or phrase

▶ Inserting commas to identify the person you are addressing

....

Go to a crowded area. Listen! What do you hear? Words, sentences, and *silence*. Yes, silence. In speech, silence separates one idea from another. In writing, commas represent silence. (So do periods. Turn to Chapter 13 for more information on periods.)

In this chapter, you examine how commas work. Then you see where to place commas, so your writing displays good "comma sense."

The Sound of Silence: Why Commas Matter

Commas are punctuation marks that begin on the line and curve underneath it:

,

Without commas, your reader may not understand what you are trying to express. Read this example aloud. (If you are too embarrassed to speak aloud, just listen to the little voice inside your head.)

> May I go mountain climbing every day. Recently I climbed with Betty Jo and Mark who were more skilled than I had imagined. From the top of the mountain trees people clouds and cars appeared very small. Oh it was a good day. Betty Jo and I would like to climb again.

You probably made sense of the paragraph, but I bet you had to work at it a little. You may have had to read it more than once! For example, perhaps you thought that the first three words were a request:

> May I go

Maybe you thought the period at the end of the sentence should have been a question mark:

> May I go mountain climbing every day?

A few sentences later, perhaps you thought that *mountain trees* were trees that grow on mountains. Instead, the word *trees* is an item on a list. Even after a few readings, you may not be sure whether *Betty Jo* is one person or two people.

Commas make this paragraph easier to understand. Read it again:

> May, I go mountain climbing every day. Recently, I climbed with Betty, Jo, and Mark, who were more skilled than I had imagined. From the top of the mountain, trees, people, clouds, and cars appeared very small. Oh, it was a good day. Betty, Jo, and I would like to climb again.

When commas are included, you immediately see that the paragraph is addressed to someone named *May*. You are not talking about "mountain trees." Instead, you see *trees* from the top of the mountain. The commas do not create meaning all by themselves, but they do add information.

If you are not too bored, read this little paragraph one more time. Do not time yourself, but pay attention to the pauses. Notice when a pause is short and when it is a bit longer.

> May, I go mountain climbing every day. Recently, I climbed with Betty, Jo, and Mark, who were more skilled than I had imagined. From the top of the mountain, trees, people, clouds, and cars appeared very small. Oh, it was a good day. Betty, Jo, and I would like to climb again.

Did you notice that longer pauses occur at periods? This punctuation mark is known as a "full stop" in Britain. I like that term because it shows that periods resemble stop signs. When you drive, you must come to a "full stop" before continuing. When you are reading and see a period, you do the same thing.

At other spots in the paragraph, you probably paused for a shorter time. Commas signal the need for those tiny gaps. Think of commas as a quick breath — a nap instead of a night's sleep.

Periods create long pauses. Commas create short pauses. Your ear — the voice you hear inside your head when you are writing — guides you to the correct punctuation *most* of the time. A few rules, explained in this chapter, help you place commas correctly *all* the time.

Making a List with Commas

The announcer says that a big storm is coming. It is time to go shopping for emergency supplies. What do you need? Here is your list:

chocolate ice cream flashlight batteries

How many things will you buy? Perhaps five:

chocolate

ice

cream

flashlight

batteries

or four:

chocolate

ice cream

flashlight

batteries

or maybe only three:

chocolate ice cream

flashlight

batteries

or just two:

chocolate ice cream

flashlight batteries

When you write a list in this way, the line breaks separate one item from another. A speaker saying this list takes a short breath at every line break. Either way, you know exactly how many items you have to buy.

In a sentence, commas take the place of line breaks or breaths. Here is the true emergency list, written in a sentence:

> At the store you should buy chocolate, ice cream, and flashlight batteries.

Yes, I do consider *chocolate* and *ice cream* essential emergency supplies! Back to grammar: The commas, as well as the word *and,* give your reader necessary information. Your list is not clear without them.

You should not place a comma before the first item in a list unless you need a comma there for another reason. (I explain other reasons to insert commas later in this chapter.)

Read these examples:

> WRONG: Charlie stuffed the turkey with a mixture of, bread cubes, sausage, celery, and seasonings.
>
> WHY IT IS WRONG: No comma should appear between *of* and the first item of the list, *bread cubes.*
>
> RIGHT: Charlie stuffed the turkey with a mixture of bread cubes, sausage, celery, and seasonings.
>
> WHY IT IS RIGHT: Now the sentence flows smoothly, with no comma separating the list from the rest of the sentence.

> WRONG: What I want is, peace, quiet, and a million dollars.
>
> WHY IT IS WRONG: No comma should appear between *is* and *peace,* which is the first item of the list.
>
> RIGHT: What I want is peace, quiet, and a million dollars.
>
> WHY IT IS RIGHT: I deserve a million dollars! Also, *peace* is the first item of the list, so no comma should separate *peace* from the rest of the sentence.

If the list is very long, you may need a colon (one dot on top of another) before the first item in the list. See Chapter 16 for more information on colons.

If the list includes only two items joined by *and,* do not place a comma before the *and.* Read these examples:

SENTENCE: The forecaster predicted strong winds, and heavy rain.

ITEMS CONNECTED: (1) *strong winds* (2) *heavy rain*

WHY IT IS WRONG: In a list of two items, no comma is needed.

RIGHT: The forecaster predicted strong winds and heavy rain.

SENTENCE: Winning the chess game was satisfying, and profitable.

ITEMS CONNECTED: (1) *satisfying* (2) *profitable*

WHY IT IS WRONG: In a list of two items, no comma is needed.

RIGHT: Winning the chess game was satisfying and profitable.

SENTENCE: Gina, and Fred played tennis for four hours.

ITEMS CONNECTED: (1) *Gina* (2) *Fred*

WHY IT IS WRONG: In a list of two items, no comma is needed.

RIGHT: Gina and Fred played tennis for four hours.

In a list of three or more items, some people skip the last comma before the word *and*, assuming that the *and* provides enough of a separation. True, at times the reader knows what you mean without a comma in that position. Occasionally, though, your meaning may not be clear without it. Look at this sentence:

Whenever he needed help, Henry phoned his brothers, Tom and Jack.

Did Henry speak to four (or more) people? Or just two? With no comma before *and, Tom and Jack* may be the names of Henry's brothers. Therefore, Henry called two people. Now look at this sentence:

Whenever he needed help, Henry phoned his brothers, Tom, and Jack.

In this version, Henry called at least four people:

his brothers (two or more)

Tom

Jack

The most important rule of writing is simple. Be clear! Do not risk being misunderstood. Make a habit of placing a comma before the *and* in a simple list of three or more items. If part of the sentence is an explanation (that Henry's brothers are named Tom and Jack, for example), do not place a comma before the *and.*

Do you know how to punctuate a list? In the first column you see a list of items. In the second, you see a sentence with an empty space. Write the list items in the blank. Be sure to punctuate the list correctly. Add *and* where it is needed.

List of Items	*Sentence*
1. umbrella raincoat boots	When John visited rainy Seattle, he packed his _____.
2. Mary' antiques the teapot six cups	As the shelf broke, _____ fell to the floor.
3. chops crushes slices purees	The new blender _____ every kind of food.
4. tomatoes carrots	Alan ordered _____ from the online food delivery service.
5. math science English history	Sandra was busy studying _____.
6. museum visits shopping trips	During their vacation, Ed and Connie set aside a few days for _____.
7. Caroline Jones Angela Ballard	Sherman will celebrate his promotion by having dinner with _____.

Here are the answers: 1. *umbrella, raincoat, and boots* 2. *Mary's antiques, the teapot, and six cups* 3. *chops, crushes, slices, and purees* 4. *tomatoes and carrots* (no comma) 5. *math, science, English, and history* 6. *museum visits and shopping trips* (no comma) 7. *Caroline Jones and Angela Ballard* (no comma).

Placing Commas before Conjunctions

My living room has several sections. In one corner stands a desk with my computer and writing materials. Near the window is a seating area lined with two sofas and a chair. A set of bookcases fills the space near the door.

Think of my living room as a sentence. It has parts, separate from each other but still a unified space. Most of your sentences have parts also. Instead of furniture, conjunctions (joining words) separate one section of a sentence from another. I must be careful when I decorate the living room. I cannot put a lamp in front of the television, for example, or behind a bookcase. You must also be careful when you insert commas near conjunctions. Placing one where it does not belong may confuse your reader. In this section, you see how to insert commas properly.

Punctuating two connected, complete sentences

Take a look at this paragraph. Pay special attention to the underlined spots.

> Dennis lived in a large city, and then he moved to a farming community. He loved the area, but jobs in his field were hard to find. Dennis could take a part time position, or he could return to his old career in the city.

Did you notice the underlined words *(and, but, or)* all have the same function? Each joins one complete sentence to another. Each follows a comma. Here is an analysis of the paragraph, sentence by sentence.

Dennis lived in a large city, and then he moved to a farming community.

First complete sentence: Dennis lived in a large city.

Second complete sentence: Then he moved to a farming community.

Joining word: *and*

Punctuation: A comma comes before the and. He loved the area, but jobs in his field were hard to find.

First complete sentence: He loved the area.

Second complete sentence: Jobs in his field were hard to find.

Joining word: *but*

Punctuation: A comma comes before the *but*.

> *Dennis could take a part-time position, or he*
> *could return to his old career in the city.*

> First complete sentence: Dennis could take a part-time position.

> Second complete sentence: He could return to his old career in the city.

> Joining word: *or*

> Punctuation: A comma comes before the *or*.

The word that joins the two complete sentences is a *conjunction*. Other conjunctions that do the same job are *nor* and *yet*. For more information on conjunctions, turn to Chapter 8.

The rule is straightforward: When you attach one complete sentence to another with the conjunctions *and, but, or, nor,* or *yet,* you should place a comma after the word that comes just before the conjunction.

A comma comes before the word preceding a conjunction that joins two complete sentences. A comma may *not* join two complete sentences all by itself. This punctuation mark is not strong enough for that task. Use a comma and a conjunction, but not a comma alone. (For more information on complete sentences, refer to Chapter 13.)

Punctuating other elements of a sentence

The conjunctions *and, but, or, yet,* and *nor* may connect other elements of a sentence. They may link two descriptions, two verbs, two subjects, and many other things that are not complete sentences. (For more information on descriptions, refer to Chapter 6. To find out more about verbs, read Chapter 5. Chapter 11 covers subjects.) Do not place a comma before these conjunctions unless they are connecting complete sentences. Take a look at these examples:

> SENTENCE: Max and his brother Josh often visit their parents.

> JOINING WORD: *and*

> WHAT THE JOINING WORD CONNECTS: (1) *Max* (2) *his brother Josh* (two subjects)

> PUNCTUATION: No comma comes before *and,* because *and* does not connect two complete sentences.

SENTENCE: Their parents cook or order takeout meals when their sons visit.

JOINING WORD: *or*

WHAT THE JOINING WORD CONNECTS: (1) *cook* (2) *order* (two verbs)

PUNCTUATION: No comma comes before *or,* because *or* does not connect two complete sentences.

SENTENCE: The brothers are tired but happy when they leave.

JOINING WORD: *but*

WHAT THE JOINING WORD CONNECTS: (1) *tired* (2) *happy* (two descriptions)

PUNCTUATION: No comma comes before *but,* because *but* does not connect two complete sentences.

See whether you can add commas where they are needed in these sentences:

1. Most of Jack's family gathered in Paris but Jack had already planned a trip to Mexico.
2. The zookeeper fed the elephants and the lions.
3. Ann Marie ordered strong coffee yet she claimed to be allergic to caffeine.
4. The chef adds milk or cream to the soup.
5. Artie's tailor measured him carelessly and Artie thinks the suit will be too large.
6. The blue silk tie and a fine leather belt complete Artie's outfit.

Here are the answers: 1. comma before *but* 2. no comma 3. comma before *yet* 4. no comma 5. comma before *and* 6. no comma.

Placing Commas after Introductory Words

Variety is the spice of life, according to an old saying. Variety is also the spice of writing. To keep the reader interested, you should play around with different sentence patterns. One interesting variation is to add an introductory word or phrase to a sentence. In this section, you see how to punctuate these introductory elements.

Single words and short phrases

<u>Well,</u> now you should think about introductory words. <u>Indeed,</u> these words spice up your writing. <u>Yes,</u> you may overuse introductory words. <u>Oh my goodness,</u> I can't believe you think you should avoid them completely!

Did you notice how each sentence in the preceding paragraph is punctuated? Each begins with a word or a phrase, followed by a comma. The words at the beginning of these sentences add meaning, but they are not really part of the sentence. If you crossed out these words, the sentence would still say the same thing. These underlined words function as an introduction to the sentence.

Here are a few more examples. The introductory words are underlined. Notice the comma placement:

> <u>Ouch,</u> that pinch hurts!
>
> <u>Okay,</u> put the toys away now.
>
> <u>No,</u> that is not a good idea.
>
> <u>Wow,</u> you did a great job.

To set off introductory words from the rest of the sentence, use a comma.

Longer introductory elements

The introductory words explained in the preceding section add little to a sentence. Sometimes, though, introductory words contribute more. Sometimes they tell you about time, location, or reasons. Read these examples:

> SENTENCE: In the garden of the house next door, tulips and roses grew.
>
> INTRODUCTORY WORDS: *In the garden of the house next door*
>
> WHAT THE INTRODUCTORY WORDS ADD: information about location
>
> MAIN PORTION OF THE SENTENCE: *tulips and roses grew*
>
> CORRECT PUNCTUATION: A comma separates the introductory words from the main portion of the sentence.

SENTENCE: Before the end of next week, John will have learned his fate.

INTRODUCTORY WORDS: *Before the end of next week*

WHAT THE INTRODUCTORY WORDS ADD: information about time

MAIN PORTION OF THE SENTENCE: *John will have learned his fate*

CORRECT PUNCTUATION: A comma separates the introductory words from the main portion of the sentence.

SENTENCE: Because of her dishonest behavior, her test scores do not count.

INTRODUCTORY WORDS: *Because of her dishonest behavior*

WHAT THE INTRODUCTORY WORDS ADD: a reason or cause

MAIN PORTION OF THE SENTENCE: *her test scores do not count*

CORRECT PUNCTUATION: A comma separates the introductory words from the main portion of the sentence.

In every example, the comma is important. It divides the introductory phrase from the rest of the sentence.

Introductory phrases containing verbs

Other introductory elements look like verbs. They give extra information, but they do not function as the main verb in the sentence. (For more information on verbs, turn to Chapter 5.) A comma always separates an introductory phrase from the rest of the sentence. Take a look at these examples:

SENTENCE: Confused by the jumbled wires, Ned read the directions again.

INTRODUCTORY PHRASE: *Confused by the jumbled wires*

WHAT THE INTRODUCTORY PHRASE ADDS: information about Ned's state of mind

MAIN PORTION OF THE SENTENCE: *Ned read the directions again*

CORRECT PUNCTUATION: A comma separates the introductory words from the main portion of the sentence.

SENTENCE: Barking and growling, the little dog seemed dangerous.

INTRODUCTORY PHRASE: *Barking and growling*

WHAT THE INTRODUCTORY PHRASE ADDS: information about the dog's actions

MAIN PORTION OF THE SENTENCE: *the little dog seemed dangerous*

CORRECT PUNCTUATION: A comma separates the introductory words from the main portion of the sentence.

SENTENCE: Having eaten and rested, Ben practiced the piano with renewed energy.

INTRODUCTORY PHRASE: *Having eaten and rested*

WHAT THE INTRODUCTORY PHRASE ADDS: information about Ben's actions

MAIN PORTION OF THE SENTENCE: *Ben practiced the piano with renewed energy*

CORRECT PUNCTUATION: A comma separates the introductory words from the main portion of the sentence.

The introductory words in these examples carry quite a bit of meaning — more than simple introductory words such as *yes* or *indeed.* The basic punctuation is the same. Cross out the introductory phrases. Read what is left. You know less, but the meaning of the main portion of the sentence does not change. The punctuation rule stays the same, too. A comma should separate the introductory words from the main portion of the sentence.

When the introductory words contain a verb form, be sure that the subject of the sentence is performing (or has performed) the action expressed by the verb. For more information, see Chapter 23.

Introductory subject–verb statements

When you see a subject–verb statement, you may think that you have a complete sentence. However, to be a complete sentence, a subject–verb statement must be able to stand alone: It must state a complete thought. (Turn to Chapter 13 for more information on complete sentences.)

Some subject–verb statements cannot stand alone. Look at these examples:

Although the presidents signed the treaty

Since the day you were born

Wherever the game is played

Because I said so

Each of these statements adds information. No statement makes sense all by itself, not even the last one, which is every parent's favorite response to a child's challenge. When these subject–verb statements appear at the beginning of a sentence, you need a comma to separate the introductory idea from the rest of the sentence. Read these examples:

SENTENCE: Although the presidents signed the treaty, neither believed that the problem was solved.

INTRODUCTORY SUBJECT–VERB STATEMENT: *Although the presidents signed the treaty*

MAIN PORTION OF THE SENTENCE: *neither believed that the problem was solved*

CORRECT PUNCTUATION: A comma separates the introductory subject–verb statement from the main portion of the sentence.

SENTENCE: Since the day you were born, Grandma has been saving for your college tuition.

INTRODUCTORY SUBJECT–VERB STATEMENT: *Since the day you were born*

MAIN PORTION OF THE SENTENCE: *Grandma has been saving for your college tuition*

CORRECT PUNCTUATION: A comma separates the introductory subject–verb statement from the main portion of the sentence.

SENTENCE: Wherever the game is played, the fans will attend.

INTRODUCTORY SUBJECT–VERB STATEMENT: *Wherever the game is played*

MAIN PORTION OF THE SENTENCE: *the fans will attend*

CORRECT PUNCTUATION: A comma separates the introductory subject–verb statement from the main portion of the sentence.

SENTENCE: Because I said so, you must take out the garbage.

INTRODUCTORY SUBJECT–VERB STATEMENT: *Because I said so*

MAIN PORTION OF THE SENTENCE: *you must take out the garbage*

CORRECT PUNCTUATION: A comma separates the introductory subject–verb statement from the main portion of the sentence.

If these introductory statements appear elsewhere in the sentence, they may not need to be set off by commas. At the beginning of a sentence, though, always insert a comma to separate these statements from the main portion of the sentence.

How are your introductory skills? Read these sentences. Insert commas where they are needed.

1. Yes I have an appointment with Mary this afternoon.

2. Really it is none of your business.

3. No she is not my first choice for the job.

4. After I have interviewed her I will make a decision.

5. Oh my you certainly will be considered for the position.

6. Having said that I am not promising anything.

Here are the answers: 1. comma after *Yes* 2. comma after *Really* 3. comma after *No* 4. comma after *After I have interviewed her* 5. comma after *Oh my* 6. comma after *Having said that.*

Talking to People: Commas in Direct Address

When you are speaking, you look at your listeners. They know that you are directing your statements or questions to them. When you are writing, readers may not always know the identity of the person you are addressing. In these situations, commas signal the name of the listener or reader. Take a look at these examples:

<u>Roger,</u> Ellie is angry at you.

Martha broke the window<u>, Ellie,</u> not Roger.

You should apologize<u>, Ellie.</u>

I hope<u>, Roger,</u> that you will forgive Ellie's mistake.

Ellie and Roger, stop fighting!

In every example, the name of the person or people you are addressing is set off from the rest of the sentence by one or two commas. These commas can be very important. In fact, they can avoid murder! Read these sentences. The meaning is quite different without a comma:

We should eat Uncle Bob.

We should eat, Uncle Bob.

Murder, of course, is extreme. However, commas can change meaning in subtle ways also:

The doctor called Max, and Eliza answered.

The doctor called, Max, and Eliza answered.

In the first example sentence, the doctor wanted to speak with Max. Eliza may have told Max about the phone message or forgotten all about it. In the second example sentence, the writer addresses Max. Max now knows about the phone call. He can get in touch with Eliza if he wants to know what the doctor said.

Try your hand at inserting commas in these sentences. To help you understand the intended meaning, I have placed additional information in parentheses.

1. Go home immediately Eric. (The speaker is addressing *Eric.*)

2. Your friend Monica is waiting for you. (The speaker is addressing *Monica.*)

3. Ann I would love to have coffee with you at the new cafe. (The speaker is addressing *Ann.*)

4. The cafe is always crowded Ann after nine o'clock. (The speaker is addressing *Ann.*)

5. Monica Eric will probably bring his guitar. (The speaker is addressing *Monica.*)

6. I hope Mr. Peterson that you like folk music. (The speaker is addressing *Mr. Peterson.*)

Here are the answers: 1. comma before *Eric* 2. commas before and after *Monica* 3. comma after *Ann* 4. commas before and after *Ann* 5. comma after *Monica* 6. commas before and after *Mr. Peterson.*

In the middle

All by itself, *mid* has no meaning. Attached to the beginning of a word, though, *mid* becomes "middle" or "in the middle of." Here are some *mid* words:

Midway means "the halfway point." "Joe stopped midway through the meeting to outline the problems."

Midday means "noon, halfway through the day." "At midday, the sun is too hot for most swimmers."

Midterm means "in the middle of the school term, usually referring to exams." "I hate midterms because I prefer to study everything at the end of the year and ace the final exam."

Midlife means "in middle age." "On his fiftieth birthday, to soothe his midlife anxiety, he made a list of his achievements and goals."

Chapter 16

Who Said What: Quotation Marks

. . . .

In This Chapter

▶ Reporting what others say or write

▶ Understanding the difference between quoting and paraphrasing

▶ Identifying the speaker

▶ Punctuating quotations

▶ Surrounding titles with quotation marks

. . . .

Type *quote* in the search box of your computer screen. Pages and pages of websites offering quotations pop up. Apparently, lots of people are interested in what others have to say about religion, love, politics, and every other topic you can imagine. For this reason, quotation marks matter. This punctuation mark encloses words that someone else said or wrote. Quotation marks always appear as a set of two, like bookends:

" "

In this chapter, you see when to insert quotation marks and when to leave them out. You also discover when to use quotation marks to enclose titles of works of literature, music, and art.

Telling the Truth with Quotation Marks

Are you a playwright? Do you type scripts for television shows, podcasts, and films? If so, you do not have to worry about quotation marks. Read this script, anexcerpt from a truly terrible science-fiction drama:

VAMPIRE (leaning toward his victim): I want to bite you.

SCOTT (standing perfectly still): Just try it! I will kill you.

VAMPIRE (smiling, coming closer): I do not think so. I am too strong.

    SCOTT: Oh, but I have a secret weapon.

    VAMPIRE (fearfully): What weapon?

    SCOTT: This magic light bulb, which is as effective as the sun. (SCOTT holds up a light bulb. VAMPIRE crumbles into dust. SCOTT smiles and grabs a vacuum cleaner.)

From this script, you learn two things. First, this film will *never* win an Academy Award. Second, you learn exactly what each character says.

What happens when you are not writing a script? Here is the same story, written as if it were in a novel:

    A vampire leaned toward his victim, declaring, "I want to bite you."

    Scott never moved a muscle. Standing perfectly still, he challenged the vampire. "Just try it!" Scott said. "I will kill you."

    "I do not think so. I am too strong," replied the vampire, who smiled as he inched closer to Scott.

    "Oh, but I have a secret weapon," Scott announced.

    For the first time, the vampire's confidence vanished. Fearfully, he asked, "What weapon?"

    Scott answered, "This magic light bulb,which is as effective as the sun." The bulb turned on, and the vampire crumbled into dust. Scott smiled and reached for the vacuum cleaner.

Once more, you know two things after you read the preceding passage. First, no one will *ever* buy this novel. Second, you know exactly what each character says. Quotation marks take the place of a script's line breaks and character labels.

Quoting or Paraphrasing: Which Is Better?

A witness swears during a trial to tell "the truth, the whole truth, and nothing but the truth." In that way, a witness is similar to a direct quotation. A reporter covering a trial may quote witnesses in an article, but much of the article is usually a summary of what was said — a *paraphrase,* in English teacher's terminology. In this section, you see the difference between quoting and paraphrasing, so you can decide which suits your needs.

Signaling exact words

Read the vampire/Scott passage in the earlier section "Telling the Truth with Quotation Marks." Compare the passage to the film script version. Notice that quotation marks enclose words that a character said — nothing more and nothing less than those words. When you see quotation marks, you are "listening" to real speech. Here are more examples:

WHAT WAS SAID: When we hit that bump in the road, my knees smashed into my chin.

QUOTATION IN A SENTENCE: Peter complained, "When we hit that bump in the road, my knees smashed into my chin."

WHAT WAS SAID: Someone should repair that road.

QUOTATION IN A SENTENCE: "Someone should repair that road," commented the police officer.

WHAT WAS SAID: My chin has a dent in it, and it may be bleeding.

QUOTATION IN A SENTENCE: "My chin has a dent in it," Peter added, "and it may be bleeding."

WHAT WAS SAID: Shall I call an ambulance?

QUOTATION IN A SENTENCE: The officer asked, "Shall I call an ambulance?"

WHAT WAS SAID: No, thank you. I am in a hurry, and I have an appointment with my doctor later. I will not wait for an ambulance. I will show these injuries to my doctor this afternoon.

QUOTATION IN A SENTENCE: Peter added, "No, thank you. I am in a hurry, and I have an appointment with my doctor later. I will not wait for an ambulance. I will show these injuries to my doctor this afternoon."

WHAT WAS SAID: The bleeding has stopped.

QUOTATION IN A SENTENCE: "The bleeding has stopped," said the officer.

Only words that are actually spoken belong between quotation marks. Do not change anything, even if you can think of more interesting comments.

A trial witness promises to tell "the whole truth." In a quotation, though, you may leave out some words. Insert three dots (. . .) in place of the deleted words. For example, you may write Peter's words this way:

Peter added, "No, thank you. I am in a hurry, and . . . I will show these injuries to my doctor this afternoon."

If you shorten a quotation, be sure not to change the meaning. Take a look at this example:

WHAT THE FILM CRITIC SAID: The acting was terrible, but the costumes were awesome.

WHAT THE QUOTATION REPORTED: "The acting was . . . awesome."

WHY THIS IS WRONG: The critic called the acting "terrible," not "awesome," so the quotation is false.

I suspect that people who write advertisements for films do not always follow these guidelines. How often have you seen an "awesome" film that was actually "terrible"?

How are you at matching quotations and the sentences they belong in? Read the quotations in the first column. Insert the quotations into the correct sentence in the second column. Be sure that you do not omit or add words. When you have finished, reread the story to be sure that it makes sense.

Don't forget to look at the punctuation marks in the second column. They may help you find the correct answer.

Quotation	*Sentence*
A. The train will arrive an hour late	1. As she bought her ticket, Margie said, "_____."
B. Oh, no	2. "_____?" she asked.
C. Track seven, on the left	3. "_____," said the clerk in the information booth.
D. Where is the train to Philadelphia	4. The conductor announced, "_____."
E. Do not worry. Your friends will wait for you	5. Another passenger replied, "_____!"
F. I have never seen such a huge train station	6. Margie comforted the other passenger by remarking, "_____."

Here are the answers: 1. F 2. D 3. C 4. A 5. B 6. E.

Paraphrasing

Sometimes quoting the exact words is unnecessary and annoying. Imagine that your friend Alex called Martha. Here is everything Alex said, word for word:

How are you? I'm calling because my aunt, the one who works for that music company, got some free tickets to the concert tonight. The seats are not in the front row, but we will be close to the stage. This band is awesome, really awesome. They are going to be superstars someday soon. Can you go with me? The tickets are free, and this is a once-in-a–lifetime opportunity. I know you have a lot of homework, but who could pass up this opportunity?

Martha wants to go to the concert, but she needs permission to go out on a school night. She sends her mom this email:

Mom, Alex called and offered me a free ticket to tonight's concert. He said that the band is great, and our seats are good. He told me that I should take advantage of his offer. May I go?

Martha'semail is short. It does not reproduce Alex's exact words. Her email does not, for example, say that "this band is awesome, really awesome" or that the free tickets are "a once-in-a-lifetime opportunity." Martha's note, though, includes the same general ideas that Alex expressed. It is a *paraphrase,* or summary, of what Alex said.

Paraphrases are not enclosed in quotation marks. The paraphrased material is not a direct quotation.

Most readers want to know the source of the information you have paraphrased. In the preceding example, the email states that "Alex called" and that he "said" and "told" the information. By including the source, you give credit to the speaker for his or her ideas. You also protect yourself, in case the information is wrong.

Take a look at these examples of paraphrasing in Table 16-1. In the first column, you see a quotation. The exact words are enclosed in quotation marks. In the second column, you see the paraphrase. Notice that the paraphrase does not use quotation marks.

Table 16-1	Examples of Paraphrasing
Exact Words	*Paraphrase*
"My feet are freezing!" moaned Harry.	According to Harry, his feet are freezing.
"Do your homework now!" ordered his dad.	His dad told him to do his homework.
"I believe that bananas will be more expensive this year," remarked Ben.	Ben said that the price of bananas will rise this year.
I asked Ella, "Are you bored?"	I asked Ella if she was bored.
"I am so relieved that I could cry," Max said.	Max said he almost cried with relief.
George inquired, "Is the contract signed?"	George asked whether the contract was signed.

Should you paraphrase or quote? The answer depends on your purpose in writing. A direct quotation is more vivid and interesting than a summary. A paraphrase is shorter and more efficient than a direct quotation. Decide what you want to accomplish, and choose accordingly.

Can you tell the difference between paraphrased and quoted words? Label each of these sentences.

Sentence	*Paraphrase or Quotation?*

1. My grandmother told me that she had forgotten how to knit.
2. "Solving this math problem is simple," Karen whispered.
3. Sheila feels that she should not be asked to do any additional chores.
4. "One more task and I will quit!" she screamed.
5. Her boss told her to take a break.
6. She needs a rest, he thinks.
7. "Who can work 20 hours straight?" he remarked.

Here are the answers: 1. paraphrase 2. quotation 3. paraphrase 4. quotation 5. paraphrase 6. paraphrase 7. quotation.

Identifying the Source of a Quotation

When you quote, you must be sure that the reader knows who said what. One way to give this information is a *speaker tag,* my term for an identification phrase containing the name of the speaker and a verb. Speaker tags are attached to the quotation. Here are some examples of speaker tags:

Sonya said

Simon responded

Oliver asked

He shouted

Roger replied

Tammy murmured

Everyone exclaimed

Now look at these speaker tags in the context of a sentence. In each example, the speaker tag is underlined:

<u>Sonya said</u>, "I was born in Russia."

<u>Simon responded</u>, "You do not have a Russian accent."

<u>Oliver asked</u>, "Have you visited Russia recently?"

"You have not seen your family for ten years!" <u>he shouted</u>.

"Airfare to Russia is expensive," <u>Roger replied</u>, "and it is hard to take time off from work."

"I hope you are not homesick," <u>Tammy murmured</u>.

<u>Everyone exclaimed</u>, "You should go this summer!"

As you see, speaker tags can pop up at the beginning, middle, or end of a sentence. They are set off from the rest of the sentence by commas.

The source of a quotation may also be identified without a speaker tag, as you see in these examples:

According to Joan

Roy's belief is that

from Elizabeth's viewpoint

Within a sentence, these labels tell you that the material in quotation marks comes from *Joan, Roy,* and *Elizabeth.*

<u>According to Joan</u>, "the flights are cheaper now."

<u>Roy's belief is that</u> "baggage fees add up."

A trip home is "essential," <u>in Elizabeth's opinion.</u>

The quotation marks tell you what *Joan, Roy*, and *Elizabeth* said. They resemble little labels, sorting out who said what.

Underline the speaker tags or labels in these sentences.

1. "The hockey team is undefeated," said the sports reporter.

2. According to the coach, the team "plays well under pressure."

3. Jamie Damico, the most valuable player, commented, "Coach Hagen inspires us to give our best effort, every game."

4. "We respect our opponents," remarked Damico, "and we know we will eventually lose a game."

5. Coach Hagen asked, "Why expect to lose?"

6. The team's defeat last night was "so sad," in Damico's opinion.

Here are the answers: 1. *said the sports reporter* 2. *According to the coach* 3. *Jamie Damico, the most valuable player, commented* 4. *remarked Damico* 5. *Coach Hagen asked* 6. *in Damico's opinion.*

Adding Punctuation to Quotations

Quotation marks, of course, are the most important punctuation in every quotation. Other punctuation, however, also appears. This section guides you to the proper placement of commas, periods, question marks, and exclamation points. You also see when a quotation must begin with a capital letter and when a lowercase (not capitalized) letter is better. (Turn to Chapter 17 for more information on capital letters.)

Quotations with speaker tags

A *speaker tag* names the person who said the quoted material. The name is attached to a verb, such as *says, asked, reply, commented,* and so on. (For more information on speaker tags, see the previous section.)

Speaker tags move around. They can show up at the beginning or end of a quotation, and even in the middle. The speaker tag's location determines where commas and other punctuation marks belong.

Speaker tag at the beginning

Here are some sentences that begin with speaker tags. What do you notice about the punctuation?

Olivia commented, "I hate surprise parties."

Don said confidently, "I bet you have never given a surprise party."

She responded, "You are wrong. I arranged a surprise party for Gina last year."

Don remarked, "Gina was probably upset."

Olivia explained with a frown, "Yes, she was. In fact, she fainted when she saw us."

These examples illustrate a couple of punctuation rules for sentences beginning with speaker tags:

- ✓ **A comma follows the speaker tag.** The comma separates the speaker tag from the quotation.

- ✓ **Quotation marks surround the quoted words.** No surprise here! The first half of the pair alerts the reader that the quotation is beginning. The second half of the pair signals the end.

- ✓ **The quotation begins with a capital letter.** You know that you should always capitalize the first word of a sentence. A quotation with a speaker tag is like a sentence. It always begins with a capital letter. (For more information on capital letters, turn to Chapter 17.)

- ✓ **The period at the end of the sentence comes before the closing quotation mark.** This rule applies to Standard American English. In Britain, the period often follows the closing quotation mark.

Speaker tag at the end

Often, a speaker tag shows up at the end of the sentence. Read these examples:

"Connie and I watched the football game together," said Ron.

"She was very emotional when her team scored a goal," he added.

"No, I was not," Connie declared.

"The tears in your eyes resulted from allergies," said Ron sarcastically.

"Okay, maybe I was a little too involved in the game," murmured Connie.

These examples show you the rules for sentences ending with speaker tags:

- ✓ **Quotation marks surround the quoted words.** The first thing you see in this kind of sentence is the opening quotation mark.

- ✓ **A comma replaces the period at the end of the quotation.** The sentence does not conclude with the quotation, so you cannot place a period at the end of the quotation. Periods generally belong at the end of a sentence, not in the middle. (The only exception is abbreviations, such as "a.m." or "p.m.")

- ✓ **The comma appears before the closing quotation mark.** Why? American custom and tradition create the rule here. (In Britain, the comma often follows the quotation mark because of different customs and traditions.)

✔ **The sentence ends with a period.** All sentences end with a punctuation mark. A sentence concluding with a speaker tag is usually a statement, so a period is what you need. If the sentence is a question or an exclamation, a question mark or an exclamation point signals the end of the sentence. (For more information on punctuation at the end of a sentence, turn to Chapter 13.)

Speaker tag in the middle

For the sake of variety, you may want to place a speaker tag in the middle of a sentence. Here are some examples of this sentence pattern:

"I am not," declared the queen, "amused or insulted."

"You looked annoyed," said the plumber, "and perhaps impatient."

"We have that pipe," added the plumber's helper, "but not the tool to install it."

The rules here are a little more complicated:

✔ **Quotation marks surround the quoted words.** Because the quotation is broken into two parts, you need two sets of quotation marks — one for the first part of the quotation and another for the second part of the quotation.

✔ **The sentence begins with a capital letter.** Every sentence begins with a capital letter, and quotations are no exception.

✔ **The second part of the quotation begins with a lowercase letter.** The logic here is that the quotation is a sentence. You do not place capital letters in the middle of a sentence, except, of course, for a name or for the personal pronoun *I*.

✔ **Place a comma after the first part of the quotation.** The comma appears before the closing quotation mark.

✔ **Insert a comma after the speaker tag.** This comma separates the speaker tag from the second half of the quotation.

✔ **Place the period at the end of the sentence before the closing quotation mark.** This rule is true if the quotation is a statement. If the quotation is a question, use a question mark. If the quotation is an exclamation, use an exclamation point. In all these situations, Standard American English requires the punctuation mark to appear before the closing quotation mark. The tradition in Britain is often different.

If you are quoting many sentences from one person, not just one, the rules change slightly. Look at this example:

"These shoes are too tight," complained Max. "Please bring me a larger size."

In this example, the speaker tag is not really in the middle of a sentence. It appears at the end of the first sentence. The second half of the quotation is a separate sentence. Be sure to punctuate separate sentences individually.

Quotations without speaker tags

When no speaker tag appears with a quotation, the punctuation changes a bit. Read these examples:

Lenny thinks that this year's election is "the most important of our era."

After seeing the exhibit, Gina called the artworks "magnificent" and "awe-inspiring."

According to the author, every new parent should "pay attention to the baby and ignore the experts."

The rules for quotations without speaker tags are simple:

✔ **Quotation marks surround the quoted words.** This rule never changes, with or without speaker tags.

✔ **Usually, no comma separates the quotation from the rest of the sentence.** As you see in the example sentences, the quotation is tucked into the sentence seamlessly.

✔ **The quotation does not begin with a capital letter.** Unless the quotation is at the beginning of the sentence, start off with lowercase. Again, the logic is that the quotation is tucked into the sentence. It is not a separate unit of thought.

Can you place periods and commas in the correct places? Insert these punctuation marks where they belong.

1. Angela said "My dog Spot ran through a mud puddle"

2. Angela complained that Spot's fur was "totally filthy"

3. "Do not worry" said the dog groomer

4. He continued "I will give Spot a bath"

5. "If you can" replied Angela "trim his nails also"

6. The dog groomer said "I will"

Quoting from written material

Quotation marks also enclose words that are reproduced from a piece of writing. For example, imagine that you are writing a report for school or for work. You see this paragraph:

> At the 2015 meeting of the Global Alternative Society (GAS), members discussed cars that run without gasoline. Lectures covered electricity, hydrogen fuel cells, and plant-based fuels. Outside, society members carefully studied models of what they called the cars of the future. One vehicle, which runs on leftover cooking oil, smelled like hamburgers and fries. Everyone who looked at this car remarked on the unusual but not unpleasant odor. A representative from GAS praised these cars for their environmentally friendly technology.

Note: The Global Alternative Society does not exist. This paragraph comes from my imagination. I do know someone whose car burns leftover cooking oil, though. It *does* smell strange!

Now take a close look at this paragraph, in which words from the written source appear:

> Petroleum is the world's most prominent fuel, but engineers from the Global Alternative Society (GAS) and other organizations are studying and promoting other energy sources. According to GAS, "cars of the future" may run on hydrogen or even on recycled cooking oil, which has an "unusual but not unpleasant odor."

Do you see that the source of every quotation is given in the text? The phrase "According to GAS" is the identifying label. You can also identify the source in a footnote or endnote. Sometimes, the source identification appears in parentheses. For more information on quoting from written material, turn to Chapter 20.

Here are the answers:

1. Angela said, "My dog Spot ran through a mud puddle."

2. Angela complained that Spot's fur was "totally filthy."

3. "Do not worry," said the dog groomer.

4. He continued, "I will give Spot a bath."

5. "If you can," replied Angela, "trim his nails also."

6. The dog groomer said, "I will."

Identifying Titles with Quotation Marks

Are you a poet? A song writer? A reporter? If so, you need quotation marks for the titles of your creations. Even if you are not the creator, you still need quotation marks to identify the titles of these works.

However, not all titles should be enclosed by quotation marks. Some titles — of longer works such as novels, newspapers or magazines, operas, and so on — should be italicized or underlined.

The rule is simple. Short works require quotation marks. Long works require italics or underlining. Read Table 16-2, which divides titles into two categories according to the way their titles should appear.

Table 16-2	Identifying Titles
Quotation Marks	*Italics or Underlining*
short poem: "Daffodils"	long poem: *The Odyssey*
song: "Gimme Some Truth"	album: *Imagine*
article: "Police Slowdown Ends"	newspaper or magazine name: *Daily News*
essay: "On Envy"	collection of essays: *The Souls of Black Folk*
television episode: "The Bizarro Jerry"	television series: *Seinfeld*
chapter title: "Who Said What: Quotation Marks"	book title: *Basic English Grammar For Dummies*

Try your hand at punctuating these titles. Enclose titles in quotation marks or underline them (for italics or underlining).

1. Birches (poem)
2. On the Road (novel)
3. America the Beautiful (song)
4. Blood on the Tracks (album)
5. Hamlet (play)
6. President Signs Peace Treaty (article)

Here are the answers: 1. quotation marks 2. italics/underlining 3. quotation marks 4. italics/underlining 5. italics/underlining 6. quotation marks.

If the title is centered on a page, alone on the line, do not enclose it with quotation marks or italicize or underline it. Being alone is enough to identify it as a title.

Many rules govern how to capitalize a title. For help with capitalization, see Chapter 17.

Colons and quotations

Usually, a comma is enough to separate a speaker tag or an introduction from a quotation. If the quotation is very long, though, you may use a colon (one dot on top of another). Check out this example:

Short quotation

Andrew remarked, "The committee is now arranging three events."

Long quotation

Andrew remarked: "The committee is now arranging three events. All these events will take place next month. Our budget has been cut, and committee members are very discouraged. They try to stretch their time, energy, and funding. No one can do everything, however. We need to examine our schedule and adjust it to assist our loyal employees."

The colon prepares the reader for a large amount of information. (Colons may also introduce lists, such as those that appear on presentation slides. For more information on presentation slides, see Chapter 19.)

Chapter 17

Big or Small? When to Write Capital Letters

*I*f you apply for a loan, what happens? Usually, the bank asks how much you earn and what you owe. One new bank checks something else. This bank looks at capital letters. That's right — *capital letters.* The bank has determined that borrowers who know the rules of capitalization are more likely to pay back their loans.

I do not believe that a bank should judge anyone's grammar skills. However, I also know that people sometimes evaluate your level of education and ability when they read your writing. For this reason, and many others, you should know the key rules of capitalization. This chapter explains those rules.

Knowing the (Capital) ABCs of Capital Letters

Many grammar rules that I explain in this book arise from logic. The rules for capital letters, though, generally do not. In this way, capitalization is similar to parenting:

CHILD: Why do I have to clean my room?

PARENT: Because.

WRITER: Why do I have to capitalize that word?

GRAMMAR EXPERT: Because.

Of course, the parent's answer could include a bit of logic. In the preceding example, the parent might say, "You have to clean your room because it smells terrible" or "You have to clean your room because the junk pile on your floor is as high as the ceiling." Those statements may be true. However, the real reason a child has to clean the room is that the parent said so. The reason why you have to write a *capital* (big) or a *lowercase* (small) letter is often simply because tradition (or a grammar expert) says so.

Here are some logical principles that govern capital letters:

- ✔ **Capital letters add importance.** When you see a capital letter, the word stands out. It appears more important.

- ✔ **Capital letters highlight specifics.** Lowercase letters appear in general terms (*river*, for example). Capital letters alert you to specific names (such as the *Nile*).

- ✔ **Capital letters separate.** Sentences begin with capital letters. Along with punctuation, a capital letter shows where a new thought begins.

Keep these ideas in mind as you look at each rule in this chapter.

Setting Up Sentences with Capital Letters

Some ancient texts have no punctuation and no capital letters. Without these two elements, readers have a hard time knowing where one idea begins and another ends. For instance, what do you understand from this message?

FRANK IS HERE IN THE STORE HE IS FINE OUTSIDE HE IS WORRIED ABOUT ROBBERS NOW

Did you read it this way?

Frank is here. In the store he is fine. Outside he is worried about robbers now.

Or this way?

Frank is here in the store. He is fine outside. He is worried about robbers now.

In the first version, Frank worries about robbers whenever he leaves the store. In the second version, Frank worries about robbers whenever he is inside the store. These two ideas are quite different. If the first version is true, Frank should hire a bodyguard. If the second is true, he should install a security alarm. (Either way, Frank should calm down!)

Sentences always begin with capital letters. I do not need to give you more examples because every sentence in this book follows the rule.

Typing with just your thumbs can be difficult. In texts and instant messages, writers sometimes break the rule requiring capital letters at the beginning of each sentence. (They often drop punctuation also.) Eliminating formal capitalization and punctuation may be fine when you are sending a message to a friend. In a business or school situation, though, a little extra effort changes sloppy communication to proper English. Consider your audience as you type. (For more information on electronic media, see Chapter 18.)

You cannot capitalize a numeral (*45,* for example). Therefore, you should not begin a sentence with a numeral. If you need a number in that spot, write the word (*Forty-five*). In other words, you may not write

14 days of vacation is too little.

Instead, you should write

Fourteen days of vacation is too little.

In the following paragraph, capitalize letters as needed. If you wish to change a numeral to a word, do so.

the subway skidded around the curve too quickly. how many people were hurt? 16 passengers had minor injuries. 2 died. transportation officials are studying what went wrong. they have questioned the driver and several riders. i think that more attention should be paid to subway safety.

Here is what the paragraph should look like:

The subway skidded around the curve too quickly. How many people were hurt? Sixteen passengers had minor injuries. Two died. Transportation officials are studying what went wrong. They have questioned the driver and several riders. I think that more attention should be paid to subway safety.

Naming Names

Human beings love to make categories. One way to do so is to give everything a name. Well, actually two names — one specific and one general. Capital letters usually appear in specific names, but not in general terms. In this section, you examine this rule in depth.

Who are you? Names for people

Write your name here: _____. You capitalized the first letter, right? People's names are always important, so they are always capitalized. Check out these examples:

Ruth Jones

Bobby Khan

Samuel Peters

Theresa Santiago

William Winfield

Annie Ellington

The personal pronoun *I*, referring to the speaker or writer, is also always written as a capital letter. Other personal pronouns — *he, they, she, you,* and so on — are not capitalized. Do you think this rule means that people always see themselves as more important than anyone else in the world?

General references to people, not names, are not capitalized:

tennis champion

ambassadors

passengers

teenager

residents

student

To sum up this rule: <u>Ruth</u> (capitalized specific name) may be a <u>passenger</u> (lowercase general term) in a car on the way to see her <u>friend</u> (lowercase general term) <u>Matt</u> (capitalized specific name).

Where are you? Names for places

Names of specific places are also always capitalized:

Columbia River

Italy

Topeka, Kansas

Main Street

Pacific Ocean

Asia

If a name has two or more parts (for instance, *San Fernando* or *Kansas City*), capitalize all the parts.

General terms for places should be written in lowercase:

mountain range

cities

oceans

neighborhood

road

coast

The names of countries are always capitalized. Sometimes, the name of a region or neighborhood is capitalized also. Read these examples:

France (country)

Midwest (region)

Upper East Side (neighborhood of New York City)

If you refer to people by naming the place they live, capitalize that term also. Take a look at these examples:

Frenchman or Frenchwoman

Midwesterners

Upper East Sider

To clarify this rule: In <u>Italy</u> (capitalized specific name), many <u>cities</u> (lowercase general term) attract tourists. <u>Venetians</u> (capitalized specific name) live in <u>Venice</u> (capitalized specific name), where the most important <u>street</u> (lowercase general term) is the watery <u>Grand Canal</u> (capitalized specific name).

What's that? Names of things

Brand names, company names, and store names are usually capitalized. However, a company can call itself and its products anything! (Apple Inc., for example, sells iPads and iMacs. The lowercase *i* is a style decision.) Here are some examples of brands, companies, and stores:

> Facebook
>
> Hecker's Flour
>
> General Mills
>
> Sony
>
> Saks Fifth Avenue
>
> Android

Once again, general terms for things, companies, and stores should be written in lowercase:

> website
>
> baking supplies
>
> cereal
>
> video games
>
> department store
>
> phone

Consider some examples in context: <u>General Motors</u> (capitalized specific name) makes many <u>cars</u> (lowercase). You can buy <u>convertibles</u> (lowercase general term) everywhere. <u>Joe's Pre-Owned Autos</u> (capitalized specific name) will offer you a good deal for this type of <u>vehicle</u> (lowercase general term).

Capital letters usually appear in specific names. Lowercase letters are best for general terms.

To see how well you understand the capitalization rules for names, add a capital letter to any word that requires one:

1. volcano

2. paul

3. i

4. oregon

5. cadillac

6. lisa simpson

7. girls

8. printers

9. yankees

10. europe

Here are the answers: 1. *volcano* 2. *Paul* 3. *I* 4. *Oregon* 5. *Cadillac* 6. *Lisa Simpson* 7. *girls* 8. *printers* 9. *Yankees* 10. *Europe*.

Mr. Mayor or mr. mayor: Capitalizing Titles

Please allow me to introduce Michael and Sally. Here are several ways I can refer to them:

<u>Mr.</u> Michael Jones

<u>Ms.</u> Sally Smith

<u>Dr.</u> Michael Jones

my <u>doctor</u>, Michael Jones

<u>Cousin</u> Michael

<u>Mayor</u> Jones

<u>Judge</u> Smith

Michael Jones, <u>mayor of my city</u>

Sally Smith, <u>judge on the county court</u>

In this list, titles for Michael and Sally are underlined. In this section, I explain why some are capitalized, and some are not.

Titles appearing before a name

A title appearing before a name usually becomes part of that name. Because names are capitalized, so are titles in this position.

First, take a look at the most common titles. Every person can claim at least one:

Mr. Peter Olson

Miss Barbara Baum

Mrs. Jean Newton

Ms. Ellen Dodge

These titles never appear in lowercase. As you see, men have one option (*Mr.*) and women have three (*Miss, Mrs.,* and *Ms.*). Do you know the difference? Traditionally, *Miss* refers to unmarried females, and *Mrs.* to married females. The title *Ms.* refers to women who are either single or married.

Do not forget to place a period after *Mr., Mrs.,* and *Ms.*

Other titles refer to someone's career or status. Read these examples:

Senator Paul Goodman

Representative Olivia Roth

Reverend Johnson

Rabbi Cohen

Lady Westfield

Lord Derek

Once again, these titles precede the names. They are part of the name, so they require capital letters.

Titles appearing after a name

Meet Edward Gower, the <u>director of marketing</u> for our company. Edward, the <u>secretary-treasurer</u> of his basketball team, plays every weekend. His teammates include Joan Dobby, <u>vice president for sales</u>, and Gene Rogers, <u>chief</u> of the accounting department.

The titles underlined in the preceding paragraph belong to *Edward Gower, Joan Dobby,* and *Gene Rogers.* (They are not real people, just examples.) The titles are not capitalized because they appear after the names. They are not part of the names. Think of these titles as a little extra information about *Edward, Joan,* and *Gene.*

Here are a few other examples of titles that are written in lowercase because of their position after the name. The titles are underlined:

Shana Porter, <u>head veterinarian</u>

Joseph Masters, <u>administrative assistant</u>

Mike May, <u>co-chair</u> of the committee

Louise Lennon, <u>webmaster</u>

Archie Goodwin, <u>private detective</u>

Linda David, <u>financial-page editor</u>

In grammar, as in life, many rules have exceptions. This rule about lowercase titles has a few exceptions. If the title is very important, you should capitalize it no matter where it appears. What is the definition of *very important?* I am glad you asked! In most American publications, these positions qualify:

President of the United States

Vice President of the United States

Secretary-General of the United Nations

the Pope

Prime Minister of Great Britain

Chief Justice of the Supreme Court

When a title includes several words, capitalize the important ones *(President, United, States).* Lowercase the unimportant words *(of, the).*

I imagine that you can name a few more positions that, from your viewpoint, are as important as those in the preceding list. If you feel strongly that a particular job is equal in rank to those appearing on this list, capitalize the position. If you are writing a report for an authority figure, ask him or her about capitalizing specific titles. With this rule, you have some room for interpretation.

Titles appearing alone

When you write about someone, you may not know the person's name. In these situations, you refer to the person by his or her title alone. Read these examples. In each, the title is underlined:

> The <u>department chair</u> ordered a review of the required textbooks.

> The sound of barking surrounds the <u>town dogcatcher</u>.

> Because the <u>publicity director</u> is out of town, we will have to write the press release ourselves.

> The <u>mayor's aide</u> responded immediately and approved their request.

> I hope to become an <u>executive vice president</u> within two years.

> Please do not inform the <u>lieutenant</u> of my late arrival.

The rule is simple. A title alone, without a name, should be written in lowercase.

This rule is not absolute. Some titles of national or international importance are always capitalized, even if no name appears with the title. For more information, look at the list at the end of the preceding section, "Titles appearing after a name."

When you speak or write to someone (a *direct address*), you may use the title, all by itself, as a name. In that case, all titles require capital letters. See Chapter 15 for more information on direct address.

See whether you can insert capital letters where they are needed in the underlined titles.

1. They say that <u>captain</u> Henry Nash has scheduled a news conference for ten o'clock.

2. Yesterday <u>general</u> Rodriguez ordered an additional thousand troops to defend that area.

3. Monica Canfield, <u>vice president</u> of that shoe company, wears her company's products.

4. Do you know <u>justice</u> Sachs?

5. The <u>ambassador</u> asked the <u>secretary-general of the united nations</u> to visit every country that signed the treaty.

6. The man standing near the door is our new <u>pastor</u>.

Here are the answers: 1. *Captain* 2. *General* 3. lowercase 4. *Justice* 5. lowercase for *ambassador, Secretary-General of the United Nations* 6. lowercase.

Mom or mom? Capitalizing Family Relationships

Like most people, you probably play many roles in your family. You may be a parent, a son or daughter, a grandchild, an uncle or an aunt, and lots of other things. Sometimes these roles should be capitalized, and sometimes they should be in lowercase.

Two rules cover family relationships:

✔ **If the relationship word is just a label, do not capitalize it.** If you refer to *my dad, her sister, his cousin, their uncle,* and so on, you are applying a label. Stay in lowercase.

✔ **If the relationship word substitutes for a name, capitalize it.** Perhaps you write about *Mom* or *Grandpa,* using those terms instead of *Mary* (the mother's name) or *Pete* (the grandfather's name). In that situation, the relationship word requires a capital letter.

Take a look at these examples:

Zena opened the package that <u>Grandma</u> had sent her. (*Grandma* = name)

Zena's <u>grandmother</u> frequently sends presents. (*grandmother* = label)

Unfortunately, <u>Mom</u> noticed that the vase was cracked in several places. (*Mom* = name)

Yesterday, her <u>dad</u> glued the pieces together. (*dad* = label)

Zena told <u>Uncle Henry</u> that the vase looked better after the accident. (*Uncle Henry* = name)

She has often remarked that her <u>uncle</u> is the kindest man she has ever met. (*uncle* = label)

Zena thanked her <u>grandmother</u> for the present. (*grandmother* = label)

If you can substitute a real name for the family relationship, you probably need a capital letter. If you cannot substitute a name without sounding strange, lowercase is most likely what you need.

Check out this method in action:

SENTENCE: Jake played five games of poker with his (Brother, brother).

SENTENCE WITH NAME SUBSTITUTED: Jake played five games of poker with his Michael.

CAPITAL OR LOWERCASE: Lowercase! The expression *his Michael* is not acceptable in formal English. Therefore, *brother* is a label in this sentence, not a name.

SENTENCE: Jake learned to play poker from (Grandpa, grandpa).

SENTENCE WITH NAME SUBSTITUTED: Jake learned to play poker from Michael.

CAPITAL OR LOWERCASE: Capital! The sentence with the name in it sounds fine, so *Grandpa* functions as a name in the sentence. Names should be capitalized.

Figure out the right way to deal with these family members. (I refer to capital or lowercase letters, of course. You will have to turn to other books for help with annoying cousins or nosy nephews and nieces.) Underline the correct term for each sentence.

1. Mabel says that (Auntie, auntie) makes the tastiest chocolate cake.

2. Although (Dad, dad) likes cake, he is allergic to chocolate.

3. When his (Sister, sister) bakes, (Dad, dad) politely refuses his slice.

4. He gives that slice to his (Wife, wife).

5. She, in turn, hands some of the cake to (Sister, sister).

6. Because my (Aunt, aunt) never pays attention, she never prepares a different dessert for (Dad, dad).

Here are the answers: 1. *Auntie* 2. *Dad* 3. *sister, Dad* 4. *wife* 5. *Sister* 6. *aunt, Dad.*

Capitalizing Creative Works

Open a newspaper or a magazine (or the website of a newspaper or a magazine). Read a few article titles. Some words are capitalized, and some are not. Take a look at these titles. Notice which words are capitalized:

"Dinosaurs: The Most Recent Discoveries in China"

"How to Reorganize Your Closet: A Guide for Messy People"

"Major Storm Hits the Northeast"

"Finding a New Career"

"The Safest Jobs in a Bad Economy"

"Fifty Recipes for Quick and Delicious Meals"

You probably noticed a pattern — the capitalization rules that the editors of these publications follow. Here is a summary of those rules:

✔ **Capitalize the first word of any title.** *Dinosaurs, How, Major, Finding, The,* and *Fifty* are capitalized because they are the first words of each title.

✔ **Capitalize the first word of any subtitle.** Subtitles show up after a colon (one dot above another). In the example list, the first two titles have subtitles. *The* and *A* are capitalized because they are the first words of each subtitle.

✔ **Capitalize nouns and pronouns.** In the example list, *Dinosaurs, Discoveries, China, Closet, Guide, People, Storm, Northeast, Career, Jobs, Economy, Recipes,* and *Meals* are capitalized because they are nouns. *Your* is capitalized because it is a pronoun.

✔ **Capitalize verb forms.** In the examples, you see capital letters for *Reorganize, Hits,* and *Finding.* They are verb forms.

✔ **Capitalize descriptive words.** *Most, Recent, Messy, Major, New, Safest, Bad, Fifty, Quick,* and *Delicious* have capital letters. Each of these words adds some information to the sentence.

✔ **Do not capitalize *a, an,* and *the.*** These last three tiny words should be in lowercase unless they appear as the first word of a title or subtitle.

✔ **Do not capitalize unimportant words.** Yes, I know. Deciding what is "unimportant" can be tough. In general, little words such as *to, for, in,* and *and* should be in lowercase. (In grammar terms, these are prepositions and conjunctions. Chapter 7 gives you more information about prepositions, and Chapter 8 discusses conjunctions.)

Editors do not always agree about which words require capital letters. The rules help, but room for disagreement exists. If you are writing for a particular teacher or supervisor, you can check what he or she prefers. If not, use your own judgment, with the preceding rules as a guide.

Apply these rules to the titles of articles and the titles of

✔ Most written work, including novels, nonfiction books, essays, and plays

✔ The titles of newspapers, magazines, and journals

✔ Works of visual art, such as paintings, photos, and sculpture

✔ Musical works, such as songs and albums

If you are a poet or a scientist, these rules may not apply to you. Poets, I am convinced, love to break rules, and most poetry readers assume that titles, like everything else in a poem, can be creative, not grammatical. (I agree with that practice, by the way, as long as the result is interesting and meaningful.) Scientific articles and reports are also different from creative works. In "science style," only the first word of the title is capitalized, as well as any proper names in the title. If a scientific work has a subtitle, the first word of the subtitle also rates a capital letter. Everything else is in lowercase. If you are a scientist, do not follow the rules in the preceding bullet points.

QUICK QUIZ

Now you can *scope out* many new words and improve your vocabulary!

Time to try capitalizing titles. Circle any lowercase letter that should be a capital.

1. a view from the executive suite

2. daily gazette

3. the polluted planet: are we in danger?

4. going for the gold medal: achieving maximum success in sports

5. the cat lover's guide

6. over the river and up the mountain: journeys on foot

Here are the answers: 1. *A View from the Executive Suite* 2. *Daily Gazette* 3. *The Polluted Planet: Are We in Danger?* 4. *Going for the Gold Medal: Achieving Maximum Success in Sports* 5. *The Cat Lover's Guide* 6. *Over the River and Up the Mountain: Journeys on Foot.*

Seeing things

The root of a word is the part that sprouts different meanings every time you add something to the beginning or the end of the word. Take a close look at the root *scope*, which means "watch" and "see":

Telescope means "a device that allows you to see things that are far away." "Through the *telescope*, I saw the moon's craters easily."

A **microscope** is "a device that magnifies." "Through the *microscope*, I saw the bacteria."

A **periscope** is "an instrument, often on a submarine, that shows the view above and on all sides." "Look through the *periscope* to check for enemy warships."

Surprisingly, the root *scope* can also refer to listening. Your doctor may use a **stethoscope** to listen to your heartbeat. ("Please warm that *stethoscope* before you place it on my chest, Doctor.") Perhaps this word comes from the idea that the doctor is "looking" for signs of health or illness. *Scope* may also be a word all by itself, with no attachments. As a verb, to *scope* is to "investigate, to look into." ("Henry *scoped* out the possible audience for that television program.") As a noun, *scope* means "extent or range." ("The *scope* of the investigation was broad, as they looked into his entire career.")

Capitalizing Abbreviations

Are you in a hurry? If so, you probably abbreviate some terms when you write. Abbreviations are generally accepted short forms, often the first letter of each word in a phrase, that take the place of the complete expression. (Abbreviations are related to contractions, a topic you can find in Chapter 14. Contractions have an apostrophe [a little hook] in place of some letters. Abbreviations generally include periods.)

Here are some common abbreviations and the long form the abbreviations replace:

Mr. (short for *Mister*)

Rev. (short for *Reverend*)

St. (short for *Street*)

Ave. (short for *Avenue*)

Jr. (short for *junior*)

Rep. (short for *Representative*)

Jan. (short for *January*)

e.g. (from the Latin phrase meaning "for example")

Fri. (short for *Friday*)

yd (short for *yard*)

kg. (short for *kilogram*)

lbs. (from the Latin word for *pounds*)

As you see, some of these abbreviations are capitalized, and some are not. Here are the underlying principles:

> ✔ **Capitalize abbreviations for people's titles.** Follow the abbreviations with periods. *Sen. (senator), St. (saint),* and *Sr. (senior)* are examples of abbreviated titles.

> ✔ **Capitalize geographic abbreviations when they are part of a name.** It's the *Mississippi R.* (the *R.* stands for *River*) but just *r.* if you are labeling a natural feature on a map without including names.

> ✔ **Do not capitalize abbreviations for most measurements.** Place a period after the abbreviation for *yd. (yard)* and *in. (inch),* for example. ***Note:*** Metric abbreviations do not always include a period. You may see *kg* for *kilogram* or *m* for *meter.*

✔ **Capitalize both letters of the abbreviation of a state name.** This rule comes to you courtesy of the United States Postal Service, which decided some time ago to create two-letter, capitalized abbreviations for every state. *NY* is *New York, CO* is *Colorado,* and so on. You can find a list at www.usps.gov.

✔ **Capitalize every letter of an acronym.** An *acronym* is a new word created by stringing together the first letter of each word in a phrase. *NATO* is the acronym for the *North Atlantic Treaty Organization. AIDS* is the acronym for *Acquired Immune Deficiency Syndrome.* Acronyms do not require periods.

Two abbreviations that come in handy are *a.m.* (morning) and *p.m.* (afternoon).These abbreviations may also be written as *AM* and *PM.* In the capitalized version, do not insert periods. You may use either, but you should not switch back and forth between capital letters and lowercase. Once you choose an abbreviation, stay with it. Are you wondering how *a.m.* turned into "morning" and *p.m.* into "afternoon"? These abbreviations come from Latin phrases, *ante meridian* and *post meridian,* which refer to the position of the sun in the sky.

I cannot list all the abbreviations and acronyms you may come across when you are reading. (If I did, this book would weigh a hundred pounds!) If you see an abbreviation or an acronym you do not recognize, check the dictionary or the Internet.

Texters love to abbreviate, maybe because their thumbs tire quickly. Be careful if you create an abbreviation, though. Someone may *lol (laugh out loud)* at your letters or, worse, misunderstand what you are trying to say. (For more on electronic media, including texting, see Chapter 18.)

Insert an abbreviation into the blank. The intended long-form is in parentheses.

1. May I introduce _____ (Senator) Smith?

2. Lola's concert began at 4 _____ (afternoon) sharp.

3. After seeing Phoenix, _____ (Arizona), Bill left for a camping trip in the _____ (mountains).

4. The _____ (United Nations) delegates applauded _____ (Mister) Johnson's speech.

5. Gene bought books, films, games, _____ (and so on).

6. Did you buy stock in Seaver _____ (Incorporated)?

Here are the answers: 1. *Sen.* 2. *P.m.* or *PM* 3. *AZ, mts.* 4. *UN* or *U.N., Mr.* 5. *etc.* 6. *Inc.*

Part V
Grammar in Action

Communication in the 21st Century

Technology changes at the speed of light. Grammar does not move along quite so quickly, but it does adapt to modern times. In this part, you look at accepted standards for writing in the 21st century, including these:

- ✓ **Electronic media:** Texts, instant messages, and emails are more common than traditional letters printed on paper and sealed in an envelope. Plus, a quick trip around the Internet reveals that half the world is blogging or commenting on someone else's blog. Check Chapter 18 to see the proper language and format for these electronic communications.

- ✓ **Presentation slides and bulleted lists:** Word processing and popular computer programs such as PowerPoint, Prezi, and Keynote rely on bullet points. Chapter 19 explains how to format slides and bullets properly, so your message comes across clearly.

- ✓ **Letters, reports, and school assignments:** Whether you are a student or an employee, you probably have to put pen to paper or fingers to keyboard to write a letter, compile a report, or fulfill a homework assignment. Chapter 20 shows you some easily adaptable formats for these types of writing.

For a bonus article on Communication in the 21st Century, go online and take a look at
www.dummies.com/extras/basicenglishgrammar.

In this part . . .

- ✔ Format emails and traditional letters.
- ✔ Communicate clearly in texts and instant messages.
- ✔ Adjust the level of formality to reach your intended audience.
- ✔ Punctuate, capitalize, and properly format presentation slides and bulleted lists.
- ✔ Follow accepted grammatical standards for reports and school assignments.

Chapter 18

Writing with Electronic Media

. . . .

In This Chapter

▶ Communicating clearly in texts, tweets, and instant messages

▶ Writing effective emails

▶ Adapting traditional grammar for blog and social media posts

. . . .

*W*ritten communication began with a stick and some loose dirt and gradually moved to pen and paper. Now you can, and probably do, click away on a full-sized computer keyboard or on a tiny phone screen. New technology means new opportunities. You can write and revise many times with very little effort, for example. Just about anyone can blog, tweet, and post on social media.

However, modern communication presents challenges. Which grammar rules stay the same? Which ones are impractical? This area of grammar is a battlefield. Grammarians defend their country (proper English) with as much passion as patriotic soldiers. Though many issues are not yet settled, in this chapter you find commonly accepted guidelines for writing in modern electronic media.

The Unbreakable Rule: Communicating Clearly in Texts, Instant Messages, and Tweets

Short. Fast. Effortless. You value these three qualities when you write. Right? Okay, sometimes you may wish to go long, to take your time, and to use every brain cell you have. Often, though, you want to say it, Send it, and be done with it.

No matter what sort of writing *it* is, one other description must apply to your work: clarity. This is the unbreakable rule:

Your readers must understand what you mean.

If they don't, why bother writing at all? (Yes, I know that many people rely on snapshots or videos to communicate, but you are reading a book about grammar, so I know that you care about writing.)

The good news is that your texts, messages, and tweets can be short, quickly and easily written, and crystal clear. This section explains how.

Omitting words

Every character counts when you are tweeting or texting. It is just not comfortable to write long paragraphs on a screen the size of a low-calorie cookie. Plus, the program you are using may limit the size of your messages. For these reasons, you may break the "complete sentence rule" that grammarians love. (For more information on complete sentences, turn to Chapter 13.)

 Before you break a grammar rule, though, you should think about the person receiving your message. Is that person a friend or a business associate? Does he or she outrank you in status, age, or authority? What sort of impression would you like to make? Chapter 2 explains when informal language is acceptable and when formal English is required.

Dropping the subject

The easiest shortcut is to drop the subject. The subject is *who* or *what* does the action. The subject may also be *who* or *what* is in the state of being the sentence expresses. (For more information on subjects and verbs, check out Chapter 11.) When you drop a subject, sometimes you may shorten the verb form also. Here are some examples of deleted subjects:

FULL SENTENCE: I will come by bus.

SHORTENED MESSAGE #1: Will come by bus.

SHORTENED MESSAGE #2: Coming by bus.

FULL SENTENCE: I need a ride to the party.

SHORTENED MESSAGE #1: Need a ride to the party.

SHORTENED MESSAGE #2: Need ride to party.

FULL SENTENCE: I will bring wine.

SHORTENED MESSAGE #1: Will bring wine.

SHORTENED MESSAGE #2: Bringing wine.

In every example, the subject dropped from the sentence is *I*. Most readers assume that *I* is the subject in texts and messages. If the subject is not *I*, you probably need to include it to avoid confusion. Take a look at these examples:

FULL SENTENCE: Henry will come with me.

SHORTENED MESSAGE: Will come with me.

READER'S REACTION: *Who* will come with you?

FULL SENTENCE: Shane and Debby need a lift to the party.

SHORTENED MESSAGE: Need a lift to the party.

READER'S REACTION: I thought you were coming by bus. Have your plans changed?

FULL SENTENCE: Mark will bring soda.

SHORTENED MESSAGE: Will bring soda.

READER'S REACTION: You are bringing wine and soda? That's too much!

Of course, your reader may understand that *Mark will bring soda* if that text is part of a longer exchange, such as this one between Sal and Wendy. Note the full version in parentheses:

SAL'S SHORTENED MESSAGE: Will bring wine. (I will bring wine.)

WENDY'S SHORTENED MESSAGE: Mark? (What will Mark bring?)

SAL'S SHORTENED MESSAGE: Bringing soda. (Mark will bring soda.)

WENDY: Good.

Because *Mark* shows up in the second message, the third line makes sense.

In commands, the subject never appears, even in normal, non-shortened writing. The subject of a command is always *you*, but the *you* is understood, not included. Because it is already missing, you do not have to delete it. Here are some examples:

COMMAND: Go home.

MEANING: You have to go home.

COMMAND: Buy milk.

MEANING: You have to stop at the store and buy milk.

COMMAND: Do your homework.

MEANING: You have to do your homework.

Dropping other words

A friend of mine was worried about her daughter, who was traveling to a party all by herself for the first time. She told her daughter to text when she arrived. This is the message my friend received:

> here

The single word communicates everything the parent wants to know, even though no subjects or verbs appear. (It also expresses the teenager's annoyance. Every parent understands that *here* contains an eye-roll and this unwritten sentence: "Mom, I'm *fourteen*. Checking in is for *babies*.")

Often, you may omit the subject and the verb and still get your point across. (To learn more about subjects and verbs, see Chapter 11.) Take a look at these examples:

> MESSAGE: On bus.
>
> MEANING: I am on the bus.
>
> WHAT IS LEFT OUT: The subject *(I)*, the verb *(am)*, and *the*.

> MESSAGE: Traffic jam. Late.
>
> MEANING: I am in a traffic jam. I will be late.
>
> WHAT IS LEFT OUT: In the first sentence, the subject *(I)*, the verb *(am)*, and two other words, *in a*. In the second sentence, the subject *(I)* and verb *(will be)*.

> MESSAGE: Meeting horrible.
>
> MEANING: The meeting is (or was) horrible.
>
> WHAT IS LEFT OUT: The verb *is* or *was*, and *the*.

In the last example, the person receiving the message probably knows which meeting you are writing about and whether that meeting is over *(was horrible)* or still going on *(is horrible)*.

Deletions work only when the person you are writing to understands the situation. For example, suppose you Send this text:

> MESSAGE: Mark sick.
>
> MEANING: Mark is not at work (or at school or somewhere else) because he is sick.
>
> WHAT IS LEFT OUT: The verb *(is)* and the place (work, school, whatever).

If the person reading the message does not know where Mark is supposed to be (or who Mark is), this message is too vague. A better message in this situation is *Mark is sick and cannot teach today* or *Mark is sick. Hire a temporary secretary* or something similar.

Dropping punctuation and capital letters

I'm a grammarian, so when I text, I take the time to insert capital letters, periods, commas, question marks, and so on. Most people are not as picky as I am. Even I must admit that it is not terrible to skip some capital letters and punctuation. However, you must be sure that your message makes sense without them. Take a look at this text:

> walk at 4

What does this text mean? I can think of a few possible interpretations:

> I am going for a walk at 4.
>
> You should go for a walk at 4.
>
> Would you like to go for a walk at 4?

You may think that the last interpretation, with a question mark, is unlikely. It *is* unlikely, but it is also possible. Why take the chance? With a period, you rule out a question and ensure that the reader knows you are making a statement.

Here is another example:

> not writing secret

Expanded, this text could be any of the following:

> I am not writing because our relationship is a secret.
>
> I am not writing the secret. Someone may be reading my messages.
>
> You are not writing to me. I do not know why. Is the reason a secret?
>
> You are not writing to me. Is there a secret you are afraid to write about?

Some *apps* (programs that run on smartphones, tablets, and other devices) automatically correct spelling, insert capital letters, and add punctuation. This extra help saves time, but be sure to read what is on the screen before you press "Send."

Why? Apps are not as smart as human beings. They can "guess" what you are trying to say, but they can be wrong. For example, when I write to my friend Pilar, the app removes the capital and changes the spelling. Instead of *Pilar,* a very nice lady, she becomes "pillar," a kind of column. Even more embarrassing changes can occur. Be careful!

One more thing about texts, instant messages, and tweets: I often receive messages with odd abbreviations, such as *U* (for *you*) and *L8* (for *late*). *IMHO* (short for *in my humble opinion*), these shortened forms are not a good idea. The reader may not understand, and *TIAS*. See what I mean? *TIAS* is an abbreviation I just made up. It means "*that is a shame.*" How could you know what I am *TTS*? (*TTS* is another abbreviation I dreamed up. It stands for *trying to say.*) Besides avoiding misunderstanding, nonstandard abbreviations are, well, nonstandard. If you wish to present yourself as educated and intelligent, proper grammar is the best means of doing so.

Check the messages in the first column. Look at the potential meanings in the second column. Circle every meaning that a reasonable person may get from the message. Then decide whether the message is clear or unclear and place your answer in the third column.

Message	Meanings	Clear or Unclear?
1. Dinner at 7:30.	a. You must attend the dinner, which takes place at 7:30.	
	b. Would you like to attend the dinner, which takes place at 7:30?	
2. Arriving early?	a. Do you expect to arrive early?	
	b. Did you arrive early?	
3. Pam here now	a. Pam is here now.	
	b. Pam was here.	
4. snow not today	a. It will not snow today.	
	b. It will snow another day	
5. Max left meeting	a. Max left the meeting.	
	b. Max left. We are still meeting.	

Here are the answers: 1. a – clear 2. a – clear 3. a – clear 4. a or b – unclear 5. a – clear.

Writing Proper Emails

This morning a radio announcer declared that "email is dead." According to this fellow, everyone texts or posts photos and updates on social media sites. I yelled at the radio, which, of course, did not yell back. "If email is dead," I said, "why is my inbox overflowing?"

Before I go any further, I should explain what I mean by *email*. I am using the term to refer to messages that are a little more formal and may be much longer than a text. Yes, I know that emails and texts overlap somewhat. A message sent from a phone may show up in my email inbox. Also, traditional emails can be very short. I once answered a two-page email from a student asking me to postpone an exam with a one-word email message: *No*.

Because just about everyone uses email (despite what the radio announcer thinks), you may be writing to an employer, a teacher, or an elderly and very strict relative. Or, you may be writing to a friend. You present yourself to these groups of people in very different ways — and that means different standards of grammar and style. Turn to Chapter 2 for guidance on adapting your writing to suit potential readers.

Exploring email structure

You have probably written and received many emails. Have you ever taken a close look at their format? In this section, I go through each part of the email, explaining do's and don'ts. Glance at the example of email format to see each element. *Note:* Depending upon the programs and device you use, your email may look a bit different. The basic ingredients of a proper email are the same, though, regardless of where everything appears.

An Example of Email Format

Subject: Repairs Completed

From: Mary Jones, Main Street Auto Repair

To: Catherine Berger

CC: Alan Smith

Dear Ms. Berger:

Your car repairs have been completed. Please call our service manager, Alan Smith, to arrange delivery. Thank you for entrusting your business to Main Street Auto Repair.

Best,

Mary Jones

Manager

To and From lines

Who is sending the message? To whom? The "to" and "from" lines of the email answer these questions. Of course, you know that the message is "to" you, if you received it. However, the "to" line informs you of other people who also received the email. (Sometimes their names appear with yours. They may also be listed separately, after "CC," the abbreviation for "copy.")

You do not have to format the "to" and "from" lines. Once you enter the email address of your reader, you are finished. If the person you are writing to is in your contact list, his or her name also appears automatically. The program inserts your own email address in the "from" line.

In the example of email format, Catherine Berger and Alan Smith received the message. (Alan's name is on the "CC" or "copy" line.) The message was sent by Mary Jones, whose name is in the "from" line.

When you add someone to your contact list, be careful how you identify him or her. If you type "annoying customer" in the first and last name boxes, that phrase appears as the name. Also, when you open an email account, pause for a moment before you choose your identifier. You may enjoy a silly (or worse than silly) label for a moment, but do you want to be stuck with it for years? Consider how your screen name will look to a potential employer or to a teacher.

Subject lines

The *subject line* is the title of the email — the line that tells the reader what you are writing about. In the example of email format, "Repairs Completed" is the subject. Check out these key points about subject lines:

- **Be sure to include a subject line in the email.** With no subject line, the person receiving your email ignores it. The time you spent writing the email will then be wasted. Also, the subject line begins the conversation with the reader, establishing what the reader should expect.

- **Make your subject line short and clear.** You want to get the point across, but you do not want the reader to turn away before checking the message. *Why You Should Hire Me to Manage Your Business* is too long. *Hiring* is too short. *Applying to Manage* is clear and may spark interest.

- **Do not attempt to shock or surprise.** No one likes spam (unwanted mass emails from strangers). Everyone is afraid of viruses. (Computer viruses, not the kind that Send you to the doctor.) If the subject line is too odd, the email will probably remain unopened.

- **Capitalize the subject line as if it were a title.** This practice is not always necessary. Some people choose to capitalize the first word of the subject line and nothing else. If you do treat the subject line as a title, be sure to do so correctly. (Chapter 17 explains everything you need to know about capitalizing titles.)

> ✔ **Update the subject line in later emails.** You can leave the same subject
> line in every reply, but sometimes an update is helpful. For example,
> suppose that the example of email format is a reply to an email asking
> about the repairs. The original subject line might be "Status of Repairs?"
> or something similar. Then the subject line of this message, "Repairs
> Completed," gives immediate and important information.

The greeting

You do not have to include a greeting line, but it is a nice touch. Greeting
lines vary. Some are very formal, suitable for emails sent to those who outrank you. Others are friendly, good for friends and co-workers. In the example of email format, the greeting line is formal (Dear Ms. Berger:) because the
person receiving the message is a customer.

Placement varies also. Some are better on the same line as the beginning of the message. Others should appear on a separate line. Here are
some examples:

GREETING: Hi, Jane.

SUITABLE FOR: friend, co-worker

PUNCTUATION: period after the name, comma between _Hi_ and _Jane_

PLACEMENT: message starts on the same line

GREETING: Hello, Andrew.

SUITABLE FOR: friend, co-worker

PUNCTUATION: period after the name, comma between _Hello_ and _Andrew_

PLACEMENT: message starts on the same line

GREETING: Dear Jane,

SUITABLE FOR: friend, co-worker

PUNCTUATION: comma after the name

PLACEMENT: message begins on the next line

GREETING: Dear Ms. Smith,

SUITABLE FOR: teacher, supervisor, someone of higher rank

PUNCTUATION: comma after the name

PLACEMENT: message begins on the next line

GREETING: To the project manager:

SUITABLE FOR: an official, storeowner, unknown person in an official capacity

PUNCTUATION: colon after the title

PLACEMENT: message begins on the next line

Can you skip the greeting entirely? Yes! However, people are attracted to their own names or titles. Including a greeting may create a connection with your reader.

The body

The *body* in an email is not part of a murder investigation. It is the message itself. Write what you wish, but be aware that any fancy touches — italics, boxed information, and the like — may be lost when you hit "Send." Various computer systems do not always communicate seamlessly. What appears to be a quotation mark on your screen may be a strange symbol on the reader's.

If you wish to ensure that your reader sees *exactly* what you wrote, you can make your message a PDF (which stands for "Portable Document File"). A PDF is a sort of picture that you Send in an attached file.

Keep your message simple and brief. In the example of email format, the writer communicates what the customer needs to know without wasting time. No matter what, take a moment to reread your message before sending it. Even careful writers can make a misstake. Er . . . I mean *mistake*.

Closing

To conclude your email, you may wish to place one of these phrases (such as "Best" in the example of email format) on a separate line above your name, followed by a comma:

Best, (short for "best regards" or "my best wishes" and suitable for both formal and informal emails)

Hope to hear from you, (suitable for informal emails, also okay for slightly more formal messages)

Sincerely, (extremely formal)

Regards, (formal)

Your friend, (informal)

Kind regards, (formal)

Love, (informal and intimate)

When the closing contains more than one word, capitalize only the first word. Lowercase the additional words.

You may conclude your email simply by typing your name or your initials on a separate line. If you rely on initials, use capital letters and do not insert periods. For example, I would type "GW" for "Geraldine Woods."

One decision every writer makes, in emails and all other forms of communication, is the proper level of formality. Turn to Chapter 2 for a full discussion of this issue.

Writing for Websites and Social Media

Every tenth of a second, it seems, a hot new app or website appears. Suddenly, thousands of users desert one medium and flock to another. Chatting, commenting, blogging, posting — how can grammar keep up?

Actually, grammar *can* keep up. The details may change, but the basic principles of communication stay the same, no matter what the medium. So when you hit the Internet, keep these ideas in mind:

- ✔ **The audience matters.** When you comment on a friend's site, slang and other types of informal language are acceptable. In a site with a large and unknown audience (say, the comments section accompanying an online article), bring out your most formal writing. (For a longer discussion of suiting your writing to the audience, check out Chapter 2.)

- ✔ **Be clear.** If you are posting a comment on a site for cat lovers, you can refer to *Manx* without explanation. Readers going to that site most likely know that *Manx* is a breed of cat. On a general site, *Manx* may require a definition. Similarly, stay away from abbreviations (except for the most common ones) when you are writing for a general audience. You have readers, not mind-readers. Why risk being misunderstood?

- ✔ **Remember that the Internet is public.** Yes, you can erect barriers that limit who can read your posts. A quick glance at the news, though, reveals that those barriers are often full of holes. More and more frequently, employers and college admissions officers check the Internet before hiring or accepting applicants. Do you want them to think that *U R* (you are) dumb *cuz* (because) you write non-Standard English? Checking up on you this way is unfair, I know. Nevertheless, it does happen!

Before you write, check out other comments or posts on the site or on similar sites (if you are starting your own). Notice what you like and dislike about others' work. Tailor your own writing accordingly.

Chapter 19

Presentation Slides and Bulleted Lists

. . . .

In This Chapter

▶ Formatting slides for presentations

▶ Writing good titles for presentations

▶ Creating matching bullet points

▶ Punctuating and capitalizing bullet points

. . . .

Do your knees shake when you have to give information to an audience? Perhaps you are worried about your presentation slides. Those slides, projected on a screen, focus the attention of your audience on key points. They also focus the attention of your audience on your grammar and punctuation skills. Any mistake you make is two-feet tall and lit up for all to see.

In this chapter, I show you how to write proper bullet points and create good presentation slides.

Ladies and Gentlemen, May I Present . . . Slides!

When someone makes a speech, how well do you listen? Be honest. Doesn't your attention wander from time to time? You hear a few sentences and then start thinking about dinner or the work piled on your desk.

Most people fade in and fade out during speeches. For this reason, presentation slides made with PowerPoint, Prezi, Keynote, and other computer programs are very popular. They give the audience a visual reference to return to after a small gap in attention.

Presentation slides come in many varieties. All have a few elements in common. Here is a sample presentation slide that shows the most common format.

Title

Introduction

    o Bullet point

    o Bullet point

    o Bullet point

As you see in the sample presentation slide, a list follows the introduction. A *bullet point* — punctuation that marks the beginning of every item on the list — is a key element of a presentation slide. Bullet points may be checkmarks, little circles, arrows, or other designs.

In the sample presentation slide, you see three bullet points. You may have two, four, or more. (You cannot have one bullet point.) In a real presentation, a slide may also feature links to video clips and other visual elements (charts, photos, drawings, graphs, and so on). Some individual slides have titles.

A title may take the place of an introduction. Then your slide looks like this.

Title

    o Bullet point

    o Bullet point

    o Bullet point

The title is centered. You may place the title on the left, if you like.

Avoid slides with bullet points but no title or introductory phrase. The audience will stare at the slide and wonder what the list is about. If people are wondering, they are not listening! You want the audience to look at the slide *and* hear what you are saying.

In this section, you find more information about titles and introductions. (To find out how to format, capitalize, and punctuate bullet points, read "Writing Bullet Points," later in this chapter.)

The title

Every presentation has a focus, the topic you are explaining. A phrase stating that focus is the *title* of the presentation. Within the presentation, the main topic divides into subtopics. Each subtopic may have a title also.

A good title fits like a tailored suit. It is not too big. (Picture a suit that you and your best friend could squeeze into together — *not* a fashionable look!)

Nor should the title be too narrow. (A suit does not serve you well if it snags on your hips.) Instead, a title covers everything you say, and nothing more.

Here is an example of a presentation with right and wrong titles:

CONTENT: Information on Germany's industry and trade, including statistics about the auto industry and general manufacturing, estimates of economic growth, and possible trouble spots

TOO-BIG TITLE: Germany: Facts and Figures

WHY IT IS TOO BIG: A presentation with this title might be about population growth, land area, climate, education, and many other things.

TOO-NARROW TITLE: Germany's Auto Industry

WHY IT IS TOO NARROW: Part of the presentation concerns the auto industry, but not all.

JUST-RIGHT TITLE: Germany's Current and Future Economy

WHY IT IS JUST RIGHT: Industry and trade are part of the economy, as are the auto industry and general manufacturing. The "current and future" part of the title takes into account "economic growth" and "possible trouble spots."

Check out one more example:

CONTENT: Examination of the reign of Tutankhamun, a ruler in ancient Egypt, including his associates and family, the change in religion during his reign, his early death, theories about the cause of his death, the discovery of his tomb in the 1920s, and public interest in his life and times.

TOO-BIG TITLE: Ancient Egypt

WHY IT IS TOO BIG: The presentation deals with Tutankhamun, one ruler of ancient Egypt. The title "Ancient Egypt" could cover thousands of years and discuss the daily life of ordinary people, other rulers, foreign relations, art, and many other topics.

TOO-NARROW TITLE: How Tutankhamun Died

WHY IT IS TOO NARROW: This title ignores associates, family, religion, and the discovery of Tutankhamun's tomb.

JUST-RIGHT TITLE: Tutankhamun: Life and Legacy

WHY IT IS JUST RIGHT: Tutankhamun's "life" includes his associates and family, the change in religion, and his death. His "legacy" takes into account his tomb, its discovery, and public interest.

When you place the presentation title on a slide, follow these guidelines:

- ✔ **The title appears on the first slide.** Usually, the title is alone or accompanied by photos or other types of illustration. It may be centered or placed so that it balances the visual material. Save the supporting text for other slides.

- ✔ **Capitalize the important words in the title.** Important words are nouns, verbs, and descriptions. Unimportant words, such as *a, an, the, to, from, by,* and so on should not be capitalized. (For more information on capitalizing titles, turn to Chapter 17.)

- ✔ **Do not enclose the title in quotation marks.** Because the title stands alone, it stands out! Quotation marks identify titles within a paragraph. You do not need them when the title is all by itself.

- ✔ **Do not place a period at the end of a title.** If the title is a question, a question mark appears at the end of the title.

Individual slides may have titles also. The title of a slide, like the title of the presentation as a whole, should refer to all the information on the slide. Stay away from titles that are too general or too narrow. Place the slide title by itself, set off from the rest of the text. You may center the title on the first line of the slide or move it to the side. Do not place quotation marks around the title of a slide. Capitalize the important words. (For more information on capitalizing titles, refer to Chapter 17.)

Test your knowledge of titles. Look at these examples. If you see an error, correct it.

1.

"Learning two languages: benefits and challenges"

2.

Our Class Trip to Peru.

3.

The Care And Feeding Of Canaries And Parakeets

4.

"How the iPod changed the Music Industry" Since the invention of the iPod, the music industry has changed in these ways:

Here are the answers:

1. Remove the quotation marks and capitalize the important words:

Learning Two Languages: Benefits and Challenges

2. Remove the period:

Our Class Trip to Peru

3. Place unimportant words within the title *(and, of, and)* in lowercase:

The Care and Feeding of Canaries and Parakeets

4. Place the title alone on a line. Center it. Remove the quotation marks. The rest of the text makes up your introduction:

How the iPod Changed the Music Industry

Since the invention of the iPod, the music industry has changed in these ways:

The introduction

Bullet points make up the bulk of your presentation. A bulleted list usually begins with an introduction, which may be just a couple of words or a complete sentence. Take a look at these sample introductions:

Entertainment supplied by

The entertainment will be

Entertainment:

The entertainment will be supplied by these bands:

Entertainment includes the following:

The first three examples are not complete sentences, but the last two are (For more information on complete sentences, see Chapter 13.) Which is better? The answer is up to you! You may use either, as long as you capitalize and punctuate properly. ***Note:*** You may see other styles of capitalization and punctuation of presentation slides. Several formats are acceptable. Here I explain one common style. Whatever style you select, be consistent. Do not change the rules from slide to slide.

Here are guidelines for the most common style of punctuation:

- ✔ **When an introduction is a sentence, place a colon at the end.** A colon is one dot atop another (:). If the sentence is a question, a question mark takes the place of a colon. A colon and a question mark should not appear together.

- ✔ **If the introduction is not a complete sentence, you may not need any punctuation at the end.** If you read the introduction and a bullet point together, do they form one sentence? Do they make sense together? If so, do not place a colon after the introduction.

- ✔ **Do not place a colon after *is, was, will be,* and other forms of the verb *be*.** When you see a form of *be,* you know that the thought is incomplete. The bullet point finishes the thought that the introduction begins. Therefore, a colon improperly interrupts the thought.

- ✔ **Capitalize the first word of the introduction.** That is the only word that is capitalized, unless the introduction includes a proper name. (For more information on capitalized names, see Chapter 17.)

- ✔ **The introduction begins at the left margin.** English words move from left to right on a line, so this placement makes sense.

Keep the introduction line short. The audience should be able to take in the idea with a quick glance. If too many words appear on the screen, the audience will not listen to what you are saying.

The rules for introduction lines are the same whether the introduction appears on the screen or on paper. If you are writing a letter or report and plan to include bullet points, follow the preceding guidelines.

Check out the first column, where you see introductions to lists of bullets. If you find a mistake, write the correction in the second column.

Introduction to List   *Corrected Introduction*

1. The fundraiser is:
2. The Marketing Campaign Will Appear In
3. Seven media outlets will participate.
4. Why do we need a fundraiser?:
5. Careers requiring college degrees include the following:

Here are the answers: 1. *The fundraiser is* (remove the colon) 2. *The marketing campaign will appear in* (only capitalize the first letter of the first word) 3. *Seven media outlets will participate:* (use a colon instead of a period) 4. *Why do we need a fundraiser?* (remove the colon) 5. correct.

Writing Bullet Points

Bullet points are punctuation marks. They appear in lists on presentation slides and also on paper. They may be plain (a simple dot) or fancy (a star or an arrow).

In this book, the bullet points at the beginning of a chapter are arrows. Within a chapter, they are checkmarks.

Bullet points are fairly new. If you look at a document that is a century old, you will not find any bullet points. They are popular now because they save time. You can read them quickly and absorb the most useful information with little effort.

Here — in a bulleted list! — are the basic principles of bullet points:

- **Each bullet point presents one idea.** A bulleted list is supposed to be easy to read. If you cram too much information into one bullet point, you lose that advantage.

- **Every list needs more than one bullet point.** Think of bullet points as subdivisions of a topic. You cannot divide a topic into one part.

- **You should introduce the bulleted list.** Occasionally, a slide has a title and a bulleted list, without an introduction. Most lists, though, benefit from a good introduction. For an example, look at the introduction to this bulleted list, which begins with the word *Here* and ends with a colon (one dot atop another).

  The introduction may also be in a different format. Read the section "The introduction," earlier in this chapter, for more information.

Bullet points on a presentation slide may be *very short.* You put a few words on the screen and add information as you speak. Bullet points on paper are often longer. Or, if they are short (as they are at the beginning of this chapter), more information appears later in the chapter or report.

Matching bullets

Police scientists examine bullets to see whether they match the gun at a crime scene. You examine bullets, too, but you do not check guns. Instead, you check grammar. The rule is simple: Every bullet point must have the same grammatical structure. In other words, if one bullet point is a complete sentence, all the bullet points should be complete sentences.

Take a look at the following lists. Notice how they match.

Beverages needed:

- soda
- water
- coffee
- tea

In this list, every bullet point is a noun (in this case, the name of a thing). The bullets on this list match. Here is another example.

The committee will

- prepare a budget
- rent space for the party
- hire the DJ
- sell tickets

Now the bullet points are actions that the committee will do. These bullet points also match. For comparison, next is a list that does *not* match.

All those attending the dance must

- pay cash
- They must show identification.
- wear appropriate clothing
- Rules must be followed.

When you read this list, do you "hear" the mismatches? The first and third items on the list begin with verbs (action words). The second and fourth items on the list are complete sentences.

Here is the corrected list:

All those attending the dance must

- pay cash
- show identification
- wear appropriate clothing
- follow the rules

Now every item on the list begins with a verb, what *those attending the dance must* do.

Check each list of bullet points. If they match, write "correct." If you see a mismatch, change the item that does not fit.

1.

Goals for next year:

- to exercise more

- to eat better

- achieving a healthier lifestyle

2.

At the next meeting, members will discuss the following topics:

- theme of the annual dinner

- outreach to the community

- how the club is perceived

- dues and fees

3.

Wound care

- Not removing the bandage for 24 hours.

- After 24 hours, remove the bandage and wash the area with soap and water.

- Cover the wound with antibiotic cream.

- Place a clean bandage on the wound.

4.

Why should you study engineering?

- many job openings

- earning good salaries

- interesting work

Here are the answers: 1. Replace *achieving a healthier lifestyle* with *to achieve a healthier lifestyle* 2. Replace *how the club is perceived* with *perceptions of the club* 3. Replace *Not removing the bandage for 24 hours* with *Do not remove the bandage for 24 hours.* 4. Replace *earning good salaries* with *good salaries.*

Capitalizing and punctuating bullet points

Do you struggle when you have to capitalize and punctuate bullet points? If so, you have a lot of company! These issues can be confusing. Some involve unbreakable grammar rules, and others are style choices. Never fear. Here is everything you need to know about capital letters and punctuation in bullet points, both for presentation slides or within a report or letter:

- ✔ **Be consistent.** In the preceding section, I discuss matching bullet points in terms of grammar. Capitalization and punctuation should also match. In other words, if one bullet point begins with a capital letter, all the bullet points should begin with capital letters. (You do not always have a choice. See the next bullet point.)

- ✔ **Begin complete sentences with capital letters.** If your bullet point is a complete sentence, you have no choice. The first word in the sentence is always capitalized.

- ✔ **Bullet points that are complete sentences must end with a period, a question mark, or an exclamation point.** This is another grammar rule you must obey. Sentences always end with punctuation marks. Statements conclude with periods. The question mark, of course, is only for bullet points that are questions. Exclamation points are rare, but if you want extra emphasis, choose this punctuation mark.

- ✔ **If the bullet point is not a complete sentence, you do not need an endmark.** Suppose that the bullet points are "cotton," "polyester," and "wool." These bullet points are not complete sentences. You should not place a period after each bullet point.

- ✔ **If a bullet point completes a sentence that the introduction begins, do not capitalize the first word.** Read the introduction to the list along with the bullet point. Do they flow together and form one sentence? If so, do not capitalize the first word. The logic here is that you should not place a capital letter in the middle of a sentence, unless you need the capital for another reason (a name, perhaps). Here is an example:

The actors must

- • attend all rehearsals

- • memorize Act I by Monday

- • wear their costumes every day

As you see, the bullet points create three sentences: *The actors must attend all rehearsals. The actors must memorize Act I by Monday. The actors must wear their costumes every day.*

- ✔ **Some bullet points may begin with capital or lowercase letters.** You get to choose capitals or lowercase letters when the bullet point is not a complete sentence and does not finish a sentence that the introduction begins. Look at these examples. Both are correct:

Director's responsibilities:

- Auditioning actors
- Selecting set designers
- Working with actors

Director's responsibilities:

- auditioning actors
- selecting set designers
- working with actors

Check these bullets. If they are correct, leave them alone. If you find a mistake, fix it.

1.

Graduation requirements:

- Two years of math
- three English courses
- at least 18 credits in elective courses

2.

Our graduates work in many fields:

- medicine
- engineering
- computer programming

3.

Why should you choose our school?

- many graduates continue their studies in the finest graduate schools
- Our placement office finds jobs for 99% of graduating seniors.
- tuition is low.

Here are the answers: 1. Capitalize the first word of every bullet point *(Two, Three, At)* or begin all three with a lowercase letter *(two, three, at)* 2. correct 3. Capitalize *Many* and add a period at the end of the first bullet point. Capitalize *Tuition* in the third bullet point.

Chapter 20

Writing at School and on the Job

In This Chapter

▶ Writing essays and research papers

▶ Creating science laboratory reports

▶ Formatting business letters and memos

*U*nless you are the ruler of the entire world, you have a boss. At school, your boss is a teacher or a professor. At work, your boss is, well, the boss! Writing done for an authority figure — a boss — requires proper English. Plus, when you are writing at school or on the job, you must conform to additional standards — traditions built up over the years.

In this chapter, you take a look at the most common types of school and workplace writing. Mastering these will help you achieve better grades or perhaps a promotion and a higher salary.

A Is for Accomplished: Writing at School

It happens every school day, sometimes more than once a day. Your teacher assigns a report, an essay, a research paper, or something similar. You sigh and wonder, "How long until vacation?" No one likes homework or tests. But grasping the *conventions* — the basic format of these assignments — can make writing them easier.

Essays and research papers

An *essay* is a written discussion of an idea. Usually, an essay expresses a point of view — your opinion on the topic or the conclusion you have drawn from the information you presented in the essay. A *research paper* generally includes information (ideas, opinions, statistics) that you gathered from books, articles, and websites. A research paper may express your own view on the subject or simply present a neutral overview of the topic. In this section are some guidelines for writing these works.

Business people write research papers, too. In the business world, these papers are generally called *reports*. Every guideline you see here applies to both academic papers and business reports.

Formal writing

Essays and research papers are formal. Slang words, a conversational tone, and most abbreviations have no place in these assignments. (You may use abbreviations attached to dates, such as *A.D.* or *C.E.* in formal papers. Both abbreviations refer to the modern or "common" era.) When you are writing an essay or a research paper, pretend that you are arguing a case before a judge or lecturing a group of scholars. The level of formality you would use in a courtroom or lecture hall is your goal. Take a look at these acceptable and unacceptable sentences for this type of assignment:

UNACCEPTABLE SENTENCE: The plot is kind of complicated, with too much stuff to keep track of.

BETTER SENTENCE: With a complicated plot, the novel challenges the reader to keep track of events.

WHY IT IS BETTER: In the first version, *kind of* and *stuff* are too informal. The wording in the second sentence is more mature.

UNACCEPTABLE SENTENCE: The general ordered his troops to attack very late in the battle. Big mistake! Lots of soldiers died.

BETTER SENTENCE: Because the general waited until late in the battle to order an attack, many soldiers died.

WHY IT IS BETTER: *Big mistake* and *lots of* are too informal. Also, the fact that soldiers died shows the mistake. The writer does not have to say *big mistake* at all.

UNACCEPTABLE SENTENCE: This painting is all about color, lots of color, and nothing else but color.

BETTER SENTENCE: The most noticeable characteristic of this painting is its color.

WHY IT IS BETTER: The original version repeats *color* and tries to be cute. Academic writing should be more formal.

Identifying others' ideas

Robbing a bank is a crime. Stealing someone else's ideas is also a crime in the academic world (and sometimes in the business world, too). This crime, *plagiarism,* is a serious offense. Luckily, you can stay on the right side of the law by crediting your sources. You can do so in several different ways.

If you insert someone else's exact words into your own writing, you must be sure that the reader knows you are quoting. Place quotation marks around short quotations and insert them into the text. Take a look at these examples:

> Historian Joan Smith said, "The economic downturn has led to lowered expectations for a better future and contributed to a rise in crime."

> According to Smith, the trade agreement signed last year "damaged many parts of the economy," bringing hardship to a large number of people.

> "Unemployment for factory workers will not improve for at least five years," she added.

> She claims that the job market is "at crisis level in nearly every area of the country."

The quotation marks tell you what Joan Smith said. If you leave them out, your reader assumes that you linked a bad economy to the crime rate, discovered the consequences of the trade agreement, and analyzed the job market. You did not do these things. Joan Smith did. (Joan Smith is just an example, not a real person.)

As you see in these examples, the quotation may appear at the beginning of the sentence, at the end, or even in the middle. (For more information on punctuating and capitalizing quotations, turn to Chapter 16.)

Quotations that are longer than three lines should be centered as a small block of words. They stand out from the rest of your paper. Take a look at this example. It is not from a real source. I created it just for you:

> Historian Alex Johnson has attempted to determine why the trial attracted so much attention. In *The Trial of Martha Martin,* he writes:

>> *Some see sexism and the narrow roles assigned to women as the cause. However, economic gain is a more likely reason why the media covered the trial in great detail. All the major television networks sent representatives, and thousands of words appeared in traditional newspapers and magazines. Millions followed the trial on various websites. All these media outlets bring in millions of dollars in advertising money.*

> Statistics provided by the Advertising Council support Johnson's view. In 2015, rates for television commercials . . . [The text continues here.]

Notice that the block quotation is not surrounded by quotation marks. The blocking takes the place of that punctuation.

If you are not directly quoting someone else's words in your paper, you may still have to give credit. Information and ideas that are not your own must be identified, even if you change the wording. If you explain Joan Dunne's ideas about the Salem Witch trials, for example, you must give credit to Joan Dunne. (Joan Dunne is not a real person. This name is just an example to illustrate the point.) When you mention statistics, identify the person supplying the statistics. You may identify the source in the text ("Joan Dunne believes that . . .") or in footnotes or parentheses.

Sometimes no name is available for a source. Instead, all you know is the name of the organization (the Advertising Council, perhaps). In this situation, give credit to the organization.

Teachers usually ask you to identify the source of a quotation, idea, or information in a *citation*. A citation is a footnote, a note at the end of a chapter, or a reference in parentheses. Several systems for formatting citations and bibliographies exist, and every teacher has a favorite. So does every subject area. Before you write, *ask* which system your teacher prefers. Then check the Internet or a reference book for the format. You may also need to attach a list of sources to an essay or research paper. You can find out how to format this list in the same place you found the format for citations.

For a longer discussion of research papers and citations, you may wish to take a look at *Research Papers For Dummies* by Geraldine Woods (Wiley, 2002).

Without identifying the source, the reader will think that the idea or information comes directly from you. Give credit where credit is due.

Other formatting issues

Your essay or research paper should have a title. Some teachers do not require this step, but a title helps you focus your ideas. For a long essay or for a research paper, place the title on a separate page. For a short piece of writing, center the title at the top of the page. Do not place quotation marks around the title.

When you write a science paper, capitalize only the first word of the title and the first word of the subtitle, if you have one. Also capitalize proper names. Everything else should be in lowercase. When you write an English, history, or art paper, capitalize all the important words. Place unimportant words — *a, an, the,* and so on — in lowercase. Follow the same system for titles of other works that you mention within your paper. The title of an article should be inside quotation marks. Titles of full length works (novels, nonfiction books, plays, and so on) should be italicized or underlined. For more information on capitalizing titles, check out Chapter 17.

Verb tense also matters when you write an essay or a research paper. In general, use past tense for history papers, except for events that are still going on. Take a look at these examples. The past tense verbs are underlined:

Rosa Parks <u>was</u> an activist for civil rights who <u>played</u> an important role in the Montgomery bus boycott.

Alexander Fleming <u>discovered</u> penicillin in 1928.

Julius Caesar <u>was</u> a Roman general and statesman whose victories <u>extended</u> the territory of the Roman Empire to modern Britain and Germany.

Spanish soldiers, <u>led</u> by Hernando Cortes, <u>defeated</u> the Aztecs and <u>colonized</u> Mexico.

If you write about a work of literature or art, present tense is best. Why? The work does not change. Every time you open the book or look at the painting, the experience begins anew. Here are some examples, with the present tense verbs underlined:

Hamlet <u>kills</u> Polonius by accident.

In Goya's painting, two women <u>stand</u> on a balcony.

The poet <u>calls</u> darkness "comforting" and "tender."

Pip, the main character in the novel, <u>meets</u> a strange man in a cemetery.

Check these bits of essays and research papers. Are they acceptable or not? You decide.

Sample	What It Is	Acceptable or Unacceptable
1. "The Role of the Narrator"	title, centered on a line above an essay	
2. Henry Peters said, The war illustrated the limitations of troops fighting without proper equipment.	sentence in a research paper	
3. The character, in my humble opinion, is way too interested in gossip.	sentence from an essay for English class	
4. The artist believed that his art was unique, but experts have identified many influences on his personal style.	sentence from a research paper about Picasso	
5. Comic Art in France: A Survey	title of a research paper, alone on a title page	
6. Hamlet was angry at his mother.	sentence from an essay for English class	

Here are the answers: 1. Unacceptable. Titles centered alone on a line should not be enclosed by quotation marks. 2. Unacceptable. Quotation marks should enclose *The war illustrated the limitations of troops fighting without proper equipment.* 3. Unacceptable. The language is too informal for an essay. 4. Acceptable 5. Acceptable 6. Unacceptable. When you write about literature, use present tense. The verb *was* should be *is.*

Science lab reports

From middle school through graduate school, most science teachers set aside time for experiments. Students follow a series of steps, observing and collecting *data* (information) along the way. Then they come to a conclusion and write a lab report. Your teacher or professor may give you a sample laboratory report and ask you to format your own work in the same way. (If you do not receive a sample, ask for one!) Science lab reports vary somewhat, but a few rules apply to all.

References to others' experiments

Some lab reports begin with a summary of others' work in the same field. If you refer to the titles of scientific papers in your lab report, capitalize the titles in "sentence style." Capitalize the first word of the title of your report, as well as the first word of the subtitle (if you have one). Capitalize proper names. Everything else appears in lowercase (non-capitals). Here are some examples:

> Pneumonia risk in newborns: The influence of nutrition
>
> Population growth of common whale species
>
> Irrigation techniques in the Gobi Desert: A comparative study

 Generally, you do not need to quote directly from someone else's scientific paper. Scientists want the information, but the exact words are not important. Summarize or state the information in your own words. Be sure to give credit to the source.

Dates are another important element in lab reports. Science constantly moves forward, extending or correcting theories as new information appears. When you refer to someone else's experiment or theory, you should supply the date. The reader then understands how current the information is. Most scientists prefer the date to appear in this order: day-month-year, or, if no day is given, month-year. No commas appear within the date. Here are a few examples of dates in the scientific style:

> 10 May 1999
>
> 26 August 2014
>
> June 2015

If you do not know the day or the month, simply write the year.

Reporting your own actions

Most of your laboratory report explains what you did, how you did it, and what results you obtained. When you report your actions, be specific. Also, write about the experiment, not about yourself. Take a look at these sample sentences:

> BAD SENTENCE: I added sodium.
>
> GOOD SENTENCE: Sodium was added.
>
> WHY IT IS GOOD: *I* is not appropriate in a lab report.

> BAD SENTENCE: We exposed the plant to sunlight.
>
> GOOD SENTENCE: The plant was exposed to sunlight.
>
> WHY IT IS GOOD: The focus of the sentence should be on the action, not on the people performing the action.

> BAD SENTENCE: After the plant flowered, Jean measured the stem.
>
> GOOD SENTENCE: After the plant flowered, the stem was measured.
>
> WHY IT IS GOOD: *Jean* is not important. Focus on the action, not the person.

Notice that the "good" sentences use past tense. The experiment is over, and the report explains what you did and what happened. Present tense does not fit this situation. For the same reason, you should also use past tense when you give information about others' experiments.

Be serious, factual, and formal when you write about an experiment. A science lab report is not the place to make a joke or to let your imagination loose. Present the information clearly. Use simple statements, and stick to formal language.

Other formatting issues

You have to present information you gathered during your experiment. Often you do so visually, in charts, graphs, tables, or diagrams. Each of these visual elements should be numbered and identified. Here is an example of a table.

In a paragraph, you may refer to "Table 1" as you analyze the information. Capitalize "Table."

Table 1	Number of flowers with and without fertilizer treatment		
Plant type	*Number of flowers without fertilizer*	*Number of flowers with fertilizer treatment*	*Average width of flowers*
Rosa abyssinica	2	8	3 cm
Rosa arkansana	0	3	2.8 cm
Rosa carolina	1	1	6 cm

Numbers often appear in lab reports. As you see in the table, scientists use metric units for size, weight, and volume. In other words, you measure *meters, kilograms,* and *liters,* not *yards, pounds,* or *quarts.* Always abbreviate metric units. Most metric abbreviations are not capitalized. (*L* for "liter" and *C* for "Celsius" temperature are exceptions.) Place a space between the number and the metric unit, and omit periods within or after the abbreviation. The same abbreviation works for both singular (one unit) and plural (more than one unit). Take a look at these examples:

> 8 cm (eight centimeters)
>
> 1.5 kg (one point five kilograms)
>
> 55 ml (fifty-five milliliters)
>
> 2 L (two liters)

Take another look at the table. The scientific names of the plants (all types of roses) are italicized. All scientific names of plants and animals require italics. Common names, such as "rose," do not need italics. Generally, the first word of a scientific name is capitalized and the rest is in lowercase. Sometimes, the first word may be abbreviated. Here are some examples, with identification in parentheses:

> *Homo sapiens* (human beings)
>
> *E. coli* (a virus)
>
> *Turdusmigratorius* (robin)

Of course, if you are writing the report with a pen, not on a computer, you cannot italicize. In that case, write the name clearly. Do not attempt to reproduce italics by hand.

Measure your knowledge of scientific style. Are these bits of lab reports acceptable or not? You decide.

Sample	What It Is	Acceptable or Unacceptable
1. Acceleration of falling objects in a vacuum	title, centered alone on a title page	
2. The fertilized rose totally won, in terms of numbers of flowers.	sentence from the conclusion	
3. The fertilizer, I think, made a difference.	another sentence from the conclusion	
4. Approximately 2 ml of fertilizer were added to the soil every day for a month.	sentence explaining the procedure	
5. Temperature was kept at 4° c.	sentence explaining the procedure	

Here are the answers: 1. Acceptable 2. Unacceptable. The language is too informal for a lab report. 3. Unacceptable. Do not use *I* in a lab report. 4. Acceptable 5. Unacceptable. The abbreviation for *Celsius* is *C*, not *c*.

Get to Work: Writing on the Job

In school, you may pay money (tuition and fees) to write. At work, someone pays you to write. That is a better arrangement, don't you think? However, writing on the job can make or break your career. If you write well, you may advance. If you write poorly, you may lose your position. In this section, you take a close look at the most common types of business writing, so every document you create is perfect.

Most word-processing programs provide templates — basic formats — for many types of business communications. When you bring one up on your screen, everything is in the right place. All you have to do is supply the content. In this section, I show you some standard formats and provide guidelines for how to use them correctly.

If your job involves writing business reports, follow the guidelines in the section "Essays and research papers," earlier in this chapter. Business reports are similar to the research papers you write (or wrote) in school.

Letters

Email and phone calls may be taking over the business world, but letters on paper are still around. When you write a business letter, you must include some important elements.

Take a look at this sample letter. Each part is labeled (all labels are in bold). Then read the instructions for each part.

NAME AND ADDRESS OF COMPANY:

Peterman Construction Company
5212 Calla Street
Anytown, New York 10021

DATE:

September 12, 2016

INSIDE ADDRESS:

Mr. George Dodge

1471 Second Avenue

Millerville, VT 05469

GREETING:

Dear Mr. Dodge:

BODY OF THE LETTER:

The repairs to your roof were completed two days ago. We hope that you are satisfied with our work. If you are, we would appreciate your sending us the final payment ($500). We look forward to working with you on future projects.

CLOSING:

Sincerely,

NAME OF SENDER:

Herman Denten

TITLE OF SENDER:

Project Manager

If you are printing the letter on official company paper, the top of the paper probably already has the company's name and address. If it does not, you can add this information yourself.

Take a look at each part of the letter:

- ✔ **The name and address of the company appears at the top of the page.** You may center the business name and do something creative, if you like. The point is to stand out! Do not include the company website or phone number at the top. Instead, place it at the bottom. That way, the reader of the letter will not confuse the two.

- ✔ **The date may begin at the right margin or in the middle of the page.** In the sample you see a month-day-year format *(September 12, 2016)*, but you may also use day-month-year *(12 September 2016)* instead. If the day comes first, do not insert commas. You may also use numbers instead of words *(6* instead of *June,* for example). Be careful, though. In some countries, the day comes before the month. In others, it follows. Your reader may see *9/12* and read it as *September 12* or *December 9.*

- ✔ **The inside address contains the name and address of the person you are writing to.** Use *Mr., Mrs., Ms., Dr.,* or any other title that fits. Capitalize the abbreviation and end the abbreviation with a period. Use both the first and last names, if you know them.

- ✔ **The greeting in a business letter is formal.** Stay away from *Hi, Hello,* and other such words. *Dear* or *To* are better choices. Generally, omit the first name of the person you are writing to. Attach the title (for example, *Mr., Mrs., Ms.,* or *Dr.)* to the last name. Follow the greeting with a colon (one dot atop another), not a comma.

- ✔ **The body of the letter should be simple and dignified.** Formality and courtesy are important when you write to an employee or customer. Steer clear of slang, and do not wander off topic. Write the message in simple, clear language.

- ✔ **The closing appears alone on a line.** *Sincerely, Yours truly, Kind regards,* and similar formal phrases are fine. Do not write *Your friend* or something similar. In business, you do not have friends! You have co-workers, supervisors, and customers. Follow the closing with a comma.

- ✔ **Your name and title, on separate lines, complete the letter.** Include both your first and last names, and a middle initial if you like. Capitalize your title: *Director of Marketing, Sales Assistant,* and so on.

You can adapt this letter format for recommendations, performance reviews, sales opportunities, and many other situations. The only portion of the letter that changes is the body, where the message appears. Everything else stays the same.

Memos

Memos are communications sent within a company — from boss to employee or from one employee to another. They are more formal than most emails. Here is a sample memo, in a popular format.

PERSON RECEIVING THE MEMO:

To: Samantha Friedman

PERSON SENDING THE MEMO:

From: Elizabeth Gordon, Vice President of Marketing

SUBJECT LINE:

Re: Performance review

DATE:

Date: June 12, 2016

MESSAGE:

All sales associates will meet with me individually during the month of July for the annual performance review. Please call my secretary (ext. 333) for an appointment.

As you write a memo, keep these ideas in mind:

- ✔ **When you fill in the "to" and "from" lines, use full names (first and last).** You may include the job title, if you wish. Capitalize the important words in the job title. Remember that *To* and *From* should be followed by colons, not commas.

- ✔ **If you send a copy to another person, include a "CC" line.** *CC* is an old abbreviation. It used to mean *carbon copy,* in the days when copies were made with carbon paper. No one uses carbon paper now, but the abbreviation remains. Most often, this abbreviation is capitalized. Lowercase is also fine. (Choose one or the other. Do not capitalize one letter and not the other.) Either way, follow the abbreviation with a colon. Then write the names of the people who should receive copies.

- ✔ **Write a clear subject line.** You must capitalize the first word. If you like, you may capitalize all the important words, or leave the rest in lowercase. The subject line should be short, just long enough to let the reader know what the memo is about.

✔ **Include the date.** Here you see the traditional month-day-year format. You can change that pattern to day-month-year. You may also drop the name of the month and insert a number (*6* instead of *June,* for example). Be careful, though. In some countries, the day always comes before the month. In others, it follows. Your reader may see 6/12 and read it as *June 12* or *December 6.*

✔ **Keep the body of the memo clear, formal, and short.** Get your message across politely, omitting unnecessary words and comments.

✔ **Initial the memo, but do not sign it.** Place your initials next to your name on the *From* line. Use a pen! A memo has no closing or signature line.

Emails and other electronic media

If you work in an office, you probably send many emails to co-workers, supervisors, and clients. You may also at times send texts or instant messages. These media are fairly new, and they may seem informal. However, you must still follow grammar rules when you write them.

In a business setting, emails and other electronic communications must be somewhat formal. Above all else, the message must be clear. A friend may understand your meaning if you abbreviate and skip some words. A client or a fellow worker may not. Turn to Chapter 18 for more information on electronic media.

See whether you understand how to write a business letter or a memo by completing the following table.

Sample	What It Is	Acceptable or Unacceptable?
1. To Mr. Carmen,	greeting line in a business letter	
2. Peterson 222 Main Street Centerton, NY 11001	inside address of a business letter (name and address of the person receiving the letter)	
3. Very truly yours,	closing of a business letter	
4. 2016 June 14	date of a memo	
5. C.C. Lorna Francis	copy line in a memo	

Here are the answers: 1. Unacceptable. A colon, not a comma, should follow the name. 2. Unacceptable. *Peterson* should not appear all by itself. Add *Mr.* or *Ms.* or whatever title fits. Also insert the first name, if you know it. 3. Acceptable 4. Unacceptable. The year should not appear first. Change to *June 14, 2016* or *14 June 2016.* 5. Unacceptable. Do not insert periods into the abbreviation *CC.* Place a colon after the abbreviation.

Part VI
Common Errors

Perfecting Your English Skills

Little things mean a lot. That is an old saying, and in writing, it's true. Paying attention to spelling, word choice, and word order pays off, convincing your readers that you have mastered the language. The best writers consider these issues:

- **Spelling:** You cannot memorize every word in the English language. There are too many! You can learn some simple rules to improve your spelling. You can also memorize some words that are frequently misspelled. Check Chapter 21 to discover the path to better spelling.

- **Confusing words:** English has many word-twins that sound alike — or almost alike — but differ in meaning. In Chapter 22, you see how to select the proper word for every sentence.

- **Common mistakes:** Descriptions add flavor to your writing. If you place a description in the wrong spot, though, you lose the intended meaning. Pronouns (words such as *he, them,* and so forth) are also useful, but only if they are clear. Chapter 23 shows you to handle descriptions and pronouns. In the same chapter, you see how to avoid double negatives, another mistake that is all too easy to make.

For a bonus article on Conquering Spelling Devils, go online and take a look at www.dummies.com/extras/basicenglishgrammar.

In this part . . .

- ✔ Discover rules that make proper spelling easier.
- ✔ See the difference between *affect* and *effect, principal* and *principle,* and other word-twins.
- ✔ Place descriptions where they belong.
- ✔ Ensure that the meaning of every pronoun is clear.
- ✔ Identify negative statements that work, and those that do not.

Chapter 21

Spelling Your Way to Perfection

*O*ne of the first things readers notice is spelling. If they see "a missteak" (a *mistake*), they may not pay attention to the message. English spelling is hard. You cannot become a perfect speller instantly, but you can improve little by little.

In this chapter, I explain some spelling rules. I also review some words that puzzle many writers. Finally, I tell you how computer programs, smartphone apps, and the dictionary help you become a champion speller.

Following the Rules of English Spelling

In some wonderful languages, what you see is what you say. The written form follows strict rules. You see a pair of letters in many different words, and you say them the same way, every time. Sadly, English is *not* one of those wonderful languages. Read these words aloud:

> th<u>ou</u>ght
>
> d<u>ou</u>gh
>
> d<u>ou</u>bt

The letters *ou* appear in every word. In *thought,* the *ou* sounds like *aw.* In *dough,* the same letters sound like *oh.* In *doubt,* the pair sounds like *ow.* Crazy, right?

You often have to memorize words or look up proper spelling. However, English does follow some patterns. Not many, but some! In this section, I explain a few rules that help you write correctly.

One spelling rule that you should memorize involves a change from *y* to *i* when you add the letters *s* or *es* to make a plural noun (more than one person, place, or thing). For example, the plural of *monkey* is *monkeys,* but the plural of *city* is *cities.* Why? In the first example *(monkeys),* a vowel (*a, e, i, o,* or *u*) comes right before the *y.* The *y* does not change in that situation. In the second example *(city),* the letter before the *y* is not a vowel. In that case, the *y* changes to *i* and you add *es.* For a longer explanation of this rule and more examples, see Chapter 3.

I before E

Do you know this little rhyme?

> *I* before *E*
>
> except after *C*
>
> unless sounded like *A*
>
> as in *neighbor* and *weigh*

The rhyme explains a spelling rule:

- ✔ **The letter *i* comes before the letter *e* most of the time.** Check out these examples: *friend, believe, field, chief, niece.* In every word, the letter *i* is first, followed by the letter *e.*

- ✔ **After the letter *c*, put the letter *e* before the letter *i*.** Take a look at these examples: *receive, ceiling, deceive, receipt.* After the letter *c* in every word, you see *ei.*

- ✔ **If the letters *e* and *i* combine to sound like the letter *a*, the *e* comes before the *i*.** Here are some examples: *neighbor, weigh, vein, reign, freight.* Do you hear the *a* sound in each? That sound comes from the *ei.*

Some words do not follow this rule. Here are a few: *ancient, their, science, efficient, fancied.* If you are not sure how to spell a word, check the dictionary.

In this table, you find some correctly spelled words and a couple of mistakes. If you see a mistake, write the proper spelling in the second column.

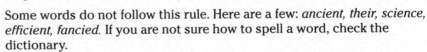

Word	Correct? Proper Spelling?
1. acheive	
2. shield	
3. breif	
4. their	
5. thief	
6. wieght	

Here are the answers: 1. *achieve* 2. correct 3. *brief* 4. correct 5. correct
6. *weight*.

Double letters

Take a look at the pairs in this table. In the first column, you see a word with
the vowel underlined. (Vowels are *a, e, i, o,* and *u.*) In the second column, you
see the word with the letters *ed* or *ing* added to the end.

Original	With ed or ing
bag	bagging
dot	dotted
hit	hitting
set	setting
cut	cutting

Did you notice that the last letter of the original word doubles when you add
ing or *ed* to the end? These words have some things in common:

- ✔ The original words are short. They have just one *syllable,* or sound.

- ✔ In the original words, the vowels are also *short.* A vowel is one of these
  letters: *a, e, i, o, u.* Any vowel can be short or long. A short vowel does
  not say its name. Say the words in the first column, and listen to the
  vowels. In *hit,* for example, you do not hear the name of the letter *i.*
  To see the difference, say these words and listen to the long vowels in
  them: *okay* (long *o,* long *a*), *be* (long *e*), *sigh* (long *i*), *cute* (long *u*).

- ✔ In the table, the original words do not end with vowels. The word *bag,*
  for example, ends with the letter *g.* The letter *g* is not a vowel. All the letters that are not vowels are *consonants.*

When you add *ed* or *ing* to a short word with a short vowel that ends with a
consonant, double the consonant.

Sometimes you double the final consonant in longer words, too, when you add *ed* or *ing*. Read these words. Pay attention to the sound of the original words in the first column:

Original	*With ed or ing*
begin	begi<u>nn</u>ing
occur	occu<u>rr</u>ed
commit	commi<u>tt</u>ing
control	contro<u>ll</u>ed

When you say the original words aloud, you hear that the accent — the stress — is on the last part of the word. You say

> beGIN, not BEgin

In this situation, the final consonant doubles when you attach *ed* or *ing*.

In this table, you find some correctly spelled words and a couple of mistakes. If you see a mistake, write the proper spelling in the second column.

Word	*Correct? Proper Spelling?*
1. claimmed	
2. planned	
3. spinning	
4. puting	
5. runing	
6. beged	

Here are the answers: 1. *claimed* 2. correct 3. correct 4. *putting* 5. *running* 6. *begged*.

Double letters cause trouble in other situations, too. See "Mastering Spelling Demons," later in this chapter, for more information.

Dropping the silent E

Read these words. Notice that the last vowel, an *e,* is silent:

> serve
>
> love
>
> compete

remove

dine

hope

rule

Many English words end with a silent *e.* Often, if you skip that last letter, you end up with a completely different word. *Hate* becomes *hat,* and *hope* turns into *hop.* Do not forget to place the silent *e* where it is needed!

Say *hate* and *hat* aloud. Do you hear the difference in the letter *a?* Often, the silent *e* is a signal that the vowel before it is long. That's why *hate* has a long vowel *(a),* and *hat* has a short vowel (also *a*).

The rule for words ending with a silent *e* has two parts:

✔ Keep the silent *e* if you add letters to the end of the word, and the first added letter is a consonant (any letter except *a, e, i, o,* or *u*):

- hate — hate<u>ful</u>
- pale — pale<u>ness</u>
- manage — manage<u>ment</u>

✔ Drop the silent *e* if you add letters to the end of the word, and the first added letter is a vowel (*a, e, i, o,* or *u*):

- arrive — arriv<u>ing</u>
- pure — pur<u>ity</u>
- nerve — nerv<u>ous</u>

You probably will not be surprised to hear that the silent *e* rule has exceptions. All English spelling rules have exceptions! Here is one:

dye (to change the color of cloth) — dyeing

As always, if you are not sure how to spell a word, check the dictionary.

See how well you know the silent *e.* If you see a misspelled word in the first column, write the correct spelling in the second column. To help you, the words you are looking at are in sentences and underlined.

Word	*Correct? Proper Spelling?*

1. A tiger's <u>bit</u> can kill you.
2. Mary is <u>givving</u> a concert this evening.
3. <u>Haveing</u> a cold is miserable, but if you <u>takcar</u> of yourself, you will heal soon.
4. Andrew was <u>driving</u> when he <u>hite</u> that tree.
5. If the soap is <u>pur</u>, it will float.
6. Play <u>nicely</u> with the other children!

Here are the answers: 1. *bite* 2. *giving* 3. *Having, take, care* 4. correct, *hit* 5. *pure* 6. correct.

Mastering Spelling Demons

You may be wondering what "spelling demons" are. No, they are not supernatural monsters. Spelling demons are groups of words that often trick writers. Many people misspell them. With a little care, though, you will always spell these words correctly.

How does the word end?

Read this paragraph. Look closely at the underlined words:

> Sandy was absent from school because she went to see the <u>doctor</u>. She was not ready for the <u>grammar</u> test. Sandy's mom, a <u>professor</u>, wrote a note to the <u>teacher</u>. "Please excuse my <u>daughter</u> from this exam," she wrote.

Every underlined word ends in *ar, er,* or *or.* These ending letters are different, but when you say the words aloud, the endings sound the same. (Isn't English great? Three ways to spell the same sound! Three spelling problems!) When you write these words, be careful. Here is a table to help you remember.

AR Endings	*ER Endings*	*OR Endings*
grammar	lawyer	doctor
scholar	plumber	tutor
dollar	builder	actor
collar	better	mentor
polar	counter	bachelor

AR Endings	ER Endings	OR Endings
burglar	writer	author
circular	kinder	director
molar	anger	editor
similar	climber	creator
spectacular	gangster	favor

The word *kinder* is a comparison: "Mary is *kinder* than Tom." When you are making a comparison, the word usually ends with *er*.

Another type of spelling demon is a word that ends with either *ant* or *ent*. These three-letter groups sound the same, so they are easy to confuse. Check this table:

ANT Ending	ENT Ending
important	different
pleasant	dependent
constant	argument
elegant	requirement
assistant	accent
instant	adolescent
irrelevant	client
immigrant	department
protestant	employment
tenant	monument

One more pair of word endings — *ible* and *able* — also confuses people. Read the words in this table:

IBLE Words	ABLE Words
visible	dependable
possible	washable
incredible	affordable
horrible	acceptable
sensible	understandable
responsible	reasonable

No rule guides you automatically to the right choice between *ible* and *able*. However, *able* generally attaches to complete words. If you cross out *able* in every word in the second column, you see a real word (*depend, wash,* and so on). If you cross out *ible,* you do not find a real word.

If you read these lists aloud once a week, gradually you will remember how to spell the words. Of course, these lists could be much longer! Many English words end the same way. If you do not know how to spell an ending, the dictionary helps.

One or two?

Are you *dissapointed* or *disappointed* or *disapointed* in your spelling skills? Deciding when to double a letter is annoying. Most often, you have to memorize the spelling. (One rule will help you figure out whether you need to double a letter when you add *ing* or *ed* to a word. See "Following the Rules of English Spelling," earlier in this chapter, for more information.)

Here are some demons that give you double trouble. I underline the spots where many people make a spelling error (doubling when one letter is needed or placing one letter where two is correct):

enroll	disgust	wedding	usually
embarrass	baggage	really	sudden
apartment	occur	commitment	excellent
opposite	unnatural	casually	lose (not be able to find)
appear	special	immediately	loose (not tight)

Two phrases are sometimes mistakenly written as one word, when two words are correct: *a lot* (many) and *all right* (fine, agreed).

Which vowel?

Vowels — *a, e, i, o, u* — can confuse spellers. Long vowels (those that sound like the name of the letter, like the *e* in *be*) are easier than short vowels (like the *e* in *wet*). Why? Short vowels often sound like each other. Also, sometimes their sound blends into the word, so you may not realize that they are present. Here are some spelling demons that cause vowel problems. The trouble spots are underlined:

separate	definite	cause	among
persuade	recognize	despair	jewelry
obey	nursery	division	officer
extraordinary	February	category	disguise

Correct or misspelled? You decide. If you find a mistake, write the proper spelling in the second column of the following table.

Word   **Correct? Proper Spelling?**

1. carpentor
2. speler
3. independant
4. catagory
5. occurr
6. calendar

Here are the answers: 1. *carpenter* 2. *speller* 3. *independent* 4. *category* 5. *occur* 6. correct.

Checking the Dictionary for Spelling Help

Rules and memory provide wonderful help with spelling. Sometimes, though, no rule applies, and you cannot remember how to spell a word. That is the time to seek help. The dictionary is the final authority on English spelling — and much more. You can turn to a book or to an online dictionary. Both give you the same information.

Dictionaries list words in alphabetical order. It is difficult to look up a word if you do not have a clue how to spell it. Try turning to the section that seems to match the first couple of letters in the word you need. (If you are working with an online dictionary, type those letters.) Look around a bit until you see a word that matches the meaning you want.

Some smartphones come with a program that recognizes speech. If you say the word, it appears on the screen. Before you use that spelling, check the word in a dictionary. The phone cannot tell the difference between many common words, so *lead* (the metal) may turn into *led* (directed, ruled). Check the definition of the word before you insert it into your writing. Be sure that the definition matches the meaning you want.

Dictionaries are great, but so are people. If a teacher or a friend who is a good speller is nearby, ask! Most people feel good about assisting others and will happily spell a word for you.

Each word in the dictionary is explained in an *entry*. Dictionary entries can be confusing because they throw in a lot of information. Here is a sample dictionary entry of the word *comfort:*

> **comfort** ˈkəm - fərt
>
> v. 1. to ease someone's worry or pain. "The doctor will comfort the injured child." 2. to help someone deal with grief. "Mourners at the funeral comfort the family."
>
> n. 1. the act of comforting. "Jane offered comfort to her friend." 2. the quality of ease. "In this car, you travel in comfort." 3. a physical feeling characterized by lack of pain or stress. "Bill valued comfort more than convenience."

Here is how to read this entry:

- ✔ **First you see the word.** I placed *comfort* in bold type. You may see it that way or in a different color or typeface.

- ✔ **Next is the pronunciation.** Online, you can listen to someone say the word. On paper, a set of special symbols tells you how to pronounce the word. The key to the symbols appears at the beginning or the end of the dictionary.

- ✔ **The part of speech appears next.** Usually, this information is abbreviated. You see *v.* for *verb* and *n.* for *noun.* Other words may be labeled as *adj.* (adjective) or *adv.* (adverb). You also find *p.* for *pronoun, prep.* for *preposition,* and *conj.* for *conjunction.* One abbreviation, *int. (interjection)* is rare because not many words fall into this category.

- ✔ **Definitions are numbered in the order of importance.** The most common definition comes first, followed by other meanings that appear less frequently.

- ✔ **Most dictionaries include sample sentences.** These sentences show you how to use the word properly.

The dictionary may also tell you the origin of the word. *Comfort,* for example, comes from the Latin language (meaning "with strength").

The format of your dictionary may be a little different. Do not worry! All the information you need should still be there.

Chapter 22

Tricky Word Traps

• •

In This Chapter

▶ Exploring sound-alike words with different meanings

▶ Knowing the difference in meaning between one- and two-word expressions

▶ Avoiding incorrect expressions

• •

Do you know any identical twins? At first, they appear to be exactly the same. After a while, you learn that Barry loves sports, and Ben hates them. Helena sings opera, and Susan cannot stay in tune. English has some identical twins also. Like humans, identical word-twins are the same in some ways and different in others. The English language also includes word pairs that are nearly, but not exactly the same.

Both types of word-twins stump many writers. In this chapter, you take a close look at them so you can choose the right word for every sentence. You also examine some common expressions that are not correct in Standard English.

Same Sounds, Different Spelling: Sorting Out Word Pairs

When you fall, are you in <u>pain</u> or in <u>pane</u>? Do you <u>accept</u> or <u>except</u> an award?

In the first sentence, the underlined words sound exactly the same. Their definitions, though, are totally different. In the second sentence, the underlined words sound nearly the same. They too differ in meaning.

In this section, you sort out these confusing words.

Homonyms

Is a <u>principal</u> or a <u>principle</u> running your school?

These words are *homonyms* — a fancy term for words that sound the same but look different and mean different things. Why does English have these confusing pairs? Just to make your life miserable. Okay, I'm joking. Your life does not have to be miserable! In this section, you learn some common homonyms, so you know which spelling expresses the meaning you want.

Study these sentence pairs. Pay close attention to the underlined word and the explanations that follow each pair.

> The ball broke a <u>pane</u> of glass.

> When the ball landed on my foot, I cried out in <u>pain</u>.

A *pane* is a sheet of glass in a window. A window may have only one pane, or it may be divided into smaller units, usually with wooden or metal strips. The piece of glass in each section is a *pane*. *Pain* is the discomfort you feel when you are hurt or sick. Both *pane* and *pain* are nouns. That is, they name things.

Now examine this pair:

> He believes in the <u>principle</u> of fair play.

> The <u>principal</u> told the students to be quiet.

A *principle* is a basic belief, a standard that guides behavior. A *principal* is a person with authority. Usually, a *principal* has power over an entire group. In a school, for example, the *principal* gives orders to the teachers and to the students. Some people remember the spelling of this word by saying, "The princi<u>pal</u> is a <u>pal</u>." *Principal* may also be a banking term. If you need money, the *principal* is the amount you borrow. If you invest money, the *principal* is the sum you invest:

> Most borrowers pay interest on a loan first, and then they repay the <u>principal</u>.

> Jean never withdrew the interest she earned from that stock. Instead, she added her earnings to the <u>principal</u>. Each year, her savings grew.

In these examples, *principle* and *principal* are nouns — names of people and things. *Principal* may also function as a description, meaning "most important." For example:

> The <u>principal</u> reason for changing careers was boredom. She hated her job!

In this example, *principal* is an adjective. For more information on nouns, see Chapter 3. Turn to Chapter 6 to learn about adjectives.

Do you know the difference between these three short, confusing words?

> Walk <u>to</u> the library.
>
> Borrow <u>two</u> books.
>
> Max needs books <u>too</u>.
>
> Do not spend <u>too</u> much time at the library.

To means "toward." *Two* is a number. *Too* may mean "also." This meaning appears in the third example sentence. Sometimes *too* means "overly." That is the definition of *too* in the last example.

Now look at another set of three:

> The <u>vain</u> actors admired their photos.
>
> The doctor injected medicine into a <u>vein</u>.
>
> There is a weather <u>vane</u> on the roof.

People who are *vain* are too proud of themselves, especially of their physical appearance. A *vain* person may also brag about intelligence, wealth, or another quality. If you call someone *vain,* you are not giving praise. *Veins* are blood vessels. A *vane* is a weather instrument. A *vane* usually sits on a roof. It turns to show the direction of the wind.

Here are still more triples:

> <u>Buy</u> a bathing suit before you go on vacation.
>
> "<u>Bye</u>!" said Sally as she left.
>
> The best suits were designed <u>by</u> Simone.

Buy means "purchase." In Standard English, *buy* is always a verb — an action. Some people also use *buy* as a noun:

> Only fifty dollars! You got a good <u>buy</u>!

This usage is fine in friendly conversations, but it is not correct in formal writing. *Bye* is short for *goodbye.* It is correct, but less formal than the full word. *By* is a preposition, a word that reveals a relationship. (For more information on prepositions, turn to Chapter 7.) In the example sentence, *by* relates *designed* to *Simone* and shows that *Simone designed the best suits. By* may also mean "near" or "past":

> Gloria rode her bicycle on the path <u>by</u> the highway.

Are you tired of triplets? Try this pair:

> I am pleased that you feel better.

> Your <u>eye</u> has healed well, and you can see perfectly.

I is the person speaking or writing. An *eye* is a body part that you see with.

I, myself, and *me* all refer to the speaker or writer. These words are not interchangeable. You cannot substitute one for another. To understand the correct usage of *I, myself,* and *me,* read Chapter 4.

Take a look at this pair:

> Drew will <u>be</u> here soon, and he will not <u>be</u> pleased with your behavior.

> Did that <u>bee</u> sting you?

Be is a verb. *Be* means "appear" or simply expresses what *is* — a state of being. A *bee* is an insect, the kind that buzzes, stings, and makes honey. *Bee* is a noun.

Check out this pair:

> Come <u>here</u> now.

> I <u>hear</u> loud music.

Here means "this place." *Hear* is "to sense sound" — what you do when you listen.

Do you have the energy for more? Look at these sentences:

> The <u>weather</u> has been terrible this winter.

> He is deciding <u>whether</u> to go away for vacation or to stay home.

Weather refers to temperature, rain, sun, and so on — the daily conditions you experience when you are outside. *Whether* sets up a choice between two actions. Sometimes both actions appear in the sentence, as they do in the second example sentence. Sometimes, a sentence with *whether* does not state two actions:

> She did not tell us <u>whether</u> she would attend the party.

In this example sentence, the words "or not" are understood. Here is the sentence again, with those words added in:

> She did not tell us <u>whether or not</u> she would attend the party.

Check this pair:

> The general <u>led</u> the troops into battle.

> <u>Lead</u> paint is dangerous.

Led is an action in the past. It means "directed." *Lead,* pronounced the same way as *led,* is a type of metal.

Lead, pronounced with a long *e* (when you hear the name of the letter *e*), is an action in the present. It means "to direct." Here is an example of *lead* (long *e*) in a sentence:

> George and Martin always <u>lead</u> the committee.

Unless you need to stop for a moment and take a break, examine these sentences:

> A driver presses the <u>brake</u> to stop the car.

> <u>Brake</u> well in advance of the railroad crossing.

> I hope the dishes do not <u>break</u> in the moving van.

> Sally needs a <u>break</u>, so she will rest now.

In the first example, *brake*, a noun, is a mechanical object that slows or stops motion. In the second example, *brake* is a verb, representing the action of slowing or stopping. In the third example, *break* is also an action word meaning "to crack or split." In the last example, a *break*, a noun, is a rest or a pause in action.

Keep your energy up! Here is the last set:

> In the <u>past</u>, only men were allowed to vote.

> She walked <u>past</u> the bank.

> Mary <u>passed</u> the other runners and won the race.

The *past* is a noun meaning "the time before the present." *Past* may also be a preposition, relating ideas. In the second example sentence, *past* means "in front of" or "farther along." In the last example, *passed* means "went in front of."

You probably noticed that *passed* and *past* can share one meaning: "in front of." *Passed* is an action that took place before the present time. It means "went in front of." *Passed* is a verb. When "Mary passed," she did something. *Past,* when it means "in front of," describes a movement. It is not an action and is not a verb. For more information on verbs, see Chapter 5.

Apostrophes — little curved hooks raised above the line — change meaning. Chapter 14 helps you decide between *your* and *you're, they're* and *there, who's* and *whose,* and *it's* and *its.*

Spell-check programs on a computer or smartphone do not detect the difference between a homonym and its partner. For example, you can write

> Eye sea the whether vain.

when what you really mean is

> I see the weather vane.

The computer accepted the first sentence, which makes no sense. If you are unsure about the spelling of a word, check the dictionary.

See whether you can choose the correct word for each blank. Your choices appear in parentheses.

1. _____ (I, eye) watched television for ten hours, and now my right _____ (I, eye) hurts.

2. What path _____ (led, lead) you to a career in medicine?

3. The decision is based on the _____ (principal, principle) of justice for all, according to the school _____ (principal, principle).

4. "I do not want to talk about the _____ (past, passed)," said Anne as she _____ (past, passed) the house she once lived in.

5. _____ (To, Two, Too) hours is _____ (to, two, too) much time _____ (to, two, too) waste on homework.

Here are the answers: 1. *I, eye* 2. *led* 3. *principle, principal* 4. *past, passed* 5. *Two, too, to.*

Similar, but not alike: Other word pairs

> Please <u>accept</u> my apology. I invited everyone <u>except</u> you to my party.

Okay, I am lying. I never give parties. If I did, I would invite you! I wrote those sentences to show you some word pairs that are spelled nearly the same. They are close in sound, also, but not in meaning.

Check out this example:

> "I <u>accept</u>!" cried Maria when we offered her the job.

> Everyone <u>except</u> Mark applied to that college.

Accept means "agree to." You can *accept* a job, a marriage proposal (congratulations!), a prison sentence (oh no!), and many other things. *Accept* is a verb, an action that someone does. *Except* is a word that places limits. It means "not including." If all the boys *accept* Roger, they like him. They let him be part of their group. If the group includes all the boys *except* Roger, they do not like him. They do not allow him into their group. *Except* is a preposition, a word that shows the relationship between one idea and another in a sentence. (For more information on verbs, refer to Chapter 5. For everything you ever wanted to know about prepositions, turn to Chapter 7.)

Now look at this pair of demons. (I say "demons" because many, many people have trouble with these words.)

> Lynn's actions <u>affect</u> the team.

> The <u>effect</u> of her laziness is obvious, because the players work harder when she is absent.

Affect is a verb. It means "to influence." In the first example sentence, Lynn's actions influence the players. Perhaps she arrives late to practice. Maybe she sits on the sidelines, complaining. Whatever Lynn does *affects* the team. In the second example sentence, *effect* is a noun. The definition of *effect* is "result or consequence." (You may have heard the expression "cause and *effect*.")

Now go shopping for the perfect outfit. Some items are available for free!

> The blue skirt and the yellow jacket are <u>complementary</u>.

> Dan gave Angela a <u>complimentary</u> scarf because she shops at his store often.

Complementary is a description. When things or people are *complementary,* they go well together. Reread the first example sentence. Picture a lovely outfit. The skirt and the jacket would each look fine alone. When they are together, however, they are even more attractive. The blue skirt makes the yellow look brighter, and the yellow jacket mellows the blue. *Complimentary* — with just one different letter — means "free." This word is also a description. In the second example sentence, Angela pays nothing for the scarf. How nice of Dan to reward a loyal customer with a free gift!

Now look at these almost-twins:

> David bought paper at that <u>stationery</u> store.

> David bought <u>stationery</u> with his company credit card.

> She rides her <u>stationary</u> bicycle every day.

Stationery may be a noun or a description. If it's a noun, it means "school or office supplies" such as paper, pens, envelopes, and so on. If it's a description, it tells you about the place where these supplies are bought, sold, or stored. *Stationary* is a description meaning "fixed in one spot, not moving or changing."

See whether you can select the correct word from the pairs in parentheses.

1. A little ____ (past, passed) the library, traffic came to a standstill because of a fallen tree.

2. The entire senior class, ____ (accept, except) for Peggy, voted to postpone the graduation ceremony until Judy could attend and ____ (accept, except) the award for "most courageous student."

3. The ____ (affect, effect) of your decision to change jobs is huge. Moving to another country will (affect, effect) the entire family.

4. The ____ (stationary, stationery) store sells paper, ink, and sticky notes.

5. Population growth is ____ (stationary, stationery), neither increasing nor decreasing.

6. When you buy eye shadow and lipstick, be sure the colors are ____ (complimentary, complementary). Also, do not forget to ask for your ____ (complimentary, complementary) lesson from our makeup artist.

Here are the answers: 1. *past* 2. *except, accept* 3. *effect, affect* 4. *stationery* 5. *stationary* 6. *complementary, complimentary*.

Together or Apart? One- and Two-Word Expressions

Read these sentences. Pay special attention to the underlined words:

Vince told his brothers that he wanted them <u>all ready</u> to go before he came home from work.

When he called them at eleven, he discovered that they had <u>already</u> left.

If you say *already* and *all ready* aloud, they sound the same. On paper, they are not the same at all. Plus, the single word and two-word expressions mean different things. *Already* means "before now" or "before a certain time." *All ready* means "completely prepared." Quite a difference!

The English language has many pairs that change in meaning depending on whether they are written as one word or two. Here is another set:

"I need <u>some time</u> alone," cried Jane.

Henry promised to visit his friends <u>sometime</u> next year.

Some time means "a period of time." You know that you need two words when you can substitute an exact amount of time in the sentence. Look at the first example sentence. Jane might say, "I need an hour alone." The meaning of the sentence is the same. As one word, *sometime* refers to a moment in time without saying exactly when that moment occurs. In the second example sentence, Henry promises a visit, but it may be in February, April, November, or some other month.

Sometimes (with an *s*) means "from time to time, occasionally." Here is an example:

<u>Sometimes</u> Peter and Rebecca go to the gym on Friday, but Monday is their usual day.

In other words, you may find Peter and Rebecca at the gym on a Friday, because they choose that day occasionally. You are more likely to find them at the gym on a Monday.

The next pair is similar:

Carl was busy and would not allow Roger <u>any time</u> to speak.

Bill said Roger could phone him <u>anytime</u>.

The two-word expression *any time* means "a period of time, no matter how short." This expression usually appears in a negative statement, as in the first example sentence. In other words, Carl will not spend even one minute listening to Roger. *Anytime,* as one word, means "at every point in time, with no exceptions." In the second example sentence, Bill has given Roger permission to call in the middle of the night, during work hours, over the weekend — whenever!

Glance at another pair:

<u>Every day</u>, Glen washes the dishes.

The <u>everyday</u> plates are good enough for Mary. Glen uses his best plates only when her mother visits.

These expressions are nearly the same, but the tiny difference in meaning is important. *Every day* means "each day, with no exceptions." In the first example sentence, Glen is at the sink on Monday, Tuesday, Wednesday, and all the other days. He never gets a break! *Everyday* means "ordinary, used all the time." In the second example, Mary does not matter much to Glen. He gives her the plates he uses when he is alone. Mary's mother, on the other hand, is special. She deserves the good dishes!

Now move from time to place. Check these sentences:

> Is there <u>some place</u> where we can speak privately?

> Tired of staying home, Louis wanted to go <u>someplace</u> for vacation.

As two words, *some place* means "a place." In the first example sentence, *some place* might refer to an empty room, a broom closet, an alley, or another location. The single word, *someplace,* is the same as *somewhere.* It refers to a location — any location, with no exceptions.

Somewhere is always one word, never two. *A lot, all right, each other,* and *even though* should always be written as two words.

Do you need one word or two? Select the correct expression from the parentheses.

1. "Stop cleaning," ordered Ellen. "The kitchen, the pantry, and the dining room are _____ (already, all ready) for the inspection. Plus, the inspector has _____ (already, all ready) given us a passing grade."

2. Don _____ (some time, sometime, sometimes) does his homework early, especially when he has _____ (some time, sometime, sometimes) to spare.

3. The secretaries deal with _____ (everyday, every day) tasks, but emergencies are the director's responsibility.

4. The announcer said, "No appointments are necessary. Come in _____ (any time, anytime)."

5. I looked for _____ (some place, someplace) to put my coat, but the closet was too crowded.

Here are the answers: 1. *all ready, already* 2. *sometimes, some time* 3. *everyday* 4. *anytime* 5. *some place.*

Staying Away from Improper Expressions

Should you <u>try and</u> learn proper English? No! I imagine my answer is puzzling. After all, you are reading a book about English grammar. The reason I answered "no" is that "try and" is an incorrect expression. You are not performing two separate actions: (1) *try* and (2) *learn*. Here is the proper wording:

Should you <u>try to</u> learn proper English?

Now the answer is yes! This sentence properly refers to an action, *to learn*, that you *should try*.

Try and is just one common, but incorrect, expression. In this section, you find many words and phrases that you see and hear all the time. The fact that many people write them, however, does not make them right.

Take a look at these sentences:

WRONG: <u>Irregardless</u> of the cost, Anne wants to buy that car.

WHY IT IS WRONG: *Irregardless* is not a Standard English word.

RIGHT: <u>Regardless</u> of the cost, Anne wants to buy that car.

ALSO RIGHT: <u>Despite</u> the cost, Anne wants to buy that car.

WRONG: <u>Being that</u> Anne is on a tight budget, she should not buy an expensive car.

WHY IT IS WRONG: *Being that* is not a Standard English expression.

RIGHT: <u>Because</u> Anne is on a tight budget, she should not buy an expensive car.

WRONG: <u>The reason is because</u> her salary was lowered.

WHY IT IS WRONG: In Standard English, the word *because* should not follow *the reason is*.

RIGHT: <u>The reason is that</u> her salary was lowered.

WRONG: This ancient vase is <u>very unique</u>.

WHY IT IS WRONG: The definition of *unique* is "one of a kind." Saying that something is "very one of a kind" makes no sense.

RIGHT: This ancient vase is <u>unique</u>.

WHY IT IS RIGHT: The sentence now states that no other vase is like *this ancient vase*. It is the only one of its kind.

ALSO RIGHT: This ancient vase is <u>very unusual</u>.

WHY IT IS RIGHT: *Unusual* means "rare." If the vase is *very rare,* only a few exist. This sentence makes sense.

Lots of people say *between you and I,* but that phrase is incorrect. The correct expression is *between you and me.* For more information, refer to Chapter 4. Three other common errors are *could of, would of,* and *should of.* In proper English, you should write *could have* or *could've, would have* or *would've,* and *should have* or *should've.* Turn to Chapter 14 for a complete explanation.

Look at the underlined words in this table. If they are incorrect, write the proper expression in the second column.

Sentence   *Correction*

1. Bert seldom washed his clothes; <u>irregardless,</u> Amy admired his wardrobe.
2. Amy always <u>tries to</u> see the best in people.
3. This quality is <u>very unique</u>.
4. The <u>reason is because</u> most people enjoy criticizing others.
5. <u>Despite</u> the fact that criticism can be helpful, Amy prefers praise.

Here are the answers: 1. *regardless* 2. correct 3. *unique* or *very unusual* 4. *reason is that* 5. correct.

Moving in the opposite direction with "dis"

Three letters attached to the beginning of a word can turn a word into its opposite. Have a look at *dis:*

Disrespectful means "not showing respect." "Charlie hated the <u>disrespectful</u> way Alice behaved. He told her that she should not refer to the teacher as "dude" and should stop interrupting the lessons."

Disconnect means "breaking a connection, unplugging." "Alice <u>disconnected</u> the hair dryer and placed it in the closet. She tried to call Charlie, but her phone had been <u>disconnected</u> because she had not paid her bill."

Disability means "not having the ability." "Roy did not think of his <u>disability</u> as a problem. In fact, he said that because he could not speak, he had more time to think."

Discontinue means "stop, not continue." "Peter <u>discontinued</u> his subscription to that magazine when they raised the price."

Dislike means "not like." "Bob <u>dislikes</u> chocolate, so he gave the candy bar to his brother."

Of course, *dis* does not always create an opposite. *Distant* is not the opposite of *tant,* because *tant* is not a word.

Chapter 23

Avoiding Common Mistakes

*W*hen you ride a bicycle, you must steer around potholes. Otherwise, you fall! When you write, you must steer around some grammar potholes — spots that can easily trip you up.

In this chapter, you find out how you can ensure that descriptions and pronouns express the meaning you intend. You also find out how to avoid *double negatives,* sentences that turn your intended meaning upside down.

Writing Clear Descriptions

In English, word order matters. To describe the color of clothing, I can write

Herb wears <u>green</u> pants.

but not

<u>Green</u> Herb wears pants.

or

Herb wears pants <u>green</u>.

or

Herb <u>green</u> wears pants.

In these examples, it is easy to see that descriptions in the wrong place make no sense. Sometimes, though, a misplaced description is harder to spot. In the sections that follow, you discover several types of description errors.

Descriptions attached to the wrong word

Take a look at this sentence. Pay close attention to the underlined description. Can you figure out why it is in the wrong place?

William hailed a taxi <u>standing on the sidewalk</u>.

The description, *standing on the sidewalk,* appears right after *taxi.* In general, descriptions apply to the closest word. Yet the *taxi* is not *standing on the sidewalk.* (If it is, the police will give the driver a ticket!) *William* is *standing on the sidewalk.* The solution is to move the description closer to *William.* Take a look at these two sentences, with descriptions placed so that *William,* not the *taxi*, is *on the sidewalk:*

<u>Standing on the sidewalk</u>, William hailed a taxi.

William, <u>standing on the sidewalk</u>, hailed a taxi.

Here are other examples:

WRONG: James read the eye chart tacked on the wall <u>with one eye covered</u>.

WHY IT IS WRONG: The *wall* does not have *one eye covered.*

RIGHT: <u>With one eye covered</u>, James read the eye chart tacked on the wall.

ALSO RIGHT: James, <u>with one eye covered</u>, read the eye chart tacked on the wall.

WHY THEY ARE RIGHT: The description *with one eye covered* appears next to *James.*

WRONG: The doctor's report described James's eyesight <u>which was typed on the computer</u>.

WHY IT IS WRONG: *James's eyesight* is not *typed on the computer.*

RIGHT: The doctor's report <u>typed on the computer</u> described James's eyesight.

WHY IT IS RIGHT: Now the description *typed on the computer* applies to *report.*

WRONG: Arthur drove to the store to buy tomatoes <u>wearing sunglasses</u>.

WHY IT IS WRONG: *Tomatoes* do not wear *sunglasses*.

RIGHT: <u>Wearing sunglasses</u>, Arthur drove to the store to buy tomatoes.

WHY IT IS RIGHT: Now the description appears in front of *Arthur,* who is the one *wearing sunglasses.*

One small word causes big trouble. *Only* must appear in front of the word or expression it describes. Take a look at this example:

WRONG: My aunt visited New York and <u>only</u> bought me a cheap tee shirt.

WHY IT IS WRONG: The description *only* belongs in front of the word it describes. The sentence says that the *aunt only bought.* With this wording, *only* describes *bought.* So the *aunt* did nothing else — no sightseeing, eating, or sleeping!

RIGHT: My aunt visited New York and bought me <u>only</u> a cheap tee shirt.

WHY IT IS RIGHT: Now the description *only* appears in front of *a cheap tee shirt.* This sentence says that the *aunt* did not buy any expensive souvenirs — just *a cheap tee shirt.*

Place descriptions as close as possible to the words they describe.

Are these sentences correct? Do you see a description in the wrong spot? In the second column, rewrite any incorrect sentences.

Sentence	*Correction*
1. The building is in my neighborhood with ten floors.	
2. Joe bought a dog with a credit card.	
3. The girl who loves to ski spends every free hour on the slopes.	
4. Paul only visits his friends on Sundays because he is busy every other day of the week.	
5. Lulu wore a gold hoop in her left ear that she had ordered from a jeweler.	

Here are the answers: 1. *The building with ten floors is in my neighborhood.* 2. *With a credit card, Joe bought a dog.* 3. correct 4. *Paul visits his friends only on Sundays because he is busy every other day of the week.* 5. *In her left ear, Lulu wore a good hoop that she had ordered from a jeweler.*

Descriptions and missing words

What do you think of this sentence?

> When only six years old, Barry's grandfather took him to the circus.

Oh my! Can you picture a six-year-old grandfather? Yet that is what this sentence states. The first part of the sentence, *When only six years old,* does not name a person. According to the rules of English, that description applies to the *subject* — normally the next person you see in a sentence like this one. The subject is *Barry's grandfather.* You can fix this error easily:

> When only six years old, Barry went to the circus with his grandfather.

Now *Barry* is the subject, so *Barry* is *only six years old,* not *his grandfather.* (For more information on subjects, turn to Chapter 11.)

Here is another way to correct the mistake:

> When Barry was only six years old, his grandfather took him to
> the circus.

By attaching the missing words (*Barry was*) to the age (*only six years old*), the proper meaning comes through.

Read through a few more examples:

> WRONG: Before painting the wall, plaster should be placed in the cracks.
>
> WHY IT IS WRONG: The *plaster* is not *painting the wall.*
>
> RIGHT: Before painting the wall, you should plaster the cracks.
>
> WHY IT IS RIGHT: Now *you* follows *painting the wall.* So *painting the wall* is what *you* are doing.
>
> ALSO RIGHT: Before you paint the wall, plaster the cracks.
>
> WHY IT IS RIGHT: Adding *you* to the beginning of the sentence takes care of the problem, because it is clear that *you are painting the wall.*

> WRONG: While wearing glasses, the sun does not bother his eyes.
>
> WHY IT IS WRONG: The *sun* cannot wear glasses! No person appears in the sentence.
>
> RIGHT: While he is wearing glasses, the sun does not bother his eyes.
>
> WHY IT IS RIGHT: Adding *he is* changes the meaning. Now *he is wearing glasses.*

WRONG: Skating on the ice, Shelly's laces broke.

WHY IT IS WRONG: *Shelly's laces* are not *skating on the ice.*

RIGHT: Skating on the ice, Shelly broke her laces.

WHY IT IS RIGHT: Now *Shelly* follows *skating on the ice,* so *Shelly* is *skating,* not *her laces.*

Skating is a verb form. The person or thing closest to that verb form should normally be the one doing the action. In the preceding example, *Shelly* is the person *skating.*

Are these sentences correct? Do missing words cause a problem? In the second column, rewrite any incorrect sentences.

Sentence   *Correction*

1. After sealing the letter, a stamp was placed on the envelope by Kathy.
2. Facing the jury, the final argument was made by the lawyer.
3. While swimming, Joe wears goggles.
4. Finished with his homework, the math book was put into Bill's desk.
5. When eating soup, a spoon is better than a fork.

Here are the answers: 1. *After sealing the letter, Kathy placed a stamp on the envelope.* 2. *Facing the jury, the lawyer made the final argument.* 3. correct 4. *Finished with his homework, Bill put the math book into his desk.* 5. *When you are eating soup, a spoon is better than a fork.*

Note: In quiz question 5, the name of any person fulfills the same role as the pronoun *you.* Just be sure to pair the name with the verb correctly. (For more information on matching people to verbs, turn to Chapter 11.)

Writing Clear Pronouns

Two things can happen when you hear this sentence:

Sally told Mary that she was an idiot.

This is the first reaction:

"How dare you call me an idiot!" said Mary as she slapped Sally.

This is the second reaction:

> "Do not say that about yourself, Sally. Everyone makes mistakes," said Mary as she hugged Sally.

These different responses are possible because the original sentence is unclear. The pronoun *she* refers to one female. The sentence names two females, *Mary* and *Sally*. The reader has no way to identify *she*. Here are clearer, better sentences:

> "You are an idiot," Sally told Mary.
>
> "I am an idiot," said Sally to Mary.
>
> Sally told Mary that Mary was an idiot.
>
> Sally told Mary that Sally was an idiot.

The goal of proper grammar is communication. You cannot reach that goal if the reader or listener is confused. To make your meaning clear, avoid vague pronouns.

These four sentences are correct, but the last two are not as good as the first two. Repeating the name makes the meaning clear, but repetition often annoys readers.

Here are a few other examples:

> WRONG: Jeff and Eddie play tennis often, and he always wins.
>
> WHY IT IS WRONG: Who wins? Who knows? The pronoun *he* is unclear.
>
> RIGHT: Jeff and Eddie play tennis often, and Jeff always wins.
>
> ALSO RIGHT: Jeff and Eddie play tennis often, and Eddie always wins.
>
> WHY THEY ARE RIGHT: Each correction clearly states who wins the tennis matches.
>
> WRONG: Marty removed the shoes from the boxes and put them in the closet.
>
> WHY IT IS WRONG: What did Marty put in the closet? The *shoes* or the *boxes?* You have no way of knowing what *them* refers to.
>
> RIGHT: Marty removed the shoes and put the boxes in the closet.
>
> ALSO RIGHT: Marty removed the shoes and put them in the closet. He threw the boxes away.
>
> WHY THEY ARE RIGHT: Both corrections are clear. (You can find other ways to correct the original sentence. Just be sure your rewritten sentence shows what *them* refers to.)

WRONG: The tomato was not ripe, and the salad had to be perfect. Fortunately, the chef replaced it.

WHY IT IS WRONG: What did the chef replace? The *tomato* or the whole *salad*? The pronoun *it* is unclear.

RIGHT: Because the tomato was not ripe, the chef replaced it. The salad had to be perfect.

ALSO RIGHT: The tomato was not ripe, and the salad had to be perfect. The chef threw out the salad and replaced it with a new one.

WHY THEY ARE RIGHT: In each correction, you know what the chef did. The pronoun *it* is clear.

WRONG: The essay was very short and very late, which annoyed the professor.

WHY IT IS WRONG: Why is the professor annoyed? Does the professor want a long essay? Is the professor strict about deadlines? Perhaps length and timing are both problems. As the sentence is written, you cannot tell.

RIGHT: The professor was annoyed because the essay was very short and very late.

ALSO RIGHT: The late essay annoyed the professor. The essay was also very short.

WHY THEY ARE RIGHT: Each correction explains why the professor is annoyed.

Take another look at the last example. The pronoun *which* does not appear in the corrected sentences. Eliminating the pronoun often solves the problem!

See whether you can spot any unclear pronouns in these sentences. If you do, rewrite the sentence. (*Note:* Because a pronoun is unclear, it may have more than one meaning. You can have more than one right answer, too. In the answers following the table, you see one or two suggested corrections. If you corrected the sentence in a different way, count yourself right if the pronoun has only one possible meaning.)

Sentence	*Correction*
1. The guards watched the boys go into the empty house, but they did not have weapons.	
2. The chair was next to a metal table, but it wobbled.	
3. The supervisor told his doctors that stress was bad for him.	
4. The wrapping was torn, and the box was ripped. This upset me.	
5. Brenda told Amanda that she loved her poem.	

Here are the answers: 1. *The guards watched the boys go into the empty house, but the boys did not have weapons.* Also correct: *The guards watched the boys go into the empty house, but the guards did not have weapons.* 2. *The chair was next to a metal table, which wobbled.* Also correct: *The chair, which wobbled, was next to a metal table.* 3. correct 4. *Because the wrapping was torn and the box was ripped, I was upset.* Also correct: *I was upset because of the torn wrapping and ripped box.* 5. *Brenda told Amanda, "I love your poem."* Also correct: *Brenda told Amanda, "I love my poem."*

No! No! Understanding Double Negatives

Lots of words are negative, including these:

no

not

never

nothing

no one

In many languages, you can pile many negative words into a sentence. In those languages, you can say

Jane did not eat no cookie

and everyone knows that Jane stayed away from the cookie jar. In English, though, two negative words cancel each other. If *Jane did not eat no cookie,* she ate the opposite of *no cookie.* The opposite of *no cookie* is one cookie, five cookies, or a whole box of cookies — any number except zero. Look at these examples:

SENTENCE: I did not do nothing.

WHAT THE SENTENCE MEANS: I did something.

CORRECTION: I did nothing.

ANOTHER CORRECTION: I did not do anything.

SENTENCE: Elizabeth never saw no one.

WHAT THE SENTENCE MEANS: Elizabeth saw someone.

CORRECTION: Elizabeth saw no one.

ANOTHER CORRECTION: Elizabeth never saw anyone.

SENTENCE: The stove didn't never work.

WHAT THE SENTENCE MEANS: The stove works.

CORRECTION: The stove didn't ever work.

ANOTHER CORRECTION: The stove never worked.

The negative word *not* often becomes *n't* when it attaches to a verb. *Didn't* is short for *did not*. English teachers call these short forms *contractions*. For more information on contractions, turn to Chapter 14.

SENTENCE: The prince won't speak to no one.

WHAT THE SENTENCE MEANS: The prince will speak to someone.

CORRECTION: The prince won't speak to anyone.

ANOTHER CORRECTION: The prince will speak to no one.

Another common double negative is *can't hardly* or *couldn't hardly*. The contraction *can't* is short for *cannot*. The contraction *couldn't* is short for *could not*. *Hardly* is a negative word. Do not put *hardly* and *not* together. If you do, you end up with a positive statement. Study these examples:

SENTENCE: Ed can't hardly speak because his throat is sore.

WHAT THE SENTENCE MEANS: Ed can speak because his throat is sore.

CORRECTION: Ed can hardly speak because his throat is sore.

SENTENCE: The politicians can't hardly agree on anything.

WHAT THE SENTENCE MEANS: The politicians can agree on anything.

CORRECTION: The politicians can hardly agree on anything.

SENTENCE: Gloria couldn't hardly believe what she was seeing.

WHAT THE SENTENCE MEANS: Gloria could believe what she was seeing.

CORRECTION: Gloria could hardly believe what she was seeing.

TIP

Have you ever heard someone say, "I cannot help but think" or something similar? The expression *cannot help but* is a double negative. The word *but* has a negative meaning. The word *not* is also negative, even when it is tucked inside the word *cannot*. When you place it in a sentence with *not,* you say the opposite of what you intend. Here is an example:

WHAT GENE SAID: I cannot help but ask for a raise.

WHAT GENE THINKS HE SAID: I have to ask for a raise.

WHAT GENE ACTUALLY SAID: I cannot ask for a raise.

WHAT GENE SHOULD HAVE SAID: I cannot help asking for a raise.

Whole and half

In the <u>United</u> States, many states come together to form one whole country. These three letters — *uni* — often mean "one" or "whole." Take a peek at these examples:

Unite means "to come together as one." "The bride and groom <u>unite</u> when they become a married couple."

Uniform means "one outfit, worn by all." "The students hated their blue <u>uniforms</u>, but they had to wear them anyway."

Unique means "one of a kind." "Collectors were willing to pay a very large amount of money for the <u>unique</u> coin."

Universal means "the same throughout the whole group." "The senator favored free, <u>universal</u> preschool, with no child left out."

You can chop a piece from the whole with *semi.* Look at these words:

Semicircle means "half circle." "The children sat in a <u>semicircle</u> while the teacher read them a story."

Semiformal means "not completely formal." "The invitation said '<u>semiformal</u>,' so Bill wore his best suit, not his tuxedo, to the reception."

Semiannual means "half-year." "George received good news during his <u>semiannual</u> job review."

Semiconscious means "not completely conscious." "The patient drifted in and out of the conversation because he was only <u>semiconscious</u>."

Part VII
The Part of Tens

For a bonus Part of Tens chapter on Ten Quick Improvements to Your Writing, go online and take a look at www.dummies.com/extras/basicenglishgrammar.

In this part . . .

✔ Discover how everyday activities can raise your English skills to a higher level.

✔ Identify which mistakes to watch out for, so you can eliminate them from your writing.

Chapter 24

Ten Easy Ways to Improve Your Writing Skills

*Y*ou are busy, right? You have work, school, family, friends, and many other things to do. Can you find time to improve your grammar? Yes! Learning grammar does not have to be an extra chore. It can be part of other things you do. This chapter explains ten easy ways to sharpen your grammar skills.

Listening

Not everyone speaks in perfect sentences all the time. Not even I do, and I am a grammarian! However, when I am in a formal setting, I bring out my best, most proper English. So do most educated people.

When you are in class, at a work meeting, or in another situation that calls for Standard English, listen carefully. Yes, listen! Very young children learn language when people talk to them. At any age, you can soak up information simply by listening to good grammar.

Learning this way is simple. You do not have to take notes. Nor do you have to memorize verbs, pronouns, or anything else. Instead, you give a little extra attention to proper English sentences. Your brain stores them away. Gradually, enough language is stored, and your brain recognizes a pattern. Good grammar sounds right, just because you have listened to it over and over again.

Be careful, though, not to confuse conversational, friendly chat with proper English. Informal language is fine in many situations, but you will not learn good habits from listening to slang and casual comments. Keep your sharpest attention for moments when language is likely to be correct.

Reading

In the section before this one, I explain how listening to good English can improve your grammar. Reading helps also, in exactly the same way. It does not matter whether you read words that are printed on paper or scrolling down your computer screen. The method of delivery is not important. What *is* important? The quality of language! If you read "Silly Things My Cat Does," you may not learn much. (Well, not much about grammar. You may learn a lot about cats.) However, a book or an article written by someone with a good grasp of proper usage will teach you many principles of grammar. By seeing complete and correct sentences, for example, you absorb the patterns of Standard English.

Of course, sometimes you want to read for fun. You should do so! Remember, though, that informal English is like ice cream. You enjoy it, but you turn to other food for nutrition and health. Have a good time with comic books, pet websites, and other entertaining material. Simply add a bit of more serious reading to your daily routine. Pay attention to language as you read. Little by little, your grammar will improve.

Writing

How often do you write? I mean *really* write — not just type some letters and numbers on your phone. Proper writing, with good grammar and spelling, comes with practice. To get in shape, athletes train and strengthen their muscles. You have to train your "writing muscles," too. You do not have to write a hundred pages at a time. Frequency is more important than quantity. Set aside a few minutes a day to compose an email, a diary entry, a letter to your grandmother, or something else. Concentrate while you write. Make an effort to create complete, grammatically correct sentences. Every day, the task will be easier, and your writing will be stronger.

Rewriting

Do you have any old school or work assignments? As you go through the chapters in this book, reread your work. Look for mistakes. For example, after you finish Chapter 13, you know the ingredients that should appear in every complete sentence. Take one paragraph that you wrote. Are the sentences complete? If not, rewrite the paragraph. Be sure that every sentence in it is correct. Do the same thing after you read Chapter 17, which discusses capital letters. Cross out misplaced capital letters and substitute with lower-case letters. Add capital letters where you need them.

Do not try to change everything at once. Your brain will explode! Instead, tackle one type of error at a time. Rewrite only small portions of your work. Investing a little time in this exercise will result in stronger writing skills.

Recognizing Your Weak Spots

Everyone has strengths. Everyone also has weaknesses. As you read this book, you may find that some chapters are harder for you than other chapters. For example, as you read Chapter 6, which deals with descriptions, you may realize that selecting the right sort of descriptive word has always been a problem for you. Do not worry! Knowing this fact is the first step toward solving that problem.

Before you write, remind yourself to be careful with descriptions. Glance at Chapter 6 again, if you wish. After you write, reread your work. Check the descriptions. Chances are more will be correct every time you do this exercise.

By the way, a topic that is easy for you may be hard for someone else. The reverse is also true. Customize your study of grammar. Concentrate on what you need and ignore everyone else's study plan!

Asking for Help

When my son was a boy, he often did his homework while I cooked dinner. As I chopped and stirred, he read and typed. From time to time, he called out a question: "Should I say *I* or *me* in this sentence? Does this sound right?" I always answered him. I was glad to do so!

This book contains a lot of information about grammar. You can learn from it. You can learn from other sources also. If you are writing and someone with strong grammar skills is nearby, take advantage of that person's knowledge. Ask for help. Most likely, you will receive it.

Note to students: Some teachers prefer that their students work entirely alone. Others require you to describe any help you have received. Check with your teacher to find out what he or she prefers.

Proofreading

No matter how careful you are, you may make an eror. (Oh, sorry, I mean *error.*) See? Your mind is quicker than your hand. As you race to express an idea, you may skip a letter or forget a punctuation mark. *Proofreading* — checking your writing for mistakes — solves this problem.

Unless you are under time pressure, take a break between writing and proofreading. The pause will give you a chance to see your work with fresh eyes. Instead of hopping over a tiping mistake (oops! I should have written a *typing* mistake), your brain will detect the error. Then you can correct it. This practice has another benefit. You will discover mistakes that you make over and over again. Soon you will remember the correct phrasing and use it automatically. Your grammar will improve.

Making Friends with a Dictionary

You probably do not know every word in the English language. Fortunately, when you are unsure about spelling, meaning, or plural forms, the dictionary provides help. Many online dictionaries even pronounce the word aloud for you, so you can say it correctly. (On paper, the pronunciation may be written out for you with special symbols. Check the front or back of the book for an explanation of the symbols.) Some dictionaries include sample sentences with each word, to help you grasp the meaning. You see the word in context and learn proper usage at the same time.

If you use a dictionary often, gradually the words you look up, as well as the sample sentences you read, will stay in your mind. Your own writing will employ stronger vocabulary and more mature sentence structure.

Using Spelling and Grammar Checkers

As I type, my computer places a wavy red line under some words. The red line alerts me to the fact that the computer does not recognize the word. A wavy green line sometimes shows up under a sentence or a phrase. The computer is programmed to detect grammar mistakes. The green line on my screen signals a possible error. (Your word-processing program may alert you in a different way.)

Pay attention to these error signs on your computer. Recheck every word or phrase the computer sees as wrong. Then — and this step is very important — use your own brain. You are much, much smarter than a computer program. Look in the dictionary or in this grammar book. Ask a friend, if you can. Then change the mistake, if it is a mistake. If your original version is correct, leave it alone. You know more than your computer does!

Solving Puzzles and Playing Games

You can have fun and improve your vocabulary and proofreading skills at the same time. Word puzzles appear in many newspapers and magazines. The Internet, too, has many sites devoted to these pastimes. Look for crossword puzzles to improve your vocabulary and help you recognize parts of speech. In a traditional crossword puzzle, clues provide a definition. When you find an answer, you may learn a new word or a different form of a familiar word. Find-a-word puzzles hide words inside a block of letters. Solving these puzzles sharpens your spelling ability. Other word puzzles rely on riddles and other tricks.

Some games are also good tools for improving vocabulary, spelling, and even grammar. Look for products that ask you to spell out words with tiles, place words in sentences, or otherwise play with language. Many word games have "beginner," "intermediate," and "hard" levels. Choose the level that is best for you, and work your way up as your skills improve.

Chapter 25

Ten Mistakes to Avoid

Turn on the television. Change channels until you find a comedy or drama. Now close your eyes and listen to the characters speak. Can you rate their level of education, just by hearing their words? Probably you can.

Television writers know that certain mistakes pop up when people have not studied much English grammar. In this chapter, you discover ten mistakes to avoid at all costs.

Substituting "Me" for "I"

I never hear "<u>me</u> will go to the beach today." Everyone seems to know that "<u>I</u> will go to the beach today" is correct. Why? The action in the sentence, *will go,* must be performed by someone. The person performing the action is the subject. The pronoun *I* is the one you want for subjects. (The pronoun *me* is reserved for objects: *Give the bill to* <u>me</u>, *she told* <u>me</u>, and so on.)

For some reason, though, I do hear sentences like this one:

<u>George and me</u> will go to the beach today.

The pair, *George and me,* causes problems! The solution is simple. When you have a pair, check each half of the pair separately. *George will go? Me will go?* The first half is fine, but the second half is not. Switch to *I* and rewrite the sentence:

<u>George and I</u> will go to the beach today.

Now you have a correct sentence. (For more information on subject and object pronouns, turn to Chapter 4.)

Switching Verb Tenses

What is wrong with this story? Hint: Look closely at the underlined words.

> My friend <u>called</u> me. She <u>told</u> me that a small fire <u>broke</u> out in her garage yesterday. Then she <u>says</u> that the fire truck <u>arrived</u> right away. The neighbors <u>ran</u> to help her.

The underlined words are all verbs — action words. They should all be past tense forms because this story is about something that already happened. Most of the verbs are in the past tense *(called, told, broke, arrived, ran).* One verb, *says,* is in the present tense. Nope! A switch to the present tense does not make sense in this story. The verb *says* should be changed to *said.* Now every verb matches.

Of course, at times you must change tenses (the "time" of the action) because the meaning requires a shift:

> Henry <u>watered</u> the lawn yesterday, and today he <u>plans</u> to weed the garden.

Watered is a past-tense verb. *Plans* is a present-tense verb. Combining them in one sentence works, though, because *yesterday* is the past, and *today* signals the present.

The lesson here is simple: Do not change verb tense without a logical reason to do so. (To find out more about verb tense, see Chapters 9 and 10.)

Adding Apostrophes to Plurals

An *apostrophe* is a little curved hook raised above the line. An apostrophe

> ✔ **Shows ownership:** Catherin<u>e's</u> painting (the painting belongs to Catherine)

> ✔ **Shortens words:** do<u>n't</u> (short for *do not*)

An apostrophe does not create plurals:

> three teach<u>er's</u> = wrong
>
> three teach<u>ers</u> = correct

When you insert an apostrophe, be sure you are indicating ownership or creating a short form. (Check out Chapter 14 to see the apostrophe in action.)

Confusing "An" and "A"

These two tiny words appear in different spots. *An* comes in front of a word beginning with a vowel sound. (*A, E, I, O,* and *U* are vowels.) *A* comes before words beginning with consonant sounds (every letter that is not a vowel):

> a apple = wrong
>
> an apple = correct
>
> an lamp = wrong
>
> a lamp = correct

Most people do fine with *a* and consonants. Problems crop up with *an* and vowel sounds. Take care not to make this mistake.

Forgetting Endmarks

Everyone sentence needs an *endmark* — a period, question mark, or exclamation point. If you write a sentence and neglect the endmark, your sentence is not complete:

> Helen sewed all night = wrong
>
> Helen sewed all night. = correct

When you are texting, you may sometimes break this rule. (Chapter 18 covers this issue.) In every other sort of writing, though, an endmark must always appear.

Pairing "You" with the Wrong Verb

The English language is not always logical. The word *you,* for example, may be either singular or plural. You refer to one person as *you* and to more than one person as *you.* How strange! Even more strange is the fact that the verb that pairs with *you* is always plural. Take a look:

> you is = wrong
>
> you are = correct
>
> you was = wrong
>
> you were = correct

This mistake is very easy to fix. Simply remember to pair *you* with a plural verb form, all the time.

Connecting Sentences with a Comma

A *comma,* a little curved hook below the line, is a useful punctuation mark. A comma signals a pause. It often helps the reader understand the meaning of a sentence. A comma cannot do every job, however. It cannot link one complete sentence to another:

> Don painted the <u>house, it</u> looks great. = wrong
>
> Don painted the <u>house. It</u> looks great. = correct
>
> Don painted the <u>house, and it</u> looks great. = also correct

When you place a comma between two ideas, say each one separately. Can each one stand alone as a complete sentence? If so, do not try to connect these ideas with a comma. Make two separate sentences or add a joining word such as *and, but,* and similar words. (For more information on commas, turn to Chapter 15.)

Omitting Capital Letters

Every name needs a capital letter. So does the pronoun *I,* which refers to the speaker or writer. Also, all sentences begin with capital letters. If you omit a capital letter in one of these spots, your writing suffers:

> <u>b</u>etty and <u>b</u>ill = wrong
>
> <u>B</u>etty and <u>B</u>ill = correct
>
> <u>i</u> am = wrong
>
> <u>I</u> am = correct
>
> <u>t</u>he bus is coming. = wrong
>
> <u>T</u>he bus is coming. = correct

For more information on capital letters, refer to Chapter 17.

Using Half a Verb

When you express action or being, you use a verb. Some verb forms are made of two words. If you leave out half the verb, you have made an error:

> Peter <u>traveling</u> to California. = wrong
>
> Peter <u>is traveling</u> to California. = correct
>
> The race <u>begun</u> already. = wrong
>
> The race <u>has begun</u> already. = correct

To see many examples of two-word verb forms, read Chapter 10.

Being Unclear

When you speak or write, you know what you want to say. Your thoughts are clear — to you! Unfortunately, many people have difficulty knowing how much information is actually expressed and how much remains inside their heads. Look at this example:

> Marty fought with his brother, and <u>his</u> hand hurt for three days.

The person who wrote this sentence knows whose hand hurt for three days. Do you? It may be Marty's hand. It may be his brother's hand. The sentence is unclear. Now read this sentence:

> Marty fought with his brother, <u>whose</u> hand hurt for three days.

Now you know that the brother's hand hurt. This sentence has a different meaning, but it is also clear:

> Marty's hand hurt for three days after he fought with his brother.

To be sure that your intended meaning comes through, pretend that you are a stranger. Reread your work. Do you understand everything? If not, make the necessary changes.

Index

• *Q* •

• R •

• S •

• *y* •

Notes

Notes

About the Author

Geraldine Woods was an English teacher for four decades. She learned grammar from very strict teachers when she was in elementary school, which, when she attended, was called grammar school.

She is the author of nearly 50 books, including *English Grammar For Dummies* (2nd Edition), *English Grammar Workbook For Dummies* (2nd Edition), *1001 English Grammar Questions For Dummies, Grammar Essentials For Dummies, Wiley AP English Language and Composition, Wiley AP English Literature and Composition, Research Papers For Dummies,* and *College Admission Essays For Dummies,* all published by Wiley. She is also the author of *Punctuation, Simplified and Applied,* published by Webster's New World.

She blogs on grammar and language at www.grammarianinthecity.com.

Dedication

To two wonderful ladies in my family: Elizabeth and Candice.

Author's Acknowledgements

I thank Iona Everson and Catherine Conley, fine editors, for their cheerful and attentive help. I am also grateful to Sophia Seidner of Queen Literary, who takes good care of me. I am always grateful to Harry Woods and Tom Woods, just for being themselves.

Publisher's Acknowledgements

We're proud of this book; please send us your comments at http://dummies.custhelp.com.
For other comments, please contact our Customer Care Department within the U.S. at 877-762-2974,
outside the U.S. at (001) 317-572-3993, or fax 317-572-4002.

Some of the people who helped bring this book to market include the following:

Acquisitions, Editorial, and Vertical Websites

Project Editor: Iona Everson

Commissioning Editor: Annie Knight

Production Editor: Kinson Raja

Copy Editor: Kerry Laundon

Technical Editor: Catherine Conley

 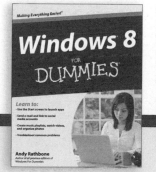  

Math & Science

Algebra I For Dummies,
2nd Edition
978-0-470-55964-2

Anatomy and Physiology
For Dummies, 2nd Edition
978-0-470-92326-9

Astronomy For Dummies,
3rd Edition
978-1-118-37697-3

Biology For Dummies,
2nd Edition
978-0-470-59875-7

Chemistry For Dummies,
2nd Edition
978-1-118-00730-3

1001 Algebra II Practice
Problems For Dummies
978-1-118-44662-1

Microsoft Office

Excel 2013 For Dummies
978-1-118-51012-4

Office 2013 All-in-One
For Dummies
978-1-118-51636-2

PowerPoint 2013
For Dummies
978-1-118-50253-2

Word 2013 For Dummies
978-1-118-49123-2

Music

Blues Harmonica
For Dummies
978-1-118-25269-7

Guitar For Dummies,
3rd Edition
978-1-118-11554-1

iPod & iTunes
For Dummies, 10th Edition
978-1-118-50864-0

Programming

Beginning Programming
with C For Dummies
978-1-118-73763-7

Excel VBA Programming
For Dummies, 3rd Edition
978-1-118-49037-2

Java For Dummies,
6th Edition
978-1-118-40780-6

Religion & Inspiration

The Bible For Dummies
978-0-7645-5296-0

Buddhism For Dummies,
2nd Edition
978-1-118-02379-2

Catholicism For Dummies,
2nd Edition
978-1-118-07778-8

Self-Help & Relationships

Beating Sugar Addiction
For Dummies
978-1-118-54645-1

Meditation For Dummies,
3rd Edition
978-1-118-29144-3

Seniors

Laptops For Seniors
For Dummies, 3rd Edition
978-1-118-71105-7

Computers For Seniors
For Dummies, 3rd Edition
978-1-118-11553-4

iPad For Seniors
For Dummies, 6th Edition
978-1-118-72826-0

Social Security
For Dummies
978-1-118-20573-0

Smartphones & Tablets

Android Phones
For Dummies, 2nd Edition
978-1-118-72030-1

Nexus Tablets
For Dummies
978-1-118-77243-0

Samsung Galaxy S 4
For Dummies
978-1-118-64222-1

Samsung Galaxy Tabs
For Dummies
978-1-118-77294-2

Test Prep

ACT For Dummies,
5th Edition
978-1-118-01259-8

ASVAB For Dummies,
3rd Edition
978-0-470-63760-9

GRE For Dummies,
7th Edition
978-0-470-88921-3

Officer Candidate Tests
For Dummies
978-0-470-59876-4

Physician's Assistant Exam
For Dummies
978-1-118-11556-5

Series 7 Exam For Dummies
978-0-470-09932-2

Windows 8

Windows 8.1 All-in-One
For Dummies
978-1-118-82087-2

Windows 8.1 For Dummies
978-1-118-82121-3

Windows 8.1 For Dummies
Book + DVD Bundle
978-1-118-82107-7

Available in print and e-book formats.

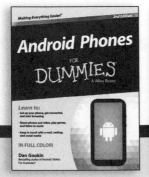

Available wherever books are sold. **For more information or to order direct visit www.dummies.com**

Take Dummies with you everywhere you go!

Whether you are excited about e-books, want more from the web, must have your mobile apps, or are swept up in social media, Dummies makes everything easier.

Leverage the Power

For Dummies is the global leader in the reference category and one of the most trusted and highly regarded brands in the world. No longer just focused on books, customers now have access to the For Dummies content they need in the format they want. Let us help you develop a solution that will fit your brand and help you connect with your customers.

Advertising & Sponsorships

Connect with an engaged audience on a powerful multimedia site, and position your message alongside expert how-to content.

Targeted ads • Video • Email marketing • Microsites • Sweepstakes sponsorship

21 Million Monthly Page Views & 13 Million Unique Visitors